MARTIN NIEMÖLLER

Martin Niemöller at a press conference in 1967, on his return from Hanoi where he talked with Ho Chi Minh. He is holding a piece of shrapnel from an American bomb.

MARTIN
NIEMÖLLER
1892–1984

James Bentley

THE FREE PRESS
A Division of Macmillan, Inc.

NEW YORK

The Free Press
A Division of Macmillan, Inc.
866 Third Avenue, New York, N. Y. 10022

Printed in Great Britain

printing number

1 2 3 4 5 6 7 8 9 10

Library of Congress Cataloging in Publication Data

Bentley, James, 1937–
  Martin Niemöller.

  Bibliography: p.
  Includes index.
  1. Niemöller, Martin, 1892–1984. 2. Lutheran Church
—Germany—Clergy—Biography. I. Title.
BX8080.N48B42 1984   284.1′092′4   84–6050
ISBN 0–02–902730–6

For
Martin and Sybil Niemöller
and in memory of Else

ACKNOWLEDGEMENTS

THIS BOOK is based first of all on conversations, some of them lasting many hours, with Pastor Niemöller between 1979 and 1983. I am deeply grateful that Pastor Niemöller was willing to give me so much of his time, and I also here thank Frau Niemöller for her invariable welcome and the food and drink she gave me. Where my text is especially dependent on these conversations, I have indicated the fact by the abbreviation MN/jb.

Secondly, this book is based on research in the archives of the Protestant Church of Hessen and Nassau. I must thank the staff of the archives, particularly the director, Herr Ekkehard Kätsch, and the archivist, Frau Eyke Schmidt-Rhode, for many kindnesses. In the text I have abbreviated references to material from the *Zentralarchiv der Evang. Kirche in Hessen und Nassau* to ZEKHN.

Next I have drawn information from the papers of Bishop George Bell in Lambeth Palace Library, and have indicated this by the abbreviation Bp. I would like to thank the Librarian and staff of the Library for their help. I am also grateful to the Provost and Fellows of Eton College for allowing me to use the Machnaghten Library. Hugh Machnaghten's practice of asking authors of books about the Great War to add not only a signature but also a message to their books makes that Library a fascinating source of insight into post-war German attitudes, and in my text I have indicated where I am dependent on it by the abbreviation ECMN.

Otherwise I have done without notes. The literature on the events I have covered in this book is vast. That appertaining to the churches' struggle against Hitler amounts to thousands and thousands of books, articles, theses and monographs. The printed material listed at the end of this book is there not principally to indicate my sources but chiefly because it would be extremely discourteous not to mention that I have used them. In Britain I worked in the British Library, the Bodleian and the Wiener Library, and I am especially grateful to the staff of the Wiener Library for their help.

The Social Science Research Council made me a small grant of money from the Federal Republic of Germany to cover part of the

viii   *Acknowledgements*

cost of my research. I am grateful to Mr Desmond Heath of Coventry-Lanchester Polytechnic for arranging the administration of this grant. Professor Jürgen Moltmann of the University of Tübingen was extremely helpful to me. But above all I must thank my wife, who worked with me in libraries and archives and went with me on all but one of my visits to the Niemöllers' home in Germany.

One last word of introduction: because this book is a biography rather than a history, it deliberately reflects Martin Niemöller's religious and secular patriotism without dwelling on the horrors of the Nazi regime (a story that has been frequently told elsewhere).

As this book was going to press Martin Niemöller died peacefully at his home in Wiesbaden on Tuesday 5 March 1984.

March 1984   JAMES BENTLEY

CONTENTS

LIST OF ILLUSTRATIONS   x

1. THE PASTOR'S SON   1

2. IN THE KAISER'S FLEET   8

3. FROM U-BOAT TO PULPIT   20

4. LOOKING FOR A FÜHRER   33

5. CHRISTIANITY UNDER THREAT   42

6. JEWS AND CHRISTIANS   62

7. FACE TO FACE WITH HITLER   81

8. BATTLE FOR THE CHURCH   92

9. HITLER'S PERSONAL PRISONER   131

10. IN SACHSENHAUSEN AND DACHAU   143

11. GUILT AND REPENTANCE   159

12. THE GOOD GERMAN   179

13. PASTOR, POLITICIAN, AND PACIFIST   199

14. TO PROVOKE PEACEFULLY   219

15. PORTRAIT OF A HUMAN BEING   229

SELECT BIBLIOGRAPHY   239

INDEX   245

LIST OF ILLUSTRATIONS

Frontispiece Martin Neimöller at a press conference on his return from Hanoi in 1967.

Between pages 118 and 119

1. Heinrich Niemöller and his family beside the Christmas tree. Martin sits at the table, left.
2. Martin Niemöller and Hermann Bremer as naval cadets.
3. The U-boat captain in World War I.
4. Niemöller and the crew of UC67, Kiel, November 1918.
5. Martin and Else Niemöller, with their children Jochen and Martin, c.1930.
6. Dora Schultz and three of Niemöller's grandchildren.
7. Martin Niemöller talks with an American soldier after his release; Tyrol, May 1945.
8. Niemöller and Bishop George Bell of Chichester greet each other on 28 October 1945 in the Marienkirche, Berlin.
9. Martin Niemöller with his wife, Else, during a press conference of the Federal Council of Churches of Christ in America, in 1947.
10. Martin Niemöller with Bishops Otto Dibelius and Hanns Lilje at a meeting of the World Council of Churches in Chichester, July 1949.
11. With Metropolitan Boris, on his return from Russia in 1952.
12. Martin Niemöller and Karl Barth.
13. The last picture of Martin with his wife Else before her death in an accident, 7 August 1961.
14. Martin and Sybil Niemöller, with Sybil's son Marc, 1979.
15. Martin Niemöller, Linus Pauling, and Sybil Niemöller in the garden of their home in Wiesbaden, 3 July 1983.

Photograph acknowledgements

Nos. 1 to 8, 10 to 13: Pahl-Rugenstein Verlag and the family of Martin Niemöller.

Nos. 14 to 15: Frau Sybil Niemöller.

Frontispiece and no. 9: Popperfoto, London.

1. THE PASTOR'S SON

On 5 July 1939 Martin Niemöller wrote a letter to his parents in celebration of the golden jubilee of their marriage. He had seen them last the previous April and hoped to see them again the following October. Alone of the Niemöller family, Martin was unable to be present at his parents' celebrations because he was lying in solitary confinement, as Adolf Hitler's personal prisoner, in Sachsenhausen concentration camp. 'In spirit I am with you', he wrote, 'not as a "Sorrowful guest" but as "partner in your joy".'

He was able to write to them only because his wife Else had given up one of the precious letters he was allowed to send her every four weeks. 'Greet the whole company', he begged his parents, 'particularly my Else, who this time for your sakes has given up a letter.' Then he spoke of all he had gained as their son, reminding them how one of his brothers, years ago, had observed, 'My mother says we are rich, not money-rich, but children-rich.' (Martin had two brothers and three sisters.) In July 1939 he summed up 'the Confession which you leave to your children, . . . the sacred legacy of your earthly life to us', as 'to be the children of God under all circumstances' and to remember that 'The Lord is our righteousness.' (Bp. 10.238f.)

Martin Niemöller's father was himself a remarkable man, married to a remarkable wife. Born in the village of Wersen, near Osnabrück, in 1859, Heinrich Niemöller was, in the words of his youngest son Wilhelm, a man of 'Westphalian stamina and doggedness'. His ancestors were for centuries small farmers in Westphalia. His father, who died at the early age of fifty-four, had broken with the family tradition to become schoolmaster and church organist at Wersen. After his death Heinrich was brought up by the efforts of his mother Christine, who survived by selling vegetables from her home on the edge of the village. She encouraged her son's early desire to become a Lutheran pastor. He succeeded in doing so at the age of 27, and by the time he was 30 was appointed pastor of the town of Lippstadt.

Secure in this position, Heinrich Niemöller took the opportunity of marrying a local girl, Paula Müller, just turned 21, whose father was a general store keeper in Westerkappeln. Though a Westphalian like her husband, Paula Niemöller never forgot that she had French Huguenot blood in her veins. Whereas Martin inherited his mother's looks and his father's doggedness (and his younger brother, Wilhelm, inherited his father's looks, as well as that same doggedness), from his mother too he learned of Protestant ancestors who had suffered for their faith.

Inevitably, Martin Niemöller's faith was Protestant, with more than a hint of anti-Catholicism. The clearest division between Christians in Lippstadt was between Catholics and Protestants. 'Protestants', Martin Niemöller remembered later, 'wore Sunday dresses on Good Friday. Catholics never did.' ('A person who was not either a Protestant or a Catholic', he added 'didn't belong to human society!') (MN/jb) In Westphalia Catholics formed a good half of the population, a proportion rising to three-fifths in the Rhineland. In consequence, most Protestants felt themselves to be in opposition to Catholics, even slightly beleaguered. This was a feeling reinforced by history, for the region had come under the jurisdiction of the Archbishops of Cologne, who had not turned Protestant at the Reformation. Since these archbishops were also secular rulers who rarely appointed Protestants to positions of governmental or departmental superiority, Martin Niemöller was born into a tradition of seeing Protestantism as in a sense part of the secular opposition to the government.

This was in contrast to the typical attitude of Lutherans, which usually strongly supported the secular powers. But Niemöller's family was by no means typically Lutheran. Although a Lutheran pastor, his father had been baptized a Calvinist (or in the 'Reformed' tradition, as Germans would say). 'All my ancestors were Reformed', Niemöller recalled, 'though since John Calvin spoke French, Zwingli, who spoke Swiss-German, was the Reformer we knew about.' (MN/jb) And Zwingli was a military chaplain who had died in battle.

Christians in the Reformed tradition were less docile than those who saw themselves as purely Lutheran. But for the most part these distinctions did not greatly exercise Martin Niemöller until much later. He was brought up as a son of the Reformation. As he told his Berlin congregation in 1933, 'Our nation would be nothing but for the Reformation – the denominational schism which we often, perhaps, feel as a burden.' His feelings for the Reformation were part of his feelings as a German. In particular, he learned from his father to reverence the embodiment of Germany, the Kaiser. Heinrich Niemöller first saw the Kaiser in 1892, when, fittingly enough, Wilhelm II was taking part in the rededication of Luther's church in Wittenberg. The young pastor was so overcome that he threw his hat into the middle of the Kaiser's guard of honour. His second sight of Wilhelm II was in Jerusalem, and he never forgot that on this occasion the Kaiser told his hearers that the gates of hell would never prevail against the Protestant church so long as it held fast to the teaching of the gospels. For the most part the Protestant religion and German nationalism went hand in hand in the household of Heinrich and Paula Niemöller.

Their first son, Gerhard Heinrich, was born in 1890. Martin followed, on 14 January 1892, then Magdalene (in October 1894), Pauline (in December 1896), Wilhelm (in April 1898), and finally Maria (in November 1901). Then, at the age of four, Heinrich died, on Martin's second birthday. Eighty-six years later Martin could still dimly recollect him and – more clearly – that he had loved his elder brother and had lived for him. On the evening of Heinrich's death, Paula Niemöller discovered Martin in the eaves of the parish house in Lippstadt. She asked what he was doing, and Martin replied, 'I am going to heaven, to bring Heinrich down.' (MN/jb)

The spiritual life was exceedingly real to the young child. His parents possessed an illustrated Bible, almost a metre high and a metre broad, filled with steel engravings – a picture of paradise, of the garden of Eden, of Adam and Eve, and so on. Noah's ark did not impress Martin; but he saw the Jesus depicted in this Bible as a friend, closely identified with the person of his lost brother Heinrich. Life in the house at Lippstadt included talking to Jesus as a friend, and as a member, tutor, and protector of the family. (MN/jb) Jesus embodied Martin's idea of God. In his old age he took up this attitude again, quoting Jesus's dictum that only those who became as little children would enter the kingdom of God.

Piety, therefore, was natural for Martin Niemöller. It arose out of this child-like devotion to Jesus. And these, in some respects, simple beliefs and attitudes sustained him throughout his turbulent life. 'Theologians and so-called scientists', he once said, 'are there only to make incomprehensible what a child can understand.' And pointing to his book-lined study, he added, 'I don't give a penny for all these volumes.'

On another occasion he observed, 'I have never cherished theologians. Take Karl Barth, my dearest friend. All his volumes are standing there. I never read any of them. I never heard a lecture by him. My first wife read some of his *Church Dogmatics*; but I have never believed in the church, and don't now.' This, too, was a stance learned in his childhood. As a boy in Heinrich Niemöller's household, 'church' was simply their whole Christian way of life. He never thought about church in terms of ecclesiastical structures. (MN/jb)

It would be wrong to suppose that Martin Niemöller's anti-intellectual attitude was a symptom of lack of intelligence. At school in Lippstadt he responded well to his mentors, and later at the Gymnasium in Elberfeld adored a superb teacher. Martin's brother Wilhelm recalled that he came first in everything: music, science, history, mathematics, languages, and sport. Martin Niemöller himself gave a slightly different memory. At school in Elberfeld it would have been easy for him to come first. But one of his closest friends there, a boy called Ernst Königs, was more conscientious than he, though not so clever. Martin was content to come second to his friend. (MN/jb) Both boys were later ordained as Lutheran pastors. Both were to find themselves at odds with Adolf Hitler.

The son of the Lippstadt pastor also learned from his father's developing interest in what was then known as the 'social question'. In the 1880s German Protestant pastors were becoming increasingly interested in politics, aware that the struggle between the propertied and the propertyless was far from acceptable in a Christian nation. In the revolutionary year of 1848, Pastor Johann Hinrich Wichern of Hamburg had founded the German 'Inner Mission', to work for the spiritual regeneration of the nation and also to apply Christianity to every aspect of social and industrial life. He set up hostels for vagrant boys, and by 1865 controlled thirty separate institutions throughout Germany – asylums, orphanages, youth hostels, and the like, all concerned to develop a Protestant social ethic capable of dealing with the new social problems thrown up by the industrial revolution in Germany.

Heinrich Niemöller became deeply interested in the work of Wichern and his followers. And whereas Wichern had eschewed political change as a solution to the 'social question', Heinrich Niemöller sought to learn from those Protestant pastors who took a different view.

One such was Adolf Stöcker, sometime court-preacher to Kaiser Wilhelm II, a virulent anti-Semite but also a man willing – for a time, at least – to describe himself as a Christian Socialist. Heinrich Niemöller was impressed by Stöcker's concern to solve the problems of the class war and the needs of the German workers. And young Martin was deeply impressed when Stöcker visited his father's parish in Lippstadt. (MN/jb)

This concern for the 'social question' no doubt prompted Heinrich Niemöller, after sixteen happy years as pastor of Lippstadt, with its 1,300 parishioners, to accept a call in 1900 to become pastor of Elberfeld, a parish of 6,000 souls in a working-class area of the Ruhr. Young Martin hated the move. He stood in the middle of the lawn, in the garden of the new pastor's house, where he did not feel at home, mumbling to himself. 'What are you saying, boy?' asked his father. 'Father', replied Martin, 'how stupid you have been to come here!' The elder Niemöller did not reprove his son. 'That is how we could be with him, this man of great natural authority', Martin later recalled. 'He never insisted on this authority.' (MN/jb)

Since Martin had no friends in the new parish, his father took the boy of eight years with him as he visited his new parishioners. (Paula Niemöller had stayed behind in Lippstadt, to arrange the transportation of their furniture and the rest of the family to Elberfeld.) They visited men working in abominable conditions. Martin Niemöller remembered a sixty-year-old man, making textiles at a loom in a basement, with two or three goats at the other side of the room. From this floor steps led down to another floor, with a kitchen and a bed.

One memory particularly affected the young boy. He and his father had lived in Elberfeld by now for two months or more. Heinrich Niemöller said he must go to pray with an old man suffering the final stages of tuberculosis. Together they entered the house, on the edge of a great city in the Ruhr in 1900, with no bell or lock on the door. The pastor went upstairs to pray with his dying parishioner. Martin stayed in the white, lime-washed basement. On one wall he discerned a frame, with glass, to the left of the sick man's loom. Never before had he seen such a thing. Inside the frame was some material, probably velvet, with glass beads stitched on it to make a sentence. The boy deciphered it with difficulty and read, 'What would Jesus say of this?' (MN/jb)

After telling that story, Martin Niemöller in his eighties declared, 'Today with regard to Christian ethics I am no cleverer than I was as a boy of eight.' In 1980 he gave as title to a collection of his speeches, sermons, and writings the question he had seen on the wall of that dying man's basement: *Was würde Jesus dazu sagen?*

By now the young Niemöller identified the figure of Jesus much more with his father than with his hazily remembered brother. Heinrich Niemöller, until his death in 1941, remained a source of strength for Martin. Forty years after his father's death, Martin Niemöller still described his father as his example and ideal. 'Even now,' he admitted, 'I put to myself the question, "What would my father say?" ' What would my father say?/*Was würde Jesus sagen?* (MN/jb)

Heinrich Niemöller, Martin recalled, 'was the head of the family and certainly the best of us'. One anecdote humorously sums up the deep relationship between the pastor and the boy who, after the death of Gerhard Heinrich, became his eldest son. In the pastor's house in Elberfeld, Martin used to work and play in the attic, from which he could see the face of his father's church clock. The boy was thirteen years old. Under the low ceiling was a gas stove, a table, and a bed in one corner. Late one evening the boy was working at his homework, when – most unusually – the door opened and his father stood there, smoking a long pipe. Martin was smoking a cigar. 'Boy, are you smoking?' asked Heinrich Niemöller. 'Yes, father', replied Martin. 'Then', said Heinrich, 'from now on we order our cigars together.' (MN/jb)

'That was his way of educating us', observed Martin Niemöller. Yet initially he did not wish to follow his father into the Christian ministry. At Lippstadt he had conceived of a different ambition. Through the pastor's huge garden there flowed the Lippe. Martin and his friends would make little boats and sail them in the river. And he determined, after his school examinations were over, to become a seaman. Nothing he experienced in Elberfeld changed this ambition, though there was scarcely a river there and he was obliged to make do with paper cut-out boats stuck on the walls of his attic.

In 1908 he sailed the sea for the first time, *en route* for England, where his parents had arranged for him to stay for over a month in London. He avidly read Shakespeare to improve his English. He learned to play billiards. He passionately explored London, with its art galleries and great buildings. He travelled to Hampton Court and to Windsor. From Windsor Castle he looked down on Eton College, and learned something more of the social structure of the western world. Seeing the sons of the British upper classes in their Eton collars, he wondered how they could bear to wear them. 'Then, later in London, on the same holiday', he noted, 'I saw boys in wing collars and realized that it signified for them, "This means that I am something in the world."' (MN/jb)

All the time he fostered his desire to be a sailor. In London he would stand by Tower Bridge and watch the ships sail down the Thames. He enormously admired the future George V, who had worked as a naval stoker. And, he observed, 'the ideal of every seaman in those days was to be like a British officer'. (MN/jb)

Two years later he took the first steps towards achieving his ambition, and began the second part of his life.

2. IN THE KAISER'S FLEET

PASTOR MARTIN Niemöller and Jürgen Moltmann, the distinguished systematic theologian, were together at the 1975 Nairobi
conference of the World Council of Churches. Moltmann
recalled that at breakfast Niemöller told many many stories.
What Pastor Niemöller liked recounting most of all, said
Moltmann, were not his struggles against Adolf Hitler but his
adventures in World War I in the Kaiser's navy.

In 1910 the eighteen-year-old Niemöller came top of the list,
or 'Primus Omnium', in his final school examinations. By March
of that year he was an officer-cadet in the German navy. He had
already learned from his parents 'the two dogmas which were
taught in the Christian church at that time – and especially in the
German Protestant church – namely that a good Christian is a
good citizen, and a good Christian is a good soldier'. He was
determined to do well and, as World War I approached, his
career was swift.

After their initial training at the Flensburg-Mürwik Naval
College, he and his fellow officer-cadets took the oath of loyalty
to the Kaiser in the Garrison church at Kiel on 7 May 1910.
Niemöller was assigned to the training vessel *Hertha*. From the
Hertha he graduated to the battleship *Thüringen*, which was
attached to the North Sea fleet. Already the abilities of Martin
Niemöller were coming to the notice of his superiors. Within a
few weeks he was taken off the *Thüringen* for training as a torpedo
officer, and rejoined the battleship early in 1913 with the rank of
Sub-Lieutenant. When war broke out in August 1914 the crew of
the *Thüringen* were soon disappointed to find her withdrawn from
active service in the North Sea and confined to the harbour at
Wilhelmshaven. Niemöller, as second torpedo officer, shared the
boredom of the rest. To his delight, in October the following year
the captain of the *Thüringen* informed him that he had been
chosen for further training as a potential U-boat officer. Captain
Michaelis observed that out of his two hundred strong crew
Niemöller was the most impudent. He added that he was also
the best.

After training, Niemöller was assigned to a submarine so much damaged and inadequately patched up that it was commonly known as the 'floating coffin'. U73 had been commissioned for mine-laying, and with her two engines working perfectly (which they rarely did) could scarcely reach a speed of $9\frac{1}{2}$ knots. Nevertheless she did her job, and occasionally even managed to sink an enemy ship. Profiting from experience on U73 as a navigating officer, Martin Niemöller took the chance to leave her at the very end of 1917 when he learned that the captain of U39 was looking for an officer with his skills. His adventures on U39 were succeeded by a spell working at the Admiralty in Berlin and then as an officer on the newly commissioned U151. Niemöller's service on this ship included the longest time spent at sea by any German U-boat throughout World War I – 114 days in all. The U151 returned to Germany on Christmas Eve, 1917.

By the end of June the following year Martin Niemöller was considered fit to command his own submarine. For eight days under his command the UC67 laid mines, evaded seaplanes and enemy vessels and sank one of them. The damage sustained by UC67 in those eight days took eight weeks to repair. In August and September 1918 UC67, commanded still by Niemöller, successfully completed a mission to lay mines off Marseilles and during the same exercise sank three enemy ships totalling 17,000 tons. On his final patrol as commander of UC67 Martin Niemöller learned that Germany had surrendered.

In company with many German officers, Martin Niemöller later wrote and published his reminiscences of the First World War, partly as an attempt to come to terms with Germany's traumatic defeat. His book, *From U-Boat to Pulpit*, was written fifteen years after the Armistice; but since Niemöller had kept a detailed log of his war service, the book possesses an immediacy surpassing most of its genre.

An English translation appeared in 1936. At that time Niemöller recalled his first visit to a British warship – HMS *Cumberland* – in the autumn of 1910. Then, 'the idea of a war to the death between out nations rose up before me as a mad fantasy', he wrote. By 1936 he had come to think that 'our generation bears a heavy responsibility to posterity . . . to seek and find a solution [to the problems of that era] which will not lead to the outbreak of further chaos.' Nevertheless, the honesty with which *From U-Boat to Pulpit* records Martin Niemöller's joy in battle prompted the reviewer of *The Times Literary Supplement* to suggest that the book was scarcely what a British reader would expect from a man who had since become a Protestant clergyman.

From U-Boat to Pulpit records the 'successes' of German naval warfare, with the exultation of those who were fighting. 'We receive joyful news of a peculiar kind', wrote Niemöller: 'Battleship *Russell*, flying the flag of Rear-Admiral Fremantle, has struck a mine in the Mediterranean; 124 men missing, 676 saved.' In 1934 he still loathed alarm-bells that rang like the ones on U73, since, whenever they shrilled through the boat, they might well have sounded his last hour. On 9 August 1917 the lookout spotted an enemy destroyer barely half a mile away. The alarm bells rang out and U73 crash dived to 60 feet. The destroyer passed over them. The following evening a small Italian schooner, the *Lorenzo Donato*, fell athwart the course of U73. 'Revenge is sweet!' wrote Niemöller. 'She was even slower than our groggy boat and thereby met her fate.' On 21 December U73 sank a large tanker and the crew triumphantly played *Deutschland über alles* on the boat's gramophone. Since U-boat commanders were in the habit of taking photographs of their sinking targets – sometimes through their periscopes – Niemöller was able to provide *From U-Boat to Pulpit* with pictures of vanquished enemy prey. Such exultation hardly endeared itself to British readers.

He also recorded the immense danger of active service. On U73, he recalled, 'The only thing we could not grow accustomed to was the fact that half the ship's company were sea-sick and the remainder had to clean up all day long.' And he noted laconically, 'A man must have luck, particularly in wartime.' A seaman was swept overboard from U73. The crew saw him swimming lustily and then, ten yards abeam, floating unconscious. One of his mates plunged into the sea to bring him on board. The drowned man was laid on the conning-tower, and for over half-an-hour the boatswain's mate tried to resuscitate him. The captain gave up hope, and U73 steamed south at half speed. Then, after fifty minutes, during which the boatswain's mate continued to pump and pump to free the man's lungs of water, he 'breathes, opens his eyes, groans and – lives! He is still very weak and corpse-like, but he is merry and bright the same night, and a sigh of relief goes up through the whole boat'.

But not all are so lucky. Another seaman is swept overboard and lost. On U151 Niemöller is reminded of the imminence of death when, asleep in his bunk he is flung to the floor as the boat is rammed by an enemy ship, leaving a gaping hole thirteen feet wide.

Inevitably the pastor's son was forced by the war to consider his deepest beliefs. Many theologians in those days, as *From U-Boat to Pulpit* observed, talked of 'a moratorium of Christianity'. The highly respected Friedrich Naumann went so far as to declare that 'One cannot wish to construct the whole of human development on sympathy and brotherly love. There are things that elude the grasp of the Christian religion. The world remains the world and power comes before compassion.' Although, he maintained, Christians individually are obliged to love their enemies, 'the struggle for existence has taught the nations to be armour-plated beasts'.

Such an amoral stance was highly congenial to many of Niemöller's fellow sailors. After the war Captain Paul Köppen, for instance, author of *Die Überwasserstreitkräfte und ihre Technik*, wrote, 'The building of Germany's fleet was the natural and necessary precaution of a people mindful of its self-preservation – and *must* become so again! For life is for every human being, every nation, every State, every animal, every plant, an unceasing struggle for existence.' (ECMN)

Such feelings did not, of course, constitute a well-thought-out moral theology. 'We junior officers', Niemöller pointed out, 'knew nothing and cared less about theological problems. But we did see that situations involving spiritual bankruptcy did arise in which it was utterly impossible to preserve a clear conscience.' One incident in particular brought this dilemma into clearest focus. On 25 January 1918, U39 sank a French destroyer. A second destroyer began to pick up survivors. U39 successfully and deliberately harassed her to prevent her picking up too many. 'What should we do?' asked Niemöller. 'We have no wish to interrupt the destroyer's work of saving lives . . . But war is war and the people being picked up out of the water are soldiers bound for the front; soldiers who are to shoot at our German brothers.'

Later there was a lengthy discussion of the whole moral problem in the ward room of U39. Niemöller concluded that 'the question whether we are to perish in despair or defiance, or survive all trials with a live conscience, depends wholly and solely on whether we believe in the forgiveness of sins'. He added: 'This 25th January was the turning point in my life, because it opened my eyes to the utter impossibility of a moral universe.'

No doubt at times the desire for sheer survival helped to quieten Niemöller's Christian conscience. After U151 had been rammed, the destroyer which had holed her blew up. Niemöller noted, 'It is a case of "You or I!" ' Throughout his life he preserved alongside courage a deep determination to survive. 'On board ship', he would say, 'when a grenade comes along, everyone ducks.' (MN/jb) But survival could not be the total purpose of life. He continually sought the meaning of his wartime experiences. Crawling cautiously through the Straits of Otranto, submerged in UC67, he asked himself, *'Is there peace anywhere?* Will peace come to us – or shall we, like the Flying Dutchman, spend year after year without rest or respite?' As ever, he noted on that occasion, 'we are faced by eternal questions: life, the universe and God'.

For one of his background, Christmas in wartime was especially poignant, and also brought searching questions. Late on Christmas Eve 1915, as he sat in his bunk in U73 reading the gospel for Christmas Day from the Bible given to him by his father on the day he was confirmed, he was touched when the boatswain's mate came in, placed a minute Christmas tree on Niemöller's chart-table, and said, 'It's Christmas, sir.'

Exactly two years later, after its cruise of 11,400 miles, U151 moored alongside the *Hannover* in safe harbour. The crew celebrated 'a German Christmas with a Christmas tree and plenty of candles'. They rejoiced at learning of the Armistice with Russia. And Niemöller noted the irony of the text chosen by a Catholic chaplain for his Christmas sermon: 'Glory to God in the highest; and on earth peace, goodwill towards men.' Niemöller himself was to preach on that same text – in a concentration camp on Christmas Eve 1944.

Those who serve in submarines are, perhaps, even more prone to think about providence than other serving men. Officers of British submarines during World War I coined the phrase, 'By guess and by God' to describe the manner of their navigating.

William Guy Carr called his account of the activities of British submarines in the war *By Guess and By God*, and observed that with all artificial aids to navigation removed, with no chance to take a sight for days on end, harassed by the enemy and with compasses often acting queerly, this was the only way to nagivate. 'Blind as bats', he wrote, 'we guessed and prayed inwardly that we guessed right: the rest was in the hands of Providence.' One of Niemöller's fellow U-boat commanders, Ernst Haushagen, summed up the message of his book *U-Boat Westwards*, with the old sailors' proverb, 'God helps the seaman in his need, but he must steer himself!' (ECMN)

Such attitudes no doubt help to account for many of Martin Niemöller's religious musings during World War I. The U-boat officer was not yet the pastor. Yet his feelings were not mere superstition. Steering UC67 at night, with his heart in his mouth, he remembered Ernst Haushagen's proverb. Who, he asked, was guiding him at that moment? 'From this time on', he wrote, 'I was instinctively conscious of a further mission of some kind awaiting me. Why, otherwise, should God Himself have directed our helm now?'

He also remembered standing with a fellow-officer, Karli Topp, on the bridge of UC67 after she had completed her first mission. Suddenly Niemöller told his friend that he was going to be a pastor. It was, he commented, no more than a passing thought. 'Since the age of five', he observed, 'I had never thought of any profession but the sea to which I was passionately attached.'

By now Niemöller was about to marry. At this time his best friend was Hermann Bremer, a former schoolfellow, now also a naval officer. During his spell at the Admiralty, Niemöller came by chance upon Bremer's sister Else, who was studying philology in Berlin. In the sunny and warm spring of 1917 they spent idyllic Sunday afternoons sailing on the Wannsee or Havel, romantic then as now. A year later they were engaged to be married.

Else Bremer's life was not to be that of a naval officer's wife, for Martin Niemöller's career at sea was soon to come to a remarkable and unexpected end. On 29 November 1918, after hearing of the Armistice while at sea, Niemöller sailed UC67 into Kiel harbour. A month earlier, fearful that the German command was planning to send out its sailors in a final, desperate act of self-immolation, a number of crews, mostly of battleships (including Niemöller's old vessel, *Thüringen*) mutinied. By 4 November the red flag was flying over German ports. It was generally held (for instance, by Admiral Reinhard Scheer) that 'The crews of the torpedo-boats and the U-boats had remained thoroughly loyal.' This was by no means the case, as Niemöller himself knew (though he chose not to reveal all the facts in *From U-Boat to Pulpit*).

News of the mutiny reached UC67 as she was leaving the Mediterranean. The navigation officer had elected to go home by train, so Niemöller alone of the whole crew was able to navigate the submarine. Calling the crew together, he announced that they were no longer obliged to serve under him. He was willing, he said, to take them to Spain, say to San Sebastian, where they might all be interned. 'Otherwise', he said, 'we go round Great Britain to Norway, where you can get your feet on the ground.' The whole crew wanted to go on. 'Sir, bring us home if you can', said a spokesman. (MN/jb) Niemöller insisted that the red flag would not be flown over his submarine and flew the red-white-and-black ensign of Kaiser Wilhelm II until they docked in Kiel harbour.

UC67 arrived at Kiel harbour and her captain ordered the ensign and pennant to be lowered. 'This was the end of our journeyings and UC67 would never again fly the German naval ensign', Niemöller recorded in *From U-Boat to Pulpit*. He packed the ensign and pennant into his suitcase to take away with him. But the revolution was not over. Every boat was obliged to elect representatives to the Soldiers' Council. It seemed to Niemöller that they were electing the noisiest and least reliable men. One morning he was told that the Soldiers' Council had discharged Lieutenant Karli Topp, since he no longer had the confidence of the crew. Niemöller replied, 'Tell your Soldiers' Council that I am not carrying on without my executive officer.' Karli Topp was reinstated.

Soon, however, Niemöller himself decided on an act of extreme insubordination – though not, in his view, either to his Kaiser or his country. After a short leave, spent chiefly in visiting the family of his future bride, he returned to Kiel on 26 January 1919. Already the notion of remaining in the German navy appeared both 'repulsive and impossible' to him, though he could not quite explain why.

On the last day of the month he received, in a sealed envelope, an order from the Inspector-General of Submarines. He was to take a dockyard tug and tow two submarines to England, to surrender them there according to the terms of the Armistice. The order scandalized his whole being. It was, it seemed, totally contrary to the traditions of his service. A fellow U-boat officer, Ludwig Freiwald, later summed up the message of his memoir *U-Boots-Maschinist Fritz Kasten* with the verses:

> You may have fallen into danger,
> You may have heavy odds to face,
> You may be vanquished in the struggle,
> And yet have fought without disgrace.
>
> Not by success is it decided
> Whether your manhood's test is passed,
> But rather, if – despite reverses –
> You have resisted to the last. (ECMN)

In this spirit Niemöller in 1919 felt that, having fought without disgrace, he must now, at the last, resist the order of his own superior officer. Indignantly, he insisted on an immediate interview with the Inspector-General. Asked why he refused to obey the order, he replied, 'I have sailed in submarines for three years, fighting against England, sir. I have neither sought nor concluded this Armistice. As far as I am concerned, the people who promised our submarines to England can take them over. I will not do it.'

After a moment's silence, the Inspector-General replied, 'Very well, I will give the order to another officer.' But Niemöller was now clearly aware that at any moment he might receive another order that would clash with his ideals of truth and honour. On 1 February he wrote home to say that he was quitting the German navy.

Niemöller's insubordination in January 1919 was not only characteristic of his own temperament – that 'impudent' spirit which Captain Michaelis had earlier discerned in him. It was also typical of the attitude of virtually the whole German officer corps at that time. Later, the Inspector-General himself told Niemöller that he was glad the U-boat commander unconditionally refused the order to surrender the two submarines. In the writings of Niemöller's fellow naval officers, it is possible to discern the same feelings. Lieutenant Johannes Spiess, who spent six years in submarines, wrote that 'their four years of battle against a whole world of enemies deserved a more honourable end'. Such men were deeply humiliated by the Armistice drawn up by the politicians. It seemed, to men like Niemöller, to cast aside as nothing four years of extreme bravery. Paul Schultz wrote *By U-Boat through the Seas of the World* because he believed that 'Simple statements of fact show more than anything else the greatness of Germany's achievements in the war.' (ECMN) Peter Cornelissen wrote *The High Sea Fleet has Set Sail!* in the conviction that 'The tragedy of the High Sea Fleet was that an ignorant government wanted to keep it safe.' He added that, 'Its only engagement with the enemy at that time proved that in leadership, personnel, and material it was far superior to its opponent.' (ECMN)

In fact the German High Sea Fleet was far *less* well equipped than the Royal Navy, whatever might be the relative merits of their fighting men. In 1897 at Queen Victoria's Diamond Jubilee celebrations, the Royal Navy assembled at Spithead off Portsmouth stretched seven miles along the coast, ships four abreast, 170 in all including over fifty battleships. Another 160 vessels of the British fleet prowled the seas of the world. By World War I Great Britain possessed in all 1,350 vessels belonging to the Royal Navy, and these included forty-two battleships and cruisers.

Nevertheless, many felt, with Niemöller, 'disappointment and helplessness' at the apparently craven capitulation of the German government after the abdication of the Kaiser. Rear-Admiral Hugo Meurer, as one British officer observed, 'was the most deathly ashy colour I have ever seen', and he seemed ready to fall down, as he agreed with the British C.-in-C., Admiral Beatty, what should happen to the German Fleet.

Initially it had been suggested that the whole High Sea Fleet sail out to mid-Atlantic to be sunk, but President Woodrow Wilson vetoed the suggestion. A second proposal was that the Fleet be taken over by neutral Spain. Finally, after a ceremony of humiliating surrender in front of 250 allied men o'war, the

German Fleet was obliged to sail, unarmed, to Scapa Flow. There, in the spirit of Martin Niemöller's own insubordination, the German navy took its cold, brilliant revenge on the British. At a pre-arranged secret signal from Admiral Lugwig von Reuter, the whole Fleet was scuttled. By 5 o'clock on the afternoon of 18 June 1919, over 400,000 tons of shipping, worth £70 million, lay on the bottom of Scapa Flow.

Scapa Flow, many German officers (including Niemöller) felt, had effaced some of the shame brought on the navy by subversive politicians who had undermined its courageous fight. Admiral Brüninghaus joined the *Reichstag* and wrote *Political Subversion and the Tragedy of the German Fleet* in the conviction, as he put it, that 'Unconquered at sea, the German Fleet found its own self-chosen honourable grave, after the miserable disintegration caused by party strife had rendered impossible the continuation of the struggle for existence which had been forced upon us.' (ECMN) Heinrich Neu's account of the revolutionary movement in the German navy in 1917 and 1918 blamed specifically the communists for the humiliation of Germany.

The tragic moment in the history of the German Fleet was in those days when the Imperial war-flag was lowered on German ships, which had co-operated for four years in the defence of their country, and the red flag, the banner of a party, was hoisted. However, the end of the once proud Fleet was not inglorious. These very ships regained their honour; the waters of Scapa Flow washed away the shame which had clung to them since those November days. (ECMN)

Sharing these views entirely, Niemöller could no longer remain an officer. He had won the Iron Cross, first class, for his service on U39. Now, when on 27 March 1919 he sent in his formal resignation, Captain Werth, flag captain of the Baltic Naval Command, and other officers too, accused him of desertion. But Niemöller was clear where his duty lay.

His farewells, to Kiel, to his friends, and to the calling which he had loved since he first aspired to it at the age of five, were, he wrote, 'painful'. He said goodbye to his old shipmates of the 1910 class at a party on 4 April 1919. Because he was about to marry, at the close of the evening he was carried round the whole mess wrapped in a table-cloth, 'to mark the burial of a bachelor'.

But in quitting the Imperial German Navy Niemöller did not renounce its old spirit. In Kiel harbour was built an eagle, with outstretched wings as an eternal U-boat memorial, testament, as one U-boat seaman wrote, 'to the enduring glory of the countless dead heroes of the U-Boat Service, a monument of faith kept and still to keep'. Niemöller wished to keep faith with those dead. Throughout World War I the Germans laid down the keels of 811 submarines, but of these fewer than 400 were put into commission. Of these 400 scarcely more than 300 did any active campaigning. Yet of those 300 or more, no fewer than 199 boats were lost. Among the dead was the brother of Niemöller's future bride, Hermann Bremer, lost with UB104. Niemöller watched Else Bremer's mother bitterly weeping at the death of her son. Hermann Bremer had been one of his two best friends. The other, Jochen Emsmann, died early in November 1918, when, as captain of UB116, he tried to steer his submarine into Scapa Flow. 'It was the last submarine to be lost', wrote Niemöller bitingly, over a decade later, 'the submarine whose crew, despite the general collapse of their country, believed in and dared to attempt the impossible.'

He believed that 'if ever there was herosim displayed in the war – apart from the contempt of death shown in its opening weeks – it was in the closing stages, when it was no longer a question of victory or honour, but just the stern sense of a warrior's duty which prompted it'. After his resignation from the navy, Niemöller's hope for the future of Germany lay in the fact that 'after four dreary years of fighting, this sense of duty was still alive'.

Martin Niemöller left the German navy a changed man. Claus Bergen, who was to edit and publish tales of U-boat heroism, wrote that 'U-boat warfare was the hardest school for the best seamen of the nations. It was also the best school for comradeship and an iron will to serve the Fatherland in ever-knightly battle.' (ECMN) Bergen had been war artist to the German High Sea Fleet between 1915 and 1918. The former captain of UC67 shared his intense patriotism. Men like Bergen and Niemöller regarded this as something they owed their dead comrades. Bergen's collaborator in collecting and editing the U-boat stories, Karl Neureuther, had commanded submarine UC55 during the war. Neureuther wrote that 'seldom can there have been so closely knit a body of men as that little company that faced their common fate within the narrow compass of a submarine. Every one of them stood at the mercy of his fellows, and the perils that beset them are only too clearly revealed by the many U-Boats that were destroyed by the enemy. No wonder, then, that the bonds that united such men have outlasted the years that followed the war.' Martin Niemöller treasured those bonds.

For many years after World War I, Martin Niemöller, in spite of his resignation in 1919, was conscious that he drew strength from his years of service in the German navy. He even derived something from his two months as an Admiralty bureaucrat in Berlin. 'I learned – as I still need and ever will need to learn – to think strategically instead of tactically', he wrote. 'At a later period of my life this experience stood me in good stead in regard to my own destiny.'

By the time he wrote those words, Niemöller's life was causing him great anxiety. Later, sometimes on occasions of very real personal danger, he would find himself drawing on what he had learned and experienced as an officer in the Imperial German Navy.

3.   FROM U-BOAT TO PULPIT

THE WOUNDS of 1919 lasted a long time with Martin Niemöller. 'We possessed a great fighting fleet and failed to use it', he wrote bitterly. News that his resignation as a naval officer had been officially received came at the end of November. It shook his composure for an entire day, and for many years he refused to visit a harbour or the seaside.

But he had other concerns now, principally marriage and the quest for a new vocation. Martin Niemöller and Else Bremer were married in his father's church at Elberfeld on Easter Sunday, 1919, having gone through the customary secular ceremony at the registrar's office the previous day. Niemöller had his naval officer's pay, followed by his naval officer's pension – not enough to live on, but something. As a result of the German revolutionary events of 1918 and his experiences on UC67 at Kiel, he now felt, he wrote, 'a stranger in my own country'. He determined to emigrate – an attitude alarmingly common among disillusioned naval officers. ('Toil and labour must start afresh to raise the honour of the German Navy,' Admiral Scheer declared in 1919. 'In this task the Fatherland will feel the lack of many capable men, who cannot live in the straitened circumstances that have been forced upon us, and so will migrate elsewhere.') Niemöller was convinced that his pension would enable him to buy a farm in Argentina, and he persuaded Else (who had planned to become a teacher) that there lay their future. Together they learned Spanish. He failed to get a job with a publishing firm in Leipzig and turned down another in the Berlin Admiralty, preferring to pay visits to the Argentine Association in the German capital and the Ibero-American Institute in Hamburg. Some of his colleagues were already living in the Argentine. Through them Niemöller learned of sheep farmers and former Argentine citizens living in or visiting Germany, and he eagerly sought them out.

All this came to nothing. Just before his marriage, Niemöller's uncle (on his mother's side) wrote from Westerkappeln, where Else was staying, to say that it was possible to be a sheep farmer in Germany as well as in Argentina. He offered to arrange with a farmer in Tecklenburg for Niemöller to be taken on as an apprentice farmhand, after which Niemöller could use his naval pension to buy his own farm.

'The scales seemed to drop from my eyes on receipt of this letter', Niemöller recalled. 'Had my ancestors not been West-phalian farmers? Should not the rebirth of Germany, if it were to take place, be founded on a healthy, free and pious peasantry?' He wrote back immediately to Westerkappeln to say that he would be ready to start work as a farmhand on 1 May.

In fact he began work on a ninety-acre farm in the village of Sennlich, Tecklenburg, four days later. His first task was to cart manure out to the fields and then spread it.

Strangely enough, there was no room for his new wife on the farm, and she was obliged to stay with Niemöller's relations in Westerkappeln. Having loyally supported his enthusiasm for Argentina, Else now nobly began to train herself for the role of a farmer's wife. By mid-July, she was working on a farm in Wersen, where she was to learn the problems of dairies and stillrooms, young livestock and poultry. The newly-married couple now lived seven kilometres away from each other. They could meet only at weekends. For the former U-boat commander this seemed entirely normal. 'I had a married life like that of a naval officer', he observed, 'on service during the week, at home from Friday to Monday.' They met at the house of an uncle who lived between the two farms. 'I walked four kilometres', said Niemöller, 'My wife walked three.' (MN/jb)

The idyll (if such it was) did not last. In September Martin Niemöller, who had scarcely found time to glance at a newspaper in the busy days of harvesting and sowing, began to make enquiries about the price of farms on the market, and was horrified. As a result of the already alarming rate of inflation in post-war Germany, an acre of land now cost over 3,000 marks. In no circumstances could the trivial capital of Else and Martin Niemöller buy a farm.

Inflation undoubtedly helped to promote Niemöller's eventual ordination. But it was not the only cause of his decision finally to follow his father's profession. Naturally enough, he and his wife had not forgotten to worship on the Sundays they spent together. Each week they went either to Westerkappeln church – where Martin's mother had been baptized, confirmed, and married – or to his father's native village, an hour's walk away – where his grandfather had been organist and schoolmaster. In short, both remained pious, godly Lutherans, but this by no means meant that Martin Niemöller wanted to be a pastor.

As he contemplated the failure of his dreams, he considered for a moment trying to become a teacher, even though this might involve some compromise with the new German state. So uncertain was he, that by 17 September 1919 he had still not brought himself to tell Else that their plan to buy a farm was now impossible. On that evening he walked to Westerkappeln to consult his uncle. *En route* he met one of the two pastors of the town, and was reminded suddenly of his talk about the future with Lieutenant Karli Topp on the bridge of U67. He asked himself whether, through the events of the past year, he had not withdrawn from his own people and his spiritual home. That evening he told Else of their new problems. And just before going to bed he wrote in his diary, 'I am going into the church!'

His problems – emotional as well as financial – were not over. For one, he had a horror of preaching to a large congregation. 'I was used to talking to fifty men or so on a ship. That was the right number for me', he said. But when he came to confide this fear to his father, Heinrich Niemöller said simply, 'Oh, you will learn.' His father added another word: 'My boy, the freest profession in the whole world today is that of a Protestant pastor.' After Martin Niemöller's recent unhappy experiences with authority, this was a decisive word. (MN/jb)

By the end of the year Martin Niemöller had not only helped to dig potatoes on the Tecklenburg farm; he had also enrolled as a theology student at the University of Münster. He learned the rudiments of Hebrew in eight weeks. Early in January 1920 he and Else moved to Münster, and for the first time set up home together, in a three-room flat at the top of the house of Pastor and Mrs Kähler. They moved in with two beds, a cupboard, a table and chairs, as well as a great many potatoes from Niemöller's former employer.

The twenty-seven-year-old student never really learned to like theology. As for philosophy, he considered it absolutely useless. 'There are no thoughts which nobody hasn't already thought,' he said. (MN/jb) German theology was in fact in a ferment after the war. Niemöller heard of and may even have read a little from Karl Barth's new, revolutionary commentary on St Paul's letter to the Romans; but he did not find Barth's complex manner of thinking at all congenial.

Nevertheless, to be ordained he needed to study and pass. And Münster possessed some able theologians – including a number who were to play their (sometimes erratic) part in the subsequent upheavals in German social, political, and cultural life. Niemöller was fortunate to be taught Christian dogma by Professor Karl Heim. Heim was the finest systematic theologian in Germany at that time, and soon moved from Münster to teach at the University of Tübingen. This move of Heim worked to Niemöller's advantage. Heim's successor at Münster, Professor Georg Wehrung, took a house virtually next door to where the Niemöllers lived. He and Martin took to walking home together after the professor's lectures, discussing theology and politics. Soon the two families were on excellent terms. In Wehrung's house in 1925 Niemöller and the great Karl Barth first met. Barth at that time came away with a distinctly unpleasant opinion of the 'Prussian' characteristics of his future friend and ally. (It happened that when Barth himself took a chair at the University of Münster, Georg Wehrung soon grew to dislike him so intensely that he moved elsewhere. Barth then took Wehrung's post!)

Niemöller's other teachers were not quite so distinguished. He learned Reformation church history from Professor Georg Grützmacher, who scarcely ever took his pipe out of his mouth. Professor Otto Schmitz taught him the theology of the New Testament, and Dr Rothstein taught the Old. Since the training was meant to be of practical use for future pastors, he was able to join the academic church choir which Professor J. Schmend directed, and also attended Schmend's classes on how to preach. He made his first attempt at preaching – before Schmend and a score of critical theological students – on 15 December 1921, and almost dried up. As a result, he asked his father whether the Elberfeld congregation, where everyone was, at least, friendly, might be willing to put up with the practice sermons of a novice. The following Sunday Martin Niemöller appeared in his father's pulpit and discovered that he had conquered his fear of preaching.

But far more fascinating – and indeed dangerous – for the ex-naval officer and for nearly every German university student was politics. Although the Kaiser had abdicated, Niemöller still felt bound to him by his oath of loyalty. Not until Wilhelm's II's death in 1941 did Niemöller feel dispensed from this oath. True, Wilhelm had dispensed everyone. But, asked Niemöller, 'how could he? The oath was a solemn pledge between three people, not two, for it was made in the presence of God. Wilhelm II could not speak for God.' (MN/jb) In consequence Niemöller's loyalties were fanatically right-wing, symbolized by the black, white, and red flag of the Kaiser which he had carefully taken away from UC67.

Again and again it is possible to see men who had fought in the naval battles of World War I on the German side seeking solace in the intense nationalism which had been the whole *raison d'être* for the sacrifice of so much. The message of an account of the last journey of the small cruiser *Dresden*, written by Petty Officer Heinrich Schneider in 1926, was:

> At all times ready with our blood
> For German honour and German good. (ECMN)

Frigate captain Georg von Hase prefaced his account of the German (partial) naval victory of Skagerrak with the words of the poet Bogislav von Selchow:

> My mind attuned to German thought,
> German by every tie and bond.
> My people first place in my heart,
> My homeland first, before all the world.

Lieutenant Captain Julius Lauterbach, navigation and prize officer of the *Emden* in 1914, a U-boat commander from 1916 to 1917, and commander of the auxiliary cruiser *Moewe* in 1918, went on a 'Fatherland world tour' after the War, to defend the proposition that, 'He who loves his Fatherland must forget his own ego and devote himself wholly and completely to his duty to that Fatherland. He must fight humanely and honourably, in order to earn the respect alike of his enemies and his fellow-men.' (ECMN).

However much men such as Lauterbach might urge their fellow officers to set aside egoism, nationalism of this kind was in part the reaction of bruised and wounded egos to Germany's defeat, and helps to explain the passion Niemöller put into his political activities at the time. Niemöller hated the Weimar Republic. 'If the Kaiser had not been forced to go to Holland by

Hindenburg and Ludendorff', he judged, 'there would have been no revolution.' In his Kaiser's absence, Niemöller remained a monarchist, hoping for the Kaiser's return and despairing of the Crown Prince as a possible substitute for Wilhelm II. He had begun to pay attention to politics in a serious way while still serving at sea, towards the end of the war, but in the elections of 1919 he felt he could cast his vote for none of the parties. 'The only choice for a naval officer was not to go to the poll.' No acting naval officer had been allowed to vote. Now, free of this restriction, Niemöller did not want to. (MN/jb)

His politics, therefore, became dangerously extra-parliamentary. At the beginning of his first term at Münster, two former officers began to enrol nationalist students in a German National Student Movement. Niemöller joined and devoted every free moment to the organization. Then, on 13 March, came news of the Kapp Putsch, the right-wing attempt to overthrow the Republic.

Niemöller, along with some of his right-wing allies, walked out of a seminar by Dr Rothert on Westphalian church history to make preparations for raising an Academic Defence Corps in support of Kapp. Kapp, however, was soon defeated by the Weimar authorities. With some reluctance the Academic Defence Corps now threw in its lot with the government, prompted all the more to do so by the attempt of the communists to profit from the disorder in Germany. Within a week the Academic Defence Corps in Münster numbered 750 men, comprising three battalions, one of which was commanded by Martin Niemöller. His brother Wilhelm, also studying for the ministry (in Bethel), hurried over from his parents' home in Elberfeld and joined his brother's troops.

Communist troops were now advancing from the Rhine, and as Easter approached Niemöller, along with the rest of the Academic Defence Corps, moved to engage them. 'On our right', he recalled, 'was the Loewenfeld Volunteer Corps, to which many of my old friends and a large part of the former ship's company of UC67 belonged.' On Good Friday Red aeroplanes were sighted and fired on as they flew over the River Lippe. All along the Lippe on that day fighting was sharp and one of Niemöller's friends, in the 1st battalion, was killed at Werne.

Meanwhile Else Niemöller was about to give birth to their first

child. On that same Good Friday, Martin's mother made a
personal telephone call to her son, at the battalion headquarters,
with the message, 'God bless you, dear boy; you have got a little
daughter; she has fair hair and blue eyes. Else is well.' Niemöller
(though he had secretly longed for a son) was delighted, though
unwilling to leave the field of battle. He promised to visit his wife
and daughter on the Sunday after Easter. On Easter Day he and
his men crossed the Lippe and occupied the village of Waltrop.
On Easter Monday they occupied the mining village of
Achenbach.

'We were greeted on all sides as liberators from the hell of
Bolshevism', Niemöller wrote later. But by now the action was
beginning to peter out. The government was anxious to reconcile
the various factions in the country. Inevitably, many deputies
were less than confident of the loyalty of the *Freikorps* such as
Niemöller's, which had only so recently come over to their side.
The three Münster battalions had to be content with house-to-
house searches for hidden arms. And on 9 April Niemöller even
managed to slip home to see his new daughter Brigitte. He
learned from Else that her brother, Friedrich Wilhelm, was
fighting in the Ruhr against the communists. And he lost no time
in returning to his battalion.

Manoeuvres and advances continued, with little result, for
scarcely more than another week. On 19 April the Münster
battalions marched to Dortmund, and there entrained for their
home town. On 23 April General von Watter took the last
parade, and the Academic Defence Corps was disbanded.

The events, however, gave Martin Niemöller much pause for
thought, especially when he learned that another friend of his
days in the Mediterranean had been killed fighting in Loewenfeld's Volunteer Corps. He asked himself why Germans were
fighting each other on their own soil, and concluded that, 'We
lacked leaders, we lacked a real goal, and, above all, we lacked the
inward and moral urge to national action.' Could it be, perhaps,
that patriotism was not enough?

With increased determination, Niemöller devoted himself to
his studies again. His family commitments were greater. In the
long vacation the three Niemöllers moved to his grandmother's
house in Wersen, where he would study in the mornings and help
his cousin with the haymaking in the afternoons. Inflation was

now seriously eroding his small pension, and Niemöller was severely tempted to take up jobs that would have deflected him from his calling. The family managed to survive, more or less, until the end of the year, but by February 1922 their situation was so bad that Niemöller tried, without success, to sell one of their most precious heirlooms – a Luther Bible printed at Wittenberg in 1545. Moreover, Else was pregnant again.

The Niemöllers' state would have been desperate had not his brother-in-law, who now had a university post, been promoted to the position of assistant medical supervisor of the clinic for nervous disorders in Göttingen. He sent Else and Martin a substantial sum of money to keep the wolf from the door. On 16 July 1922 their first son was born. They baptized him Hans Jochen, in memory of Niemöller's old shipmate, Emsmann. Hans Jochen Niemöller was to be killed fighting for Germany in World War II.

Without the doggedness inherited from his father, Martin Niemöller could never have completed his theological studies. It was the custom for students to study at more than one German universty, but the Niemöllers were far too poor to leave Münster. In his father's home in Elberfeld money was never mentioned. 'An honourable man doesn't speak of money', decreed Heinrich Niemöller. 'Short of it he goes to the bank for a loan. He doesn't speak of it at table.' In those pre-war years, in a working-class district of the Ruhr, the Niemöller household included a housemaid, a children's maid, and an au pair maid. (MN/jb) Now with the German government unable to control inflation, Martin was increasingly anxious about how he and his family were to survive. 'I began to realize', he wrote, 'that I was up against the toughest years of my life.' Without giving up his studies, he needed to find a job. On 29 July 1922 the future Pastor Niemöller started work as a platelayer on the German state railways.

He learned the job within six weeks. It was dirtier and harder than coaling the naval vessel *Thüringen*. And his fellow workmen were coarser than his shipmates. Niemöller was accepted by them only because he fought a young lout who tried to take away his pick.

It also gave him the invaluable opportunity of coming closer than ever before to working men. After they had accepted him, these platelayers, who were Roman Catholic to a man, gave him tips on making the arduous work lighter. And during the dinner hour they questioned him closely about his earlier life and the reasons for his future vocation. Niemöller, for his part, learned something of their politics. They distrusted the bourgeoisie, he concluded, but their extreme left-wing 'veneer' had nothing of the international Marxist about it. (At this time Niemöller had a lively animosity against the leftists for the personal reason that they had caused him difficulties by mounting a hunger demonstration in front of Elberfeld town hall on the day Martin and Else wished to ratify their marriage with the registrar. The couple were obliged to enter through the back door.)

Although he made permanent friendships among the platelayers, Martin was soon moved first to workshop duty and then to the railway station accountants' office. There the apparently unending inflation made the calculation of pay sheets, pension arrangements and so on a daily nightmare. Niemöller was obliged to work from 8 a.m. till noon and again from 3 p.m. till 7 p.m., with scarcely a moment for his theological studies.

With enormous determination, he succeeded. Early in October 1922 he managed to arrange leave to attend a fascinating 'theological week' at Bethel. The lecturers included Adolf Schlatter, later to become a fanatical Nazi and anti-Semite, and Paul Althaus, who, though never a National Socialist, developed a theology well in accordance with many of Hitler's views. But in 1922 Niemöller found himself most impressed with Althaus's lecture on the cross of Christ.

By the middle of January 1923 Niemöller had completed the work for his crucial first examination by the Münster Consistory Board. The platelayer and railway accountant had written two acceptable theses, on the subjects, 'Was Paul a true witness of Jesus Christ?', and 'The mysticism of Meister Eckart and Bernard of Clairvaux'. But his work was not over. The following April he would be examined in the history of philosophy.

The French occupation of the Ruhr had meant that the railways now could call on very many displaced workers. Niemöller lost his job. It enabled him and his brother Wilhelm to wander through the fields in February and March, swotting up philosophy from a crammer written – happily – by the man who was to examine them. In spite of the difficulties, both brothers remembered these years as happy ones. 'We didn't drink much', recalled Wilhelm, 'for how should we have paid for it?' Instead they sang, particularly the ditties of Gustav Falker:

> We are two cherries on a stem,
> Singing a canon together . . .

'It was a happy time', said Martin in 1980, 'working at night for my examinations and during the day on the railways for my wife and children. As a young fellow you can stand it.' (MN/jb)

Yet Niemöller, in spite of his success in examinations, continued to insist that during these years he learned most from the Protestant preachers of Münster, from personal contact with Christians in his native Westphalia, from his landlord, Pastor Kähler, and from the Bishop of Westphalia, Dr Zoellner. These last were to give him his first jobs as a clergyman.

After his oral examination in April 1923, Pastor Kähler invited Niemöller to become curate in the parish where he was living. As a preparation for the long-desired parish of his own, this was precisely what Niemöller wanted. As a curate he could preach and instruct confirmation candidates, but not conduct burials, marriages, the service of Holy Communion, or (except in emergencies) baptisms. Niemöller preached not only in Pastor Kähler's church but also in a camp for refugees from Posen and West Prussia situated on the old race track to the south of Münster. He also – fittingly for an ex-platelayer – preached to a tiny congregation that met once or twice a month in the house of the station-master of Telgte, a small town just outside the gates of Münster. Here Niemöller's earlier attitudes to Roman Catholicism were inevitably reinforced, for this congregation comprised the tiny Protestant minority in a town consisting almost entirely of Catholics and containing a famous Catholic shrine. Meanwhile Niemöller also continued his studies.

Almost immediately life became less pleasant. First, his friend and guide, Pastor Kähler, was appointed Bishop of Stettin and in August left the work of the entire parish to the Niemöllers. Secondly, inflation began to soar again. The Niemöllers obtained permission to carry on living in the Kählers' old house. To his deep chagrin, he could support his family only by parting with some of the most prized possessions from his days as a submariner. Else picked the gold lace off all his carefully preserved uniforms, and took it to a jeweller who bought it to melt down. Next he was obliged to sell a chronometer, which he had taken as prize from an Italian vessel during his time on U151.

They lived on the money from the chronometer for a fortnight. Martin unsuccessfully tried to find work with the Westphalian Bank. For a couple of weeks the superintendent of the Münster railway accountants' department found him work, but so many trade unionists were unemployed that their organizations soon put a stop to the employment of men in Niemöller's position. For a fortnight he was saved by the offer of work, after all, with the Westphalian Bank, where he found he had absolutely no time for his studies. Then the railway accountants' department was bold enough to find him work again until, on 13 November 1923, he received his second and final dismissal.

In these circumstances, how he ever managed to complete a thesis on 'The rights and limits of religious psychological method' remained a puzzle to Niemöller for the rest of his life. Yet, he believed, the whole experience of anxiety and poverty was a valuable part of the preparation for his vocation as a pastor. 'I discovered and still know what it feels like', he wrote, 'to have no fixed employment and means of existence and sustenance.'

These circumstances also deflected him from his deepest desire at that time, namely to have a parish of his own. On the day of his final dismissal from the railway accountants' department, he returned home deeply anxious about the financial survival of his family. The last instalment of his naval pension had been enough to purchase exactly half a loaf of bread. As he explained their precarious situation to Else, she said, 'By the way, the bishop sent a message asking you to come to see him after supper.' Dr Zoellner had already discussed with Niemöller the possibility that after his first curacy he might take a post with the Westphalian 'Inner Mission', part of the remarkable structure set up by Pastor Johann Hinrich Wichern which had so much impressed Niemöller's father. On that occasion, much preferring the idea of taking a country living, Martin had found the proposition uncongenial.

Now Dr Zoellner repeated the offer – which had come, in fact, partially at the prompting of Heinrich Niemöller – with the further proviso that Martin should start work for the Inner

Mission not at the end of a first curacy but on 1 December. Niemöller had no choice. His work for the railways was to end on 30 November. His final church examination was not due until 24 April the following year. The bishop was in effect offering him a secure position before his ordination, without knowing what might be the results of his final exam.

Moreover, Else was pregnant again. (Heinz Hermann was born on 6 January 1924.) Their means of support was frighteningly small. Niemöller replied, biblically, 'Jacob served his Leah for seven years. I'll take the job for seven years, not a day more.'

The following day the board of the Westphalian Inner Mission offered him the post of manager. Niemöller insisted that they pay him only the difference between his naval officer's pension and the church salary. 'I wanted to serve persons', he said later, 'not an organization.'

For very many young men, such a position would have seemed an enormous step upwards. For the Niemöllers it was certainly a step into financial security. During 1924 the Westphalian Inner Mission built a house for their use and to serve as Niemöller's offices. The family moved into the large basement in 1925, and there their next three children were born. Jan Heinrich arrived on 11 December 1925. A second daughter, whom the ex-submariner took the opportunity of naming after his old ship *Hertha*, was born on 8 July 1927. Jutta arrived on 15 November 1928.

And Martin's work was extremely successful. Used to concentrating on several diverse jobs at once, he passed his final church examination without difficulty at the beginning of May 1924. 'In actual fact', he wrote, 'they merely constituted an interlude, which interrupted my regular duties for three days.'

On 29 June 1924, assisted by Heinrich Niemöller, the Rt Revd Dr Simon ordained Martin Niemöller and two other pastors in the church of the Redeemer, Münster. Martin preached, as the senior ordinand. He chose a text of humility, from St Paul: 'Not as though I had already succeeded, or were already perfect, but I follow after, so as to take hold of that for which Jesus Christ has already taken hold of me.' The same afternoon, in the attic of Pastor Kähler's old house, Martin Niemöller performed his first baptism, that of his son Heinz Hermann. The baptismal water was placed on Niemöller's desk, which carried not only a crucifix and candles but also the black-white-and-red ensign of submarine UC67. Heinz was a contraction of the name of the boy's grandfather. Heinrich. Hermann was the name of Else's brother, who had fallen on active service on submarine UB104.

4.   LOOKING FOR A FÜHRER

HOWEVER RELUCTANT Niemöller was to start working in the offices of the Inner Mission, the experience was invaluable for him. He developed powers of organizing people and institutions that were later to be of immense value to the church under Hitler. He also became far more aware of the 'social gospel'.

In 1948, one hundred years after Pastor Hinrich Wichern had founded the German Inner Mission – and with it the first great meeting, or *Kirchentag* of lay and ordained representatives of the whole German church – Martin Niemöller described him as a man who approached social problems in the spirit of an Old Testament prophet as well as that of a disciple of Jesus Christ. 'As we would put it today', observed Niemöller, 'the responsibility of the church was social and political.' Her task was not simply to care for the sick and wounded but also to serve as the salt of the earth and the light of the world. This was Wichern's vision.

Bishop Wilhelm Zoellner, who had brought Niemöller to work in the Westphalian Inner Mission, shared Wichern's vision and communicated it to his protégé. Zoellner envisaged the Inner Mission as a reform movement within the church itself, as well as part of the church's fulfilment of its social responsibilities. He strove to set up under the auspices of the Inner Mission youth and welfare organizations in every parish of his diocese. By the time Niemöller began to work for the Inner Mission in 1924, forty-nine such organizations existed in Westphalia. To co-ordinate their work was one part of Niemöller's task, a task which kept him away from home at least every other day of the year.

'In those days', Niemöller recalled, 'the churches were properly concerned about their responsibility to the *people*, but far less about their attitude to the *neighbour*. They concerned themselves about individual members of their congregations, about children, confirmands, and so on – but that was not really what we now recognize and feel to be the meaning of the commandment, "You must love your neighbour as yourself".' The Inner Mission seemed both to offer one way of fulfilling this commandment and to be a means of reminding the German churches of their neglected responsibilities.

Wichern was also well aware that large classes of human beings were outside and virtually untouched by the German Protestant churches. He longed to make contact with them and bring them to Christ. His social analysis was by no means revolutionary. In 1948 Niemöller noted the irony of the fact that the Inner Mission was founded in the year of the appearance of *The Communist Manifesto*. The followers of Wichern and the followers of Karl Marx often saw their aims as diametrically opposed. In one notable clash at a meeting in the 1880s, members of the Christian social movement inspired by Wichern sang Luther's hymn *Ein' feste Burg*, while rival Marxists tried to drown their music by singing the *Marseillaise*. Yet both groups were passionately concerned to ameliorate the lot of the growing numbers of alienated working men and women, together with their families, in a Germany that was rapidly becoming industrialized.

In consequence, as he put it at the end of his seven-year stint with the Westphalian Inner Mission, Niemöller had no difficulty in discovering a 'programme' under the inspiration of Wichern. Since Wichern had been concerned with those outside the churches, as well as with those inside them, part of that programme involved inspiring German Protestantism to become once again truly a people's church, a *Volkskirche*.

The task seemed all the more difficult because of the precarious relationship between church and state in the Weimar Republic. In the end (as Dr J. R. C. Wright concluded in his detailed study of the German Protestant church leadership between 1918 and 1933) the churches had every reason to be pleased with the settlement made between them and the secular authorities. Even the right of the churches to collect taxes remained virtually unmodified. But between 1919 and 1931 Pastors Reinhard Moeller and Hermann Kapler (successive presidents of the Berlin Oberkirchenrat) worked tirelessly and sometimes anxiously to preserve the independence of the churches whilst striving to reach an amicable agreement with the Republic. In this work new men like Niemöller and Wilhelm Zoellner had their part to play.

In Westphalia the Inner Mission had a particularly strong tradition of independent social action. There at the end of the nineteenth century, Freidrich von Bodelschwingh the elder had set up a system of social work in Bethel concerned especially to care for epileptics, and now directed by von Bodelschwingh's son,

Friedrich. Niemöller built up a friendship with Friedrich von Bodelschwingh that was to be particularly important in the earlier conflicts of the Protestant churches with Adolf Hitler. But in the late twenties Niemöller looked to the example of the Bethel sanatoria in putting the charitable works of the Inner Mission on a secure financial footing again, while making sure that they were not absorbed by the state welfare authorities which might deprive them of their individual Christian impulse. He succeeded.

Fortunately, inflation was at last abating, but the years of financial chaos had played havoc with the property of the Inner Mission, much of which was in disrepair. Niemöller founded a Protestant Savings Society which by 1931 had a capital of 15 million marks. Formed in 1927, it survived the economic disaster of 'Black Friday', 1929, when it was the only such society not to have to close its doors. Niemöller kept its finances entirely separate from any sort of state subsidy. He refused to allow it to lend money to private individuals, even though this was legally possible. The income was used to build new sanatoria, as well as to repair old ones.

The Weimar authorities were in fact unwilling to recognize the Inner Mission institutions as adequate to care for orphans and similar needy persons – which in its turn helped Niemöller and his like-minded colleagues to keep them independent of state subsidies. In truth, a good number of the sisters who worked for the Inner Mission were ill-trained – if trained at all. Fortunately, many of these were due for retirement. Niemöller set up a school to train new recruits in the rudiments of welfare work, and even taught there himself once or twice a week.

He also made his first entry into politics in these years. Partly he was inspired to do so for personal, family reasons. In 1927 his eldest daughter, Brigitte, started school, and Niemöller discovered the inadequacies of Protestant education in Catholic Münster. By the end of November 1929 he had been elected to the city council, as leader of a seven-man faction committed to Protestant welfare in the city, owing allegiance to no political party. Niemöller was wise enough to build up good relations with Catholic delegates who, like him, were anxious not to allow the socialist Republic to undermine their own educational institutions.

Yet none of this work made him entirely happy. Both he and Else had hoped that, 'after years of continual uneasiness and worry, uncertainty and constantly changing occupation, we should be able to devote ourselves to the peaceful and orderly work of a parish', he wrote. 'Now we were doing the very opposite thing: conferences, meetings, journeys and addresses, dealings with clergy and officials, organization and financial matters.' He acknowledged that he learned much from the work. Pastor Kähler's appointment as Bishop of Stettin had left a vacancy on the board of the Westphalian Inner Mission, and Niemöller was nominated in his place. There his influence was felt, and he learned the arts of committee work and tactical compromises; but, he wrote, 'I used to ask myself whether I would not have done better to have studied economics and law.'

He stuck it out for his promised seven years. He enormously expanded the work involved in his post. When he began, his office was a room in the Deaconesses' Institute in Münster. His staff consisted of a sixty-year-old, ready for retirement, and Fräulein Kuhtze, who could not spell properly but had been taken on because her father was a high-ranking official in the diocese. He left his department in 1931 with new offices of its own and a staff of ten.

In January of that year, in spite of Heinrich Niemöller's protests, he gave the Inner Mission six months' notice and began to look for a parish. He turned down an invitation to work as pastor in Essen. He would have accepted an offer to work in Bielefeld, when he discovered that the other pastor of the parish disliked him. Finally (partly because of work behind the scenes by his father, who had accepted Martin's determination to leave the Inner Mission), he was invited to become third pastor of the parish of Dahlem, one of the most fashionable suburbs of Berlin. Niemöller visited Berlin, found that he liked the two other pastors of Dahlem, and agreed to begin work there when his notice expired on 1 July 1931. Leaving their children in the care of Paula and Heinrich Niemöller, Martin and Else went on holiday.

'Dahlem', which means 'settlement on the mountain', had possessed a church certainly since the thirteenth century. St Anne's was visited by pilgrims in the later Middle Ages, and had been re-ordered and extended in 1420 and later. From the

Reformation onwards, the parish was dominated by the von Wilmersdorf family. Members of this family were pastors in Dahlem until the line ran out in 1770.

At the beginning of the twentieth century, the parish began to expand, helped by the building of the Berlin underground railway. Dahlem prospered, and St Anne's became rich. In 1926, with a Protestant population of 9,500 souls, Dahlem drew church taxes worth 403,628 marks. The ancient granite church was proving too small for its congregation, and in 1930 work began on building another – the Church of Jesus Christ – in the parish. Three years earlier the parishioners had built a new parish hall, capable of seating 400 persons in one large room and 100 in a smaller one. By 1931 Dahlem's population had risen to 12,000.

In the last week of June 1931 Martin and Else Niemöller and their six children moved into a pastor's house, number 20 on Pobbleskiallee, Dahlem. The parishioners had felt numerous enough to start their own parish magazine in 1924. It now carried a welcome to Niemöller, his wife and children from his new colleague Pastor Eberhard Röhricht, offering him God's blessing, friendship, and strength for his new work. On 28 June, with the fraternal presence of Herr Superintendent Diestel of Berlin, the parish met its new pastor. At 11.45 a.m. he introduced himself to the children. At one o'clock the whole congregation took lunch with him in the parish hall. It was an inspiring occasion, Niemöller recalled. None present, certainly not Niemöller himself, realized how soon meetings in that same parish hall would be occasions fraught with extreme political danger. The following evening, at another homely occasion to which the whole parish was invited, Martin Niemöller's other colleague, Pastor Gerhard, introduced him to the congregation over cups of tea. Having achieved his heart's desire, Martin Niemöller then set to work in what was to prove his one and only parish. (ZEKHN 62, Vol. 1064)

Dahlem, he recalled, contained 'very rich and cultivated parishioners, with, at the same time, the lowest class of workers from the Dahlem estate'. (MN/jb) These last lived in the cellars of the rich in a rigid hierarchy of servants. Niemöller set himself the task of visiting every one of them, rich and poor alike. Ten times a week he ran confirmation classes in the new parish hall, and soon he started fortnightly classes to strengthen the faith of any adult parishioners who might care to come. Although Niemöller was technically third of his colleagues, the pastors took the presidency of the parish in rotation. And after six months, the death of his senior colleague left him with greater responsibility. In 1932 Pastor Fritz Müller, son of the rector of Berlin and three years older than Niemöller, joined the team of clergy in Dahlem. Martin, in spite of his own recent arrival, was now acknowledged as leader of the three and he and his family moved into the large pastor's house, number 61 in Cecilienallee, adjoining the ancient church of St Anne.

In Berlin he soon made contact with other pastors besides his Dahlem colleagues Eberhardt Röhricht and Fritz Müller. One such was Gerhard Jacobi, a Christian of Jewish stock, a year older than Niemöller and now pastor at the Kaiser Wilhelm I Memorial church in the centre of the city. Another was Hermann Ehlers, whom Niemöller met through his work for the Berlin Bible study circle. This remarkable organization had been set up in the winter of 1883, along with a sister organization in Elberfeld. Niemöller therefore had youthful connections with the movement, which soon spread to other towns and cities of Germany. In Münster he had found time to work for the Bible study circle there. Now he became a leader of the group in Berlin, which enrolled at the beginning of the 1930s some 1,300 students. And as well as meeting influential Protestant colleagues and making friends with them, Niemöller was making a name for himself, in demand as a preacher and also a practised broadcaster.

There were two sides to Martin Niemöller's personality at this time. In spite of his obviously sincere yearning to be a simple pastor, he had also grown used to a bigger role. At the time of the abortive offer of a parish in Bielefeld, he had toyed with the idea of combining the work there with a continuation of his job at the Inner Mission.

And in spite of his commitment to the 'unpolitical' task of caring for the souls of his parishioners, Martin Niemöller was at this time a man of deep political passions. Fifteen years after the Armistice the ex-naval officer still bitterly resented Germany's humiliation at the hands of the allies. He despised both those who had unconditionally signed the peace treaty of Versailles and the 'socialist agitators' who made promises they could not possibly keep. He and his family had suffered anxiety and near starvation in part because of the impossible burden of reparations laid upon Germany by her conquerors. On the day he handed in his two theological theses in 1923, the French occupied part of the Ruhr, and he recorded the 'wave of resentment' and the 'growing spirit of opposition' which swept over the German people. 'Living as we did on the borders of the newly "Occupied Territory"', he noted, 'we felt it at first hand.' Nor did he scruple to keep his feelings to himself. At the 'theological week' at Bethel, when Professor Samuel Jäger hinted in a sermon that Germany might bear some responsibility for the outbreak of World War I, both Martin and Wilhelm Niemöller walked out. Martin looked upon democracy as contributing to fragmentation and excessive individuality. He yearned for the comradeship of war, and his nostalgia for the Kaiser was in part a longing for a lost symbol of national unity. He lectured students in Münster on honour and the Fatherland.

The men who had fought so bravely for Germany during the naval battles of World War I did not regard the German surrender in 1918 as the last word. Their determination to rise again was reinforced by their country's sufferings in the 1920s. 'We Germans are faced with a cruel fate', wrote Frigate Captain Georg von Hase in 1928. 'Our German youth will grow up in an enslaved Germany in which foreign powers are compelling us to work for them. We shall see how the Anglo-Saxon will look scornfully down on us. Even Frenchmen, Italians, and representatives of other races which are inferior to us intellectually, morally and physically, will pluck up courage to regard us Germans as brute barbarians, rightly punished for our crimes.' Hase, however, declared himself to be 'firmly convinced that our German youth will not allow all this to close its eyes to the truth'. In his view it was 'the duty of us elders to give young Germany the benefit of our advice and help in its approaching struggle'. With this aim in mind he wrote his memoirs of active service, just as Niemöller lectured and preached and wrote *From U-Boat to Pulpit.* When ten thousand French troops (together with African mercenaries) brutally revealed the extent of Germany's humiliation by occupying the Ruhr for over a year (incidentally throwing Niemöller out of work), they shot and killed one German resister, Albert Leo Schlageter, in Düsseldorf. The whole Niemöller family attended a great memorial service for Schlageter in Elberfeld town hall, and Martin and Wilhelm were pall-bearers as his coffin was carried in honour to the railway station on its way to his hometown.

Georg von Hase had been first gunnery officer on the battle-cruiser *Derfflinger*, which sank at Scapa Flow. Admiral von Reuter, who was responsible for that great act of defiance, wrote on a copy of his *Scapa Flow, Das Grab der deutschen Flotte* ('The Grave of the German Fleet') which is now in Eton College Macnaghten Library, the significant words, 'After Good Friday comes Easter'. (ECML) Niemöller belonged to that company who strongly believed in the resurrection of the German navy, and with the same religious intensity. One who, unlike Niemöller, had participated in surrendering a U-Boat to England, Leading Seaman O. Wehner, insisted that, 'never again should we have to face so shameful a voyage'. Wehner added that even the surrender of the High Sea Fleet had been a sign of German honour. On 2 November 1918 the whole fleet, battle-cruisers, cruisers, and destroyers, had passed his U-Boat in the small hours of the morning, steaming at 15 knots to Scapa Flow. 'We could not take our eyes off these proud, undefeated veterans of the sea', he recalled. 'As they gradually disappeared northwards, tears came into our eyes, for we were sure we should never see them again.' But Leading Seaman Wehner was convinced that a new Germany would arise. 'Our faith in the spirit of the German nation, that will guide it out of the pit of humiliation', he wrote, 'enables us to look with steady eyes to the future.'

Men of this stamp did not look to the democratic regime of Weimar for Germany's salvation, to the 'three hundred pacifist deputies in the Reichstag', as Ludwig Freiwald put it in his account of the last days of the German High Sea Fleet. Admiral Hopman, in the preface to his war diary, published in 1925, looked forward to the day when Germany would no longer be led by 'average men'.

In 1923 a possible saviour appeared. Adolf Hitler's National Socialist Party held its first national rally in January. In November Hitler's Putsch in Munich appeared to have been a complete disaster. Fourteen Nazis and four policemen were killed. Hitler and some of his accomplices were put in prison. The National Socialist Party was banned in Bavaria.

But Hitler had made his mark. Where other right-wing parties remained indecisive. Hitler had acted. He was now known throughout Germany, not just in Bavaria. To ex-soldiers, his credentials seemed impeccable. 'In 1923', Niemöller recalled, 'Hitler appeared as an ally of Ludendorff. We didn't know then that Ludendorff had broken with Hindenburg, and we looked upon Hindenburg as an honest follower of the Kaiser.' With hindsight, he added, 'All this was nonsense.' And, he explained, 'naval officers who were politically inclined felt themselves to be opposed to the state authorities [i.e., the revolutionaries] and behind their superiors', i.e. those who were attempting to take power as loyal officers of the Kaiser. (MN/jb)

In the 1924 *Landtag* elections, Niemöller voted National Socialist. In 1931 he was avidly reading Hitler's *Mein Kampf.* He voted National Socialist again in Spring 1933, the last free German elections of the decade. As Corvette Captain Karl Neureuther wrote in June of the following year, it seemed that 'the successes of our U-Boats had presaged the success of National Socialism, for already they decisively united the workers and the soldiers at the front'. And Ludwig Freiwald's laudatory biography of the U-Boat engineer Fritz Kasten ended with the picture of the Hitler youth, marching through the Brandenburg Gate, singing defiantly:

Raise high German toil, away with the Red Flag,
Bringing the light of freedom, the Swastika must triumph.
For a better time the men of Germany shall fight,
None of us shall rest, till Germany be free.

In these heady times Martin Niemöller, who had striven to keep the charitable work of the Inner Mission independent of the Weimar Republic, now sought the renewed alliance between the church and the German nation which men like Wichern and Wilhelm Zoellner had long desired. Bishop Zoellner longed for 'a Protestant church of the German nation'. In 1933 Niemöller told his Berlin congregation that the dream was coming true. 'Among many sections of our people the hope has sprung up that there will now be a new meeting between our nation and the Christian church, between our nation and God. And we hope from our hearts that through the movement which is at present developing in our church, obstacles will be swept away and the way made clear.'

He was to be tragically disappointed.

5. CHRISTIANITY UNDER THREAT

IN THE autumn of 1931 Martin Niemöller broadcast a 'Call for the Führer'. 'Where is the leader?' he asked. 'When will he come? Our seeking and willing, our calling and strivings fail to bring him. When he comes, he will come as a present, as a gift of God. Our call for a leader is a crying for compassion.'

The religious tone was entirely appropriate. As Albert Speer (Hitler's architect and later Minister for Munitions) came to realize, 'One major secret of dictatorships, from Stalin to Hitler, lies in their ability to provide moralistic dressing for coercion and so transform it into a satisfying experience.' In 1937 the Marxist philosopher Ernst Bloch wrote a satirical article on Hitler's 'piety', noting that the word 'Providence' was rarely far from his lips. Hitler managed to bring religion into militarism and the German quest for *Lebensraum*. 'If a man is not ready to fight for his existence', he declared, 'righteous Providence has already decreed his fate.'

Moreover, article 24 of the Nazi party programme, declared unalterable by Hitler in 1926, not only insisted on freedom for all religious denominations ('provided that they do not endanger the existence or offend the sense of decency and morality of the German race'); it also declared that the party stood for 'positive Christianity'. Hitler's *Reichstag* speech of 23 March 1933 reassured doubters by stating that the new government regarded both Catholics and Protestants as 'important factors in the preservation of our nationality', adding that the churches had their part to play in 'the task the government has set itself, namely the moral and ethical renewal of the German nation'. Small wonder if many were deceived, and not only inside Germany. In Britain the Archbishop of Canterbury himself professed a 'boundless admiration for the moral and ethical side of the National Socialist programme, with its clear-cut stand for religion and Christianity'.

Helmut Thielicke, a Christian who later came to oppose Hitler, has described how Hitler's apparent piety pulled the wool over the eyes of many in those years.

He made free use of the Christian vocabulary, talked about the blessing of the Almighty and the Christian confessions which would become pillars of the new State, he rang bells and pulled out all the organ stops. He assumed the earnestness of a man who is utterly weighed down by historic responsibility. He handed out pious stories to the press, especially the Church papers. It was reported, for example, that he showed his tattered Bible to some deaconesses and declared that he drew the strength for his great work from the Word of God. He was able to introduce a pietistic timbre into his voice which caused many religious people to welcome him as a man sent from God.

Because of all this, Thielicke concluded, 'one had to look very closely and read his terrible book *Mein Kampf* very carefully to see the cloven hoof beneath the angel's luminous robes'.

For many it seemed that a new age of piety had dawned. For Paul Althaus, for instance, the coming to power of Hitler was 'the hour of the church'. After so many years of anxiety, recalled Martin Niemöller, 'it was a kind of liberation when Hitler came'. (MN/jb) Hitler himself asserted that, 'Today Christians, not international atheists, stand at the head of Germany.'

Martin Niemöller's sermons at the beginning of 1933 leave no doubt not only of his hopes of the new regime but also that he was influenced by some of its doctrines. On the first Sunday in Lent he echoed point 24 of the Nazi party programme by asserting that the German nation had been built on 'the positive Christianity of the Lutherans and the Calvinists and the Catholics'. In this sermon Niemöller expounded the mystical nationalism that Hitler so brilliantly exploited. 'When our German nation became a nation', he said, 'God gave it as soul the Christian faith; . . . and from this Christianity of the German national soul have come all the forces which made our nation develop and grow.' By the time of his Harvest Thanksgiving sermon the following autumn, Niemöller had developed serious doubts about the direction being taken by the new Reich. None the less, he was still espousing Hitler's notions of 'race' and 'nationality', which, said Niemöller, 'make demands on us that we cannot escape'.

For Hitler, however, exaltation of the German nation had a viciously negative side – the denigration of other races, and in particular the Jews. *Mein Kampf* perversely denied that Judaism was a religion at all. 'The phrase "religious community" has been stolen from other non-Jewish religiously minded communities and is employed by the Jew for tactical reasons', Hitler wrote. 'Its purpose is to conceal his carefully laid and tenaciously pursued plans for world domination.' Jews were a people with definite and in Hitler's view inalienable racial characteristics. Since he held that a divine mission had been mediated through the German race and German 'blood', he insisted that Germans must do their utmost not to mingle their blood with Jews (or with the blood of any other of the races he held to be inferior). Here, as elsewhere in *Mein Kampf*, Hitler displayed a bizarre ability to mix religious phraseology, notions of the survival of the fittest and an extraordinary vulgarity:

There is one sacred human right, and this right is also a sacred obligation, namely to see to it that the blood remains pure, so that the preservation of the best of humanity will give to the species the possibility of a nobler stage of evolution. A pure German (*völkischer*) state will thus have as its first task the raising of marriage from its low state of being a permanent source of racial defilement and to consecrate it as an institution called to create images of the Lord and not monstrosities that are halfway between man and ape.

Niemöller by no means shared this fanatical racism. But he did recall fifty years later that the whole atmosphere of the first decade of the century in which he had come to maturity was anti-Semitic (an atmosphere only slightly changed by the fact that the Kaiser had a great many Jewish friends). (MN/jb)

Many Christians automatically condemned the Jews for the death of Jesus Christ. Some went further. In 1928 Niemöller's fellow pastor, Otto Dibelius, who was later to play his own courageous part in the church struggle against Hitler, declared, 'It cannot be denied that in all the manifestations of disintegration in modern civilization, Jewry has always played a leading role.' Martin Niemöller would not have shared views so extreme as this. But it was the common coinage of much of the Christian world that the Jews had played an extremely discreditable role in the early years of Christianity. In 1929 the Dahlem parish magazine carried an account of a performance by the Deutsches Theater of Franz Werfels of a play called 'Paul and the Jews', remarking that the 'truly tragic and apprehensive conflict' between Paul and his Jewish opponents arose because whereas Rome threatened the outer existence of the Jews, Christianity now threatened their very inner existence.

All this, offensive though it undoubtedly was to the Jewish people, was very far from *Mein Kampf*, with its descriptions of the Jew as germ, leech, devil, and symbol of all evil. Hitler's viciousness was the black side of the nationalistic pride which had sustained men like Niemöller after Germany's defeat – though this too could become tinged with a more or less harmless hint of racism. Freiherr Spiegel von und zu Peckelsheim, who had commanded U202, wrote after the war, 'British and Germans are cousins and should be friends'. Commander Georg von Hase wrote in 1928 that 'The Germans and the Anglo-Saxons ought in future never to forget that they are of the same stock, originally members of one and the same noble race.' And Paul Kagelmann added to his account of U-Boat minelaying in World War I the hope, 'may Fate forbid that in the future people of the sound, strong, chivalrous Germanic race, possessing such a high degree of culture, should be opposed to each other in murderous strife'. Kagelmann wrote this in 1935, and he added a sentence that reveals the baleful influence of Hitler's doctrine of the master race: 'I wish all Germanic people to realize that only by keeping their race pure and by mutual respect of their national commonwealth as a people can they live together in peace.' (ECML)

Niemöller's intense nationalism took him along this dangerous trail far enough for him to suggest in the 1930s that there were more Jews holding high office in the German liberal professions than their total numbers with respect to the rest of the population warranted. This was a prejudiced statement he later came much to regret. In spite of his undiminished pride in both his upbringing and his naval career, Niemöller admitted that both his early life in Elberfeld (where Jewish money-lenders were simultaneously utilized and resented) and his environment as a German naval officer had encouraged in him an undoubted anti-Semitism. Such feelings initially helped to blind him to the virulence of Adolf Hitler's views.

He soon began to change. Within a few months of Hitler's coming to power Martin Niemöller had emerged as a leading enemy of Hitler's most fanatical Christian supporters. Niemöller's warmth towards the ideologies of the new Führer was as nothing compared with that shown by other religious propagandists. As early as 1927 the Gauleiter of Thüringia, Artur Dinter, put forward the notion of a special 'Aryan' religion – a mixture of Christianity and German nationalism – which he hoped Hitler might officially adopt. Since Hitler wished to prove himself a friend to all sections of German opinion (in order to persuade the Bavarian authorities to rescind the ban on his party after the Munich *Putsch*), he expelled Dinter from the ranks of the National Socialists.

Either out of self-interest and ambition or out of genuine conviction, some Christians continued to support an amalgam of German nationalism (and even racism) and Christianity. As the times became increasingly propitious for the Nazis, these groups received more support from Hitler and his lieutenants. In January 1932 Wilhelm Kube, leader of the National Socialists in the Prussian *Landtag*, started a campaign to win over the leadership of the Prussian Protestant church at the synodical elections which were to take place the following autumn. His chief ally was Pastor Joachim Hossenfelder, of Christ Church, Berlin, who had been a member of the Nazi party since 1929. Hossenfelder set to work uniting the various right-wing factions of the Protestant church into one 'German Christian' movement. On 23 May 1932 he was officially commissioned by Gregor Strasser to organize election campaigns on behalf of the Nazis in all the regional Protestant churches.

Three days later the 'German Christians' published their first manifesto. It affirmed 'positive Christianity . . . in the Germanic spirit of Luther and heroic piety'. It recognized race, nation, and the German cultural inheritance as orders of existence given by God, a sacred trust to be stringently preserved from any racial miscegenation. The programme specifically condemned the work of the Inner Mission amongst Jews as 'a grave danger to our culture'. Any mission to Jews inside Germany was opposed 'so long as the Jews have a right to citizenship and there is in consequence a danger of bastardization and an obscuring of racial differences'. These 'German Christians' wanted specifically to prohibit marriage between Germans and Jews. They opposed 'the spirit of a Christian cosmopolitanism' which might threaten 'faith in our nation's God-given mission'. They looked for a unification of the separate German regional churches in one Protestant Reich church. 'We want', said the programme, 'a dynamic national church [*Volkskirche*], which expresses the living faith of our people.'

The 'German Christians' could draw on the support of a number of German Protestant theologians, some of them lightweight, like Professor Karl Fezer of Tübingen University, others far more substantial and distinguished, like Professor Emmanuel Hirsch of Göttingen and Professor Gerhard Kittel of Tübingen. Kittel, for example, had made himself an international reputation as editor of the *Theological Dictionary of the New Testament*, a superb work of scholarship, incorporating the biblical insights and discoveries of the previous fifty years. His own writings were distinguished from those of most other New Testament scholars by their emphasis on rabbinic studies, and he had once gone so far as to assert that every part of the ethical teaching of Jesus had its counterpart in Jewish literature.

In 1933, however, he seemed completely won over to Hitler. He welcomed National Socialism as a 'renewal movement based on a Christian moral foundation', an antidote to the decadence and immorality he had detected in the Weimar Republic. In a public lecture on the Jewish question, Kittel defended Hitler's anti-Semitism – now expressed in legislation against the Jews of Germany. He argued that the Scriptures teach a history of rejection, as well as forgiveness. By rejecting Jesus Christ, the Jews had themselves incurred rejection. More: Kittel argued that the Old Testament itself teaches that the mixture of races leads inevitably to decadence. He believed that the relatively pure Israelites of the Old Testament had been replaced by a racially-mixed world Jewry which, having threatened civilization at the time of Jesus, now threatened Germany. Then, as now, the enemy was the assimilated and emancipated Jew, along with all who supported him.

In *Mein Kampf*, Hitler had complained of the shallowness and lack of scholarly argument in much of the available anti-Semitic literature, and he repeated the complaint at the Nuremberg party convention of 1933. Kittel agreed with him: only those who were masters of the Jewish question ought to make pronouncements on it. He helped to make anti-Semitism respectable.

The struggle between those Christians who – for whatever reason – were prepared to support Hitler and those such as Niemöller whose consciences in the end made them draw back was not initially fought over anti-Semitism. Throughout the struggle very few saw that racism was an attack on humanity in general, a denial of the solidarity of the human race. At the beginning of 1933 few saw the Jewish question as the central problem of the Hitler regime.

What Niemöller and his allies did see in 1933 was initially a squalid bid for power in the German Protestant church by a group of people who were adulterating the Christian faith. Whatever distinguished (if perverse) support academics gave to 'German Christians', their attempt to take over the Old Prussian church with the help of Adolf Hitler was bound to cause a stiff reaction. The church leadership insisted that the forthcoming elections were and ought to be non-political. Although all Nazi party members were instructed to vote for 'German Christian' candidates (regardless of whether or not the voter went to church), the followers of Hossenfelder won only a third of the seats.

But they were ready to reap the benefit of Hitler's coming to power in January 1933. Hitler appointed Bernhard Rust minister of education for Prussia, and Rust appointed Hossenfelder as his adviser in matters pertaining to the church. The first National Assembly of 'German Christians' was held early in April, when Hossenfelder declared that his movement comprised 'the storm troopers of Jesus Christ'.

Hitler himself, however, was wary of Rust's impetuous adviser on religious affairs. On 25 April he nominated as his own special adviser another, less extreme 'German Christian', Ludwig Müller. 'He has', Hitler announced, 'a particular responsibility to promote in every way a German Protestant Reich church.'

Hitler had chosen his Protestant allies. Soon Niemöller would identify them as his enemies. Why did he turn against them? One curious fact is that these two 'German Christian' leaders, Joachim Hossenfelder and Ludwig Müller, possessed strikingly similar backgrounds to the man who would shortly emerge as their leading opponent. Seven years younger than Martin Niemöller, Hossenfelder had enlisted as a soldier in 1917. He too had fought and served in an extra-parliamentary *Freikorps* between 1919 and 1921. He had been ordained pastor in 1925. And Müller, who was military chaplain to the Königsberg when Hitler appointed him adviser in 1933, had been a naval chaplain throughout the war. All three had been drawn to Adolf Hitler before his electoral success. As early as 1927 Müller had promised Hitler that he would use all his strength to bring about a united German Protestant church.

As Westphalians Müller and Niemöller were fellow-countrymen. Niemöller had come across him as a naval chaplain and grown to despise him as an opportunist with few religious principles. 'He was very ambitious', Niemöller recalled, 'and extremely well-loved in the navy for making the garrison church at Wilmershaven into a First World War naval museum. Many welcomed the opportunity of visiting it', added Niemöller, sarcastically, 'not for an act of worship but to look at First World War remains.' (MN/jb)

And yet in spite of Niemöller's mockery of Ludwig Müller's spiritual coarseness, he was too much out of the same mould to find it easy to formulate his objections to 'German Christians'. The best religious argument for the 'German Christians' was that God can speak to mankind through his wonderful creation. In 'creation', in nature, in human beings themselves, we see his mighty hand and divine wisdom, partially concealed but visible to those with insight. Niemöller had been taught this theology at Münster by his friend Professor Georg Wehrung. What 'German Christian' theologians like Emmanuel Hirsch added was that the finest part of all God's creation could be recognized in such Hitlerite concepts as 'race', 'nation', and 'honour'.

In spite of his deep reverence for his nation and its honour, Niemöller's kind of Christianity forced him to question this. November 1933 was the 450th anniversary of the birth of Martin Luther. Luther had pointed to Scripture alone as the witness to God. The 'German Christians' were denying this uniqueness. Niemöller came under the influence of a revived Lutheranism, partly as a result of the coming 450th anniversary. He needed to affirm the uniqueness of the biblical witness. At the same time he longed to participate in the spiritual revival of Germany. Could these two aims be reconciled under Hitler?

In this perplexity he gained help from a group of Christians who began meeting in the house of his friend Gerhard Jacobi in 1932. In May 1933 they designated themselves as the 'Young Reformation Movement'. Although Karl Barth mocked the Young Reformation Movement as a middle-of-the-road compromise, offering on the one hand independence for the church and on the other a 'joyful yes to the new German state', those whom Niemöller met in Jacobi's Berlin home during these critical months gave him the support he needed to clarify and reorder his views. They included men whom he was to work with in the difficult years to come: Hanns Lilje (then secretary of the Student Christian Movement, and editor of the Young Reformation Movement's journal *Junge Kirche*); Walter Künneth (who ran the church's apologetical centre in Spandau); and the future martyr Dietrich Bonhoeffer.

Oddly enough, it was through Jacobi that Niemöller also came to know the worth of Barth. As a Swiss, this fierce, brilliant, independent, theologian had no truck whatsoever with German nationalism. As a Calvinist, his theology derived (Barth insisted) solely from the Word of God, and not from any word of men. Barth lumped Hitler with Nero, Diocletian, and Louis XIV as promoting an 'anti-God' movement by means of a new state-religion. The 'German Christians', Barth believed, grievously sinned by affirming 'the German nationhood, its history and its contemporary political situation, as a second source of divine revelation, and thereby betray themselves to be believers in "another God"'. When Gerhard Kittel told Barth he perceived the sovereign sway of God not only in the sacred history of Israel, but also in the sparrow on the rooftop, the lily in the field, in the history of the Greeks and the Palestinian zealots, in the Roman empire, and in Mussolini and Hitler, Barth suggested that the right-wing theologian ought also, then, to see the hand of God in the Bolshevik revolution! When Professor Karl Fezer asked Barth to agree to a memorandum that gave support to 'German Christian' teachings, Barth replied publicly, 'We have different beliefs, different spirits and a different God.' Many Germans were scandalized by Barth's comment.

Barth and Niemöller were soon on the way to cementing a firm and lasting friendship. On Niemöller's seventieth birthday, Barth described him, in naval terms, as 'a compass needle which, for all its mobility, infallibly pointed forwards in the direction of the gospel'. But in Berlin in 1933, Barth noted that he still had 'very little confidence' in his new friend. Niemöller's theology seemed dangerously close to compromise with what Barth was now passionately attacking. As Barth, in another naval turn of phrase, humorously told Helmut Gollwitzer, Niemöller should put his theology in a boat, sail out to sea, and sink it.

In fact, Niemöller was growing as anxious about the progress of the 'German Christians' as Barth, At the beginning of April 1933 he noted in his diary, 'The "German Christians" are coming to the fore. The prognosis is not happy.' And it was from the Young Reformation Movement, not the Swiss theologian, that a practical way of combating them offered itself.

Hermann Kapler, who had spend so many anxious hours as president of the Berlin *Oberkirchenrat* attempting to negotiate a reasonable settlement for the church with the Weimar Republic, now faced a new regime. Aided by Lutheran Bishop August Marahrens of Hanover and the Reformed Pastor Hermann Albert Hesse of Elberfeld, Kapler set himself and his two colleagues the task of working out a new church constitution that would be acceptable to the Hitler regime and the various German Protestant churches. The task was ultimately impossible.

Their chief problem arose over who should head the united German Reich church that Hitler was known to desire. This person would have powers hitherto unthought of in German Protestantism. Even so, the appointment of a 'Reich bishop' was advocated not solely by Hitler's allies, the 'German Christians'. Niemöller's old patron, Wilhelm Zoellner, was one who demanded a bishop as head of the church, instead of an ecclesiastical parliament, which he called the 'false adaptation to the democratic principle of Weimar'. The committee of three recommended, therefore, that a Lutheran Reich bishop be appointed, but he must share the direction of the church with a 'spiritual committee'.

The question now arose, who should be appointed to this office? Hitler's personal religious adviser, Ludwig Müller, let it be known that both the Führer and he himself considered that he, Müller, should take the post. The Young Reformation Movement, and Niemöller in particular, had other views. Believing neither in Weimar democracy nor in the subservice of the church to the state, they simultaneously supported with enthusiasm the call for a united *Volkskirche* – and this, it seemed, needed a Reich bishop. The Berlin leaders of the Movement (whose existence had only just been made public) demanded that such a bishop be appointed immediately.

In a second manifesto they insisted that his appointment must result 'neither from a popular democratic election, nor from a government appointment, but should be made solely by the church itself'. The Young Reformers added that the Reich bishop 'should be a pastor who enjoys the confidence of active, worshipping congregations'. The right person for such a high office, they suggested, was a man like Niemöller's former colleague at the Westphalian Inner Mission, the director of Bethel, Friedrich von Bodelschwingh.

On 22 May the committee of three met again in Berlin. There Pastor Hesse suggested that either Bishop Hans Meiser of Bavaria or Bishop Marahrens should take the post of Reich bishop. Marahrens and Hermann Kapler, however, threw their lot behind the Young Reformers' candidate, Bodelschwingh. Having made their support for Bodelschwingh public, they were extremely disturbed when the following day the 'German Christians' nominated Müller as a rival candidate.

Bodelschwingh had asked Martin Niemöller and the West-phalian Pastor Gerhard Stratenwerth to act as his 'adjutants' if he were either nominated or elected Reich bishop. On 26 May delegates from each regional Protestant church were to meet at Eisenach and now would have to choose between Bodelschwingh and Ludwig Müller. In the few days available Niemöller was intensely busy lobbying support for Bodelschwingh. On the first day of the Eisenach conference, Bishop Heinrich Rentdorff of Mecklenburg (a member of the National Socialist party since 1930) nominated Müller for Reich bishop. On a close vote, eleven church delegates voted for Müller, thirteen against. On a second vote, Bodelschwingh was elected by eleven votes to eight.

Müller had lost. Niemöller was now bound by his promise to Bodelschwingh to serve as his adjutant, should he be elected Reich bishop. 'I said I would serve him', recalled Niemöller, 'but it must be a service which did not hinder me from being pastor in my congregation at Dahlem, because I regarded that as being my main task and my real profession.' In truth Niemöller was far more committed to Bodelschwingh's candidacy and success than this undoubtedly honest recollection suggests. Bodelschwingh would not have reached Eisenach to be elected but for Niemöller. He carried his objections to the *Führerprinzip* to the point of extreme diffidence. 'If I had my way', he said, 'I would rather be called Reich deacon than Reich bishop.' When he learned of the divisions among the committee of three, he would have withdrawn from the election had not Niemöller passionately pressed him to continue.

In any case Niemöller's phenomenal energy made it perfectly possible for him to serve his Dahlem parishioners and act as Bodelschwingh's adjutant at the same time. He had already, in one-and-a-half years, visited all the homes in the parish. (MN/jb) He rose in time to run a confirmation class at 8 a.m. several times a week. At 9 a.m. a secretary would come to take letters, to be followed by a meeting before lunch and visits in the afternoons. His father once reported to the rest of the family seeing Martin with two telephones on his desk in the pastor's house. Into one he shouted, 'Yes', into the other, 'No'.

In saying 'Yes' to Bodelschwingh Martin Niemöller publicly declared himself for the first time concerning the church politics of the Third Reich. Passions were running high. In the foyer of the church meeting house at Eisenach, Niemöller had an open and heated argument with Bishop Hans Meiser of Bavaria, who had voted for Müller. Nor did Müller take his defeat well. In a broadcast on the evening following the election, he declared that the church delegates had not listened to the call of the hour. 'The solution they have proposed to us in the matter of the Reich bishop', he added, 'has nothing to do with the belief and hope and love now stirring among the hitherto apathetic millions.' Müller determined to reverse the result of the election. Hermann Kapler decided to resign as soon as possible.

First Müller let it be known that in Hitler's opinion events had taken a decidedly unacceptable turn – news reinforced when Hitler absolutely refused to receive Bodelschwingh. Next he obtained a legal opinion that the election at Eisenach had been irregularly conducted. Niemöller and his lieutenants set about rallying support for Bodelschwingh, fighting as they were against the Nazi propaganda machine, which could foster 'dissension' at will, and against an order banning the discussion of Protestant affairs. Müller alone was allowed to broadcast. The Young Reformation Movement tried to counter with cyclostyled news-sheets, and with parish meetings. Niemöller's colleagues Eberhard Röhricht and Fritz Müller flung themselves into the fray alongside him.

The next meeting of the leadership of the German Protestant churches was to be at Eisenach on 23 June. On 21 June Niemöller begged Bodelschwingh to stand firm. It was now, he believed, a question of asking who stood for the faith of the Reformation and who represented another creed. Should the church leadership now reject Bodelschwingh, he ought to offer himself as leader of those true Christians, who would be forced to secede from the ones who had taken up an alien faith. Whatever happened, Niemöller was certain that a struggle lay ahead: 'the last word will not be spoken at Eisenach'.

Bodelschwingh did not stand firm, nor did others in the Protestant church leadership. On 22 June Kapler resigned. Bernhard Rust (Hitler's minister of education for Prussia) took the opportunity of declaring a state of emergency. On Saturday 24 June he appointed a Wiesbaden magistrate named August Jäger as state commissar for the Protestant churches in Prussia, to 'put an end to the religious strife. A 'German Christian' himself, Jäger appointed 'German Christians' to almost every important office in the Prussian churches. Ludwig Müller was appointed head of the Old Prussian church and put in charge of the federal church offices. He instantly dismissed all his high-ranking church opponents.

On the Saturday of Jäger's appointment, Bodelschwingh resigned as Reich bishop. 'By the appointment of a state commissar for the Protestant churches in Prussia', he said, 'I have been deprived of the possibility of carrying out the task entrusted to me.' His position had been difficult from the start. At the Eisenach conference, Kapler had hoped to have his election ratified by a large majority, but even after Bodelschwingh was elected, Heinrich Rentdorff, along with Bishops Theophil Wurm of Württemberg and Simon Schöffel of Hamburg, still publicly refused to come over to his side.

As a Nazi, Rentdorff's behaviour is explicable. Bishop Schöffel, for his part, was newly-elected, on the wave of enthusiasm connected with the coming to power of Hitler. But Wurm was a person of different stamp, who was to show considerable courage in opposing Hitler. 'He was a hero', Martin Niemöller conceded. (MN/jb) But Wurm very much disliked what he called 'the false walling-off of theology from life', advocated by the Young Reformation Movement. And more important than this was his judgement on Bodelschwingh. The director of Bethel, he judged, lacked leadership qualities. (Wurm went so far as to say that his election as Reich bishop would mean 'the death of our church'.) He was right. Bodelschwingh was too weak for the job. His cautious temperament later even obstructed Martin Niemöller's attempts to force changes in Hitler's policies. As events shortly revealed, it was by no means necessary for him to resign so precipitately (after only four weeks in office) in 1933.

His adjutant Niemöller could now return to parish work. But for Niemöller the fight was not over. And some of the church officials dismissed by August Jäger were ready to fight back, including Otto Dibelius, General Superintendent of the Kurmark. Hossenfelder, Müller, and the new authorities ordered that the Sunday following their coup should be a day of rejoicing. In each congregation, they directed the pastors to read a proclamation offering thanks that the state now had assumed, 'in addition to all its tremendous tasks, the great load and burden of reorganizing the church'.

Otto Dibelius and his dismissed colleagues, on the other hand, recommended a service of atonement and prayer for the disgrace that had fallen on the churches. The Young Reformation Movement passed the message to all the Berlin congregations. Pastor Grossman of Steglitz was arrested by storm troopers for obeying Dibelius's recommendation. (This was the first arrest of the German church struggle.) And in the church of Jesus Christ in Dahlem, a new pattern of protest was forged in defence of the untainted Christian gospel and the liberty of the churches. As senior pastor, Niemöller read the recommendation of the new church authorities, followed by that of Otto Dibelius and his dismissed colleagues. Next he, Eberhard Röhricht and Fritz Müller read a selection of texts from Luther about the true relationship between the secular and the religious powers. Then, as the pastors began the words of the Christian creed, the whole congregation in an affirmation of the historic Christian faith, unprecedentedly joined in. They did the same as the final Lord's Prayer was being said. The struggle for Christian freedom was by no means over. And Martin Niemöller knew that he had his congregation behind him.

August Jäger, by contrast, seems to have offended most of those he came into contact with, even 'German Christians'. His techniques were brutal and high-handed. When he offered Kapler's old post of president of the Berlin *Oberkirchenrat* to the former vice-president, a lawyer and a National Socialist named Ernst Hundt, even Hundt declined, on the grounds that yet another lawyer (rather than a pastor) in the highest offices of the church would have been absurdly provocative. Jäger later was to set up the notorious 'church' of the Warthegau, where a German-speaking minority lived in occupied Poland. There he proceeded to abolish churches as such, allowing their continued existence only as private religious clubs. He was condemned to death for war crimes by a Polish court in 1948.

In 1933 he and his lieutenants proved far too aggressive to be accepted by the churches. Brownshirts marched into the offices of the churches. Jäger appointed commissars to take over the headquarters of the Inner Mission. He appointed Joachim Hossenfelder as Otto Dibelius's successor without even telling Dibelius.

Karl Barth's reaction was characteristically fierce. The day after Jäger's appointment he wrote his *Theological Existence today*, in which he roundly declared that 'This leadership principle is absolute rubbish'. He sent a copy to Hitler, with the explanation, 'This is a word to the German Protestant pastors. I am recommending that they should reflect on their special position and their particular work in the light of the most recent events in church politics.' So many copies were sold that a second edition came out on 8 July. By the time *Theological Existence today* was banned (less than a month after the Eisenach meeting) 37,000 copies were in print.

Hitler, perhaps, paid little attention to theological pamphlets from Swiss professors, but he deeply disliked a huge disturbance in the churches. And he was obliged to listen to the aged President Hindenburg, who was now receiving an enormous number of protests from the Protestant churchmen. Even Bodelschwingh was prevailed on to write a letter to Hindenburg. Martin Niemöller sent a circular to friendly pastors, urging them to write not only to Hindenburg but also to the minister of the interior (Wilhelm Frick) and to Bernhard Rust, the Prussian minister of education. He himself wrote to Hindenburg, signing his letter 'Former Captain-lieutenant Niemöller of UC67'. He told the aged president that the recent events could destroy the churches and severely shake the state.

On 29 June Hindenburg warned Hitler that he needed to check his more extreme supporters. Hitler by now was claiming ignorance of the activities of the 'German Christians'. He delegated to Frick the task of settling the problem. Frick accordingly sought the assistance of church leaders to co-operate with Ludwig Müller in drawing up and agreeing to a new constitutional arrangement with the state. Four Lutheran bishops, four 'German Christians', one member of the Young Reformation Movement and a representative of the church of the Old Prussian Union agreed to work not only with Müller but also with the odious Jäger in this task. Their final proposals did in fact give to the Reich bishop *more* powers than the constitution proposed by the former committee of three. Now he would be able to issue authoritative decrees without the concurrence of any 'spiritual committee'. Even Bishops Meiser and Schöffel considered this too much. But before the church leaders was the carrot of an end to Jäger's reforms, if only they could agree to a new constitution acceptable to the Reich. They stifled their doubts and approved the constitution, which became law on 14 July.

The opening sentence of the new constitution specifically connected the proposal for a united German Protestant church with the coming to power of Hitler. It read: 'At this time when Almighty God is letting our German people pass through a new historical era, the German Protestant churches unite in continuing and perfecting the unity brought about by the federation of German Protestant churches, by forming with one accord one German Protestant church.' The law promulgating the constitution ordered new church elections for 26 July, leaving men such as Niemöller no more than twelve days to organize themselves to take on their 'German Christian' opponents.

In exchange for this, the church leadership gained, if only temporarily, the freedom of the church again. This was the principal aim of Niemöller, Walter Künneth and the leaders of the Young Reformation Movement. They did not set themselves up against the new German regime in any way. A. S. Duncan-Jones, the British Dean of Chichester Cathedral, who was already taking care to make himself an expert in what was going on in the German churches, wrote that Niemöller 'was still a convinced supporter of National Socialism as far as the political position of Germany was concerned, but he had become a determined opponent of State interference in the affairs of the Church'. This was the stance of the Young Reformation Movement, set out in its first manifesto. 'The church must remain the church', joyfully affirming the new German state, committed 'irrevocably' to the German people, but fulfilling 'the commission given to her by God in complete freedom from all political influence'.

Even this marked a development in Niemöller's thinking. His sermon on the first Sunday in Lent, 1933, asserted as a fact 'that it is simply impossible for us today to accept the comfortable formula that politics have no place in the church'. Naïvely enough, he trusted to Hitler (influenced by Hindenburg) to preserve the church's independence. Hitler's *Reichstag* speech of 23 March had promised to respect the rights of the Christian denominations. In the opinion of Niemöller's old mentor Wilhelm Zoellner, in that speech Hitler once again had 'laid down the *magna carta* of the independence of church life'. What Niemöller was never foolish enough to believe was that spiritual renewal came from Adolf Hitler rather than Jesus Christ. On the third Sunday after Easter, 1933, he spoke of the returning spring, observing that, 'In Christendom, too, there are signs of a returning spring, other than that which the seasons bring us.' But, he warned, 'When I say that, I am not thinking of the lively and, to some extent, passionate interest with which the transforming of the Protestant church into a state church is today being pursued and carried out, but of the desire to become acquainted with Jesus, to get in touch with him and to be guided by him, which is again making itself felt.'

Just before the new constitution of the state church was approved by the *Reichstag*, Hitler acted to restore the freedom of the Protestants. On 12 July he telegraphed Hindenburg to say that negotiations had been concluded on the settlement of the Prussian church conflict in a manner satisfactory both to church and state. 'The internal freedom of the church, for which I am specially concerned', said Hitler's telegram, 'will doubtless be assured by the withdrawal of the commissars and assistant commissars of the state.' Two days later the commissars were dismissed. Dibelius and his colleagues were reinstated. Bodelschwingh had clearly given up too soon. August Jäger, however, managed to retain his post in the Prussian ministry of education.

Martin Niemöller soon perceived that the belief that Hitler treasured the freedom of the churches was an illusion. By 28 June 1936 he was observing (to a Frau Buddenbrook of Heiden) that since the destructive activities of Müller and Jäger, there had been no legitimate church leadership in Prussia. (ZEKHN 62, Vol. 1002) Nevertheless he now flung himself vigorously into the campaign for the new church elections. The Young Reformation Movement set up a list of candidates under the slogan 'Gospel and Church' to compete against the 'German Christian' candidates. Karl Barth would not support either list, since he believed that the Young Reformers went much too far in their support for Hitler's ideologies. 'For the sake of the freedom of the gospel, no-one can vote for these two lists', he judged. 'The "Gospel and Church" group is saying in secret what the "German Christians" are saying openly, loudly and uninterruptedly.' This was massively unfair. Niemöller campaigned for a church that would be 'grounded on the word of God and free from state control'. The 'German Christians', by contrast, relied heavily on state support in their campaign. Joachim Hossenfelder urged every Nazi Gauleiter to help them in the campaign. The National Socialist newspaper, *Völkischer Beobachter*, urged every party member to vote for them. August Jäger, with typical brutality, even ordered the Gestapo to raid the offices of the 'Gospel and Church' group and confiscate their election material.

Finally, Hitler himself came out into the open. On the eve of the election he broadcast on behalf of the 'German Christians'. Still supposedly supporting the freedom of the churches, he argued that in return the churches ought to support the state which guaranteed that freedom. Those who did not perceive the greatness of the political events of the hour would petrify and die. The only positive Christian forces in the state, he declared, were those 'marshalled in that section of the Protestant population which, taking their stand on the basis of the National Socialist state, were to be found in the "German Christians"'.

On the evening of this broadcast Niemöller was listening to the radio with Bishop Marahrens of Hanover in a little room in the Wilhelmstrasse in Berlin. To some extent the scales fell from his eyes. For one reason, Hitler, he knew, was by birth and upbringing a Roman Catholic. Niemöller was appalled that a person of his denomination – however nominal his beliefs – should interfere in a Protestant election. Roman Catholic or not, he later recalled, 'I was absolutely disgusted that a head of state should act in this way. From that moment onwards, I didn't believe that there would be any support for the autonomous existence of Protestant churches so long as Hitler had the say.' (MN/jb)

The results were, however, totally predictable. Hitler always drew more support from Protestant voters than from Catholics. In many areas, seeing where Hitler's preferences lay, no election was held at all, since no one opposed the 'German Christian' candidates. Where agreed lists were drawn up between the parties, the 'German Christians' took around 70 per cent of the seats. Where the election was fought, they generally won 75 per cent of the seats. Only in Westphalia was there a 'Gospel and Church' majority, of 55 per cent. And such had been the influence of Hitler and the National Socialist campaign for the 'German Christians' that, where elections did take place, voting was two or even four times heavier than usual. Hitler, it seemed, was winning the churches for himself.

On 4 August the senate of the Old Prussian church elected Ludwig Müller to Hermann Kapler's old post as president of the *Oberkirchenrat*, and gave him the title of bishop. At the beginning of September the first meeting of the synod of this church became known as the 'Brown Synod' because of the many Nazis wearing brownshirts who sat among the delegates. Niemöller, ostentatiously dressed in a grey suit, protested during the opening act of worship (along with Pastor Karl Lücking, an associate of his brother Wilhelm) at the introduction of worldly matters and techniques into the affairs of the church. The chairman of the 'Gospel and Church' minority in the synod, President Karl Koch, was shouted down as he attempted to make a similar protest during the proceedings, and at this Niemöller and the group left the meeting. Undeterred, the synod proceeded to introduce the *Führerprinzip* into church affairs by abolishing the office of general superintendent throughout the province and substituting in its place ten bishoprics. Joachim Hossenfelder was elected Bishop of Brandenburg. From this moment dated Martin

Niemöller's lifelong hatred of the title of bishop in the German churches.

He continued to fight for the freedom of the church, using the agency of the Young Reformation Movement, writing an article 'On the fundamental review of the situation of the church' which appeared in the journal *Junge Kirche* in November. Whereas Hitler's election broadcast for the 'German Christians' insisted that 'The strong state must welcome the chance to lend its support to those religious groupings which, for their part, can be useful to it', the 'Gospel and Church' election manifesto had declared, 'We fight for a *free church*. The church must be independent from the state and from the pressure of all political powers. It can only serve the German people as it should if it *declares the Word of God in complete freedom.*' Niemöller's article elaborated and defended this manifesto. Agreeing that the renewal of the German nation demanded a religious basis, he insisted that 'If the Protestant church wishes to understand properly its responsibility to the people and the Fatherland – and not to misunderstand it, as often happened during the War – then she must discover the humility and the courage to think on the Gospel given to her, to confine herself to it, and decisively renounce every erroneous teaching which undertakes to blur or deny the boundaries between the world and the church.' In this article Niemöller was openly rejecting some of his own past, as well as the teachings of the 'German Christians', the deliberate mixing of the gospel with German mythology, and the pretensions of the state. He was not renouncing the notion of a special mission of the Protestant churches to the German people, but the God-given gospel was, he maintained, the 'pre-requisite' of any discussion of this mission.

This was not, however, the whole problem. Niemöller's sometimes frenzied activities in the conflicts over the freedom of the church, over its new constitution, and over who should lead it were bound up with an issue of far greater human importance: the attitude of the Third Reich to the Jews.

6. JEWS AND CHRISTIANS

AT THE beginning of April 1933 the Nazis ordered a boycott of Jewish (or 'non-Aryan') shops and businesses. Placards in Jewish-owned shops urged Germans not to patronize them. Storm-troopers humiliated and maltreated Jews in the streets. On 7 April a law was passed to dismiss all state officials of 'non-Aryan' descent, unless they had served Germany before August 1914, or fought in the front line during World War I, or had lost either a father or a son in that same war. This was entirely acceptable to the 'German Christians', whose views were soon to be given a spurious theological undergirding by men like Emmanuel Hirsch and Gerhard Kittel. At the 'German Christian' mass rally in Berlin, anti-Semitic sentiments were rife, soon to be collected in the official report of the occasion, which Joachim Hossenfelder edited. Ludwig Müller, whose whole career depended on keeping Hitler's favour, was more than content to go along with these views, and when the Old Prussian senate made him a bishop on 4 August, took particular care to reassure the congregations that from now on they should be preached to only by men of their own race.

Some members of the academic world were all too willing to support Müller and Hossenfelder. Gerhard Kittel argued that Jews – converted or not – can avoid divine judgement neither by seeking assimilation into modern secular society nor by finding a land of their own. His solution was to bring assimilation to an end, to make mixed marriages illegal, and to set up a separate Jewish-Christian church for Jews converted to Christianity. He claimed to have no quarrel with individual Jews, only 'world Jewry'. But he admitted that some of his proposals would cause hardship, perhaps even complete mental breakdown, for some Jews. However, he pointed out, even rabbinic Judaism accepted that because of their failure to keep the law of Moses, the Jews had been designated universal strangers.

Martin Niemöller himself toyed with the notion that 'non-Aryan' Christians might set up their own separate congregations. It is important to realize two things about Niemöller's willingness to consider this idea. First, he was not contemplating joining

Kittel's camp. When he chaired a discussion of the whole subject in his parish hall on the evening of 29 April 1933, he raised the suggestion not of a separate church for 'non-Aryan' Christians but that independent Jewish-Christian congregations might be set up. These, if set up at all, would come about not as the result of any imposition by the state or by the church leadership, but as the free choice of the Jewish-Christians themselves. He was convinced (as he told Jürgen Schmidt in 1968) even in those early months of 1933 that neither the churches nor the state had the right to force such a church on unwilling 'non-Aryans'.

It is, secondly, important to realize that Martin Niemöller *was* prepared to contemplate such proposals. This makes all the more impressive his development as a defender of the Jews – a development that was not complete until the end of World War II.

Niemöller's hesitations and qualifications in 1933 reveal that what he had hitherto accepted almost unthinkingly about Jews was now being severely tested by the anti-Semitism of the Third Reich. His reading of the Acts of the Apostles had led him (and many other Christians at that time) to the conclusion that, as he said, 'the original strife between Jews and Christians arose not from the persecution of Jews by Christians but from the persecution of Christians by Jews'. (MN/jb)

For centuries Christian churches had dedicated the tenth Sunday after Trinity to remembering the destruction of the Jewish temple and the fate of the Jewish people. Niemöller habitually preached on this theme on the appointed day, introducing into his sermon such notions as that of the 'Wandering Jew', who has no home and cannot find peace. He spoke (in 1935) of 'a highly gifted people which produces idea after idea for the benefit of the world, but whatever it takes up changes into poison, and all that it ever reaps is contempt and hatred'. The reason, he explained, was not hard to find. The Jew was cursed for crucifying Jesus, and Jews since then have carried about with them 'as a fearsome burden the unforgiven blood-guilt of their fathers'.

The assumptions behind this thinking not only offered no practical guidance for coping with the Jewish question during the Third Reich but actually played into Hitler's hands.

In September 1933 the 'Brown Synod' accepted the law of 7

April and decreed that from henceforth it should apply to all who held office in the churches. This decree, henceforth known as the 'Aryan paragraph', ran: 'Anyone who is not of Aryan descent or who is married to a person of non-Aryan descent may not be appointed as a pastor or official. Pastors or officials of Aryan descent who marry non-Aryans are to be dismissed. The only exceptions are those laid down in the state law'.

Some of the church leaders present did not wish to apply the Aryan paragraph to those already in office. They were, however, willing to see it applied to any future appointments. On behalf of the 'Gospel and Church' group, President Koch tried to complain about the introduction into church affairs of secular legislation without any theological discussion; but he was shouted down. And – in one form or another – similar Aryan legislation was adopted by the other regional Protestant churches.

As a former senior official in the Inner Mission, Martin Niemöller was already well aware that the question of evangelizing Jews was a point of conflict between himself and the National Socialists. In 1931 the Inner Mission had argued, in an official volume widely circulated amongst the Protestant clergy, that it ought to continue its mission to the German Jews, in spite of Nazi objections. Niemöller's friendship with Dietrich Bonhoeffer in the Young Reformation Movement also helped to stiffen his resolve against the introduction of the Aryan paragraph into the church. After the defeat of the Young Reformers in the July church elections, Niemöller had suggested that the best counter-attack might be a confession of faith, to be presented to the whole church, designed to counteract the errors of the 'German Christians'. Bonhoeffer and others had gone into retreat with Bodelschwingh at Bethel in order to draw up such a confession. Bonhoeffer's own opposition to racism in the churches was reinforced by the views of some of the very few 'non-Aryan' Germans who had not only accepted Christianity but also become Protestant pastors. These included in particular Pastor Franz Hildebrandt and Pastor Hans Ehrenberg.

Dietrich Bonhoeffer wished to make the Bethel confession a powerfully biting document. 'It is becoming ever more evident to me', he told his grandmother, 'that we are to be given a great popular national church, whose nature cannot be reconciled with Christianity . . . The question is really: Christianity or Germanism? and the sooner the conflict is revealed in the clear light of day, the better.' Unfortunately, his draft of the confession was sent round to twenty so-called experts, who so emasculated it – especially the section on the Jewish question – that Bonhoeffer in the end refused to sign the final draft. One of his friends told Niemöller that Bonhoeffer was 'wholly opposed to publication in its present form'. Bodelschwingh characteristically tired of the effort to keep his group of collaborators together. Finally, Karl Lücking, Gerhard Stratenwerth and a few others persuaded Niemöller to bring the toothless document out in his own name, with the rider, 'Submitted for consideration by a group of Protestant theologians'.

There were, in fact, only a tiny number of Protestant pastors to whom the Aryan paragraph could apply. Leaving aside those married to 'non-Aryans', only twenty-three pastors were of Jewish extraction. But the issue raised very deep theological considerations. The Aryan paragraph essentially denied that any person could cease to be a Jew and become a Christian. The motive of the Inner Mission to Jews was nullified at a stroke. Baptism, as entry into the membership of the church, was rendered inferior to 'race'. Whatever Niemöller's personal feelings towards Jews, he was obliged by his very faith to attack the application of the Aryan paragraph to the officers of the church.

This led to a curious situation: the church's opposition to Hitler seemed ungenerously confined to defending its own members against anti-Semitic legislation, and not the Jewish people in general. The criticism could be levelled at Dietrich Bonhoeffer as well as at Martin Niemöller. At times, for both men, the question seemed more one of the independence of the church than the rights of man. 'The church cannot allow its actions towards its members to be prescribed by the state', wrote Bonhoeffer. 'The baptized Jew is a member of our church. Thus the Jewish problem is not the same for the church as it is for the state.' Was the implication that the *unbaptized* Jew could legitimately be victimized by the state?

In the context of the time, such a criticism appears unjust. On the so-called *Kristallnacht* of 9 November 1938, 119 synagogues in Germany were set on fire, 76 destroyed and 20,000 Jews arrested. Niemöller was by then in a concentration camp. 'It became clear only then', he recalled, 'that the Jews were to be eliminated not simply from the church but from human society.' In the early days of the church struggle it seemed only that the National Socialists were against the church as he and men like Bonhoeffer understood it. 'We acted', said Niemöller, 'as if we had only to sustain the church. Afterwards from the experience of those bygone years, we learned we had a responsibility for the whole nation.' (MN/jb)

On the evening of 6 September 1933 Bonhoeffer, Franz Hildebrandt, and several Berlin theological students, tacitly acknowledging Niemöller's increasing prominence in the opposition to the 'German Christians' and the Nazi legislation in the church, called on him in his Dahlem home. Their intention was to formulate further tactics against the Aryan paragraph. The three pastors drew up an uncompromising document, to be issued in the name of the two 'non-Aryans'. To Niemöller it seemed that the Aryan paragraph threatened to cut the Prussian Protestant church off from the rest of Christendom. The document declared that 'Anyone giving his consent to such a confession of faith thereby excludes himself from the fellowship of the church. We demand therefore that this law, which separates the Protestant church in Prussia from the rest of the Christian church, be immediately repealed.' Both Niemöller and Bonhoeffer hoped to collect a great many other signatories for the document. They were saddened to find that Bodelschwingh himself would not go along with the notion that those who supported the Aryan paragraph should be excluded from the church.

Aware at least that a new situation required some new answers, the Protestant church leaders had asked the theology faculties of the universities of Marburg and Erlangen if the Aryan paragraph was acceptable to Christians. Marburg replied 'No'. Erlangen equivocated, replying that there might be circumstances in which a Jewish-Christian pastor could not successfully minister. But no serving pastor, said Erlangen, should be dismissed.

At this moment Niemöller sided neither with Erlangen nor Marburg. 'The Jew who confesses Christ as being his Lord is certainly my brother', he judged, 'and I cannot deny him membership of the Christian congregation and the Christian church.' But he thought it wise that 'non-Aryan' pastors should work only in congregations 'where they would cause no offence'.

Gone, however, was the suggestion that Jewish-Christians should form their own churches. Niemöller recognized that, just as Germans for the most part are best served by German pastors, so (for example) in the mission field the aim should be to ordain converts who would eventually minister to their own people. But he now saw that this was not in any way a parallel to the situation of Jewish converts in Germany. 'The Christian Jew forfeits membership of his people, when he becomes a Christian', Niemöller wrote.

After many hesitations he published (in the same issue of *Junge Kirche* as contained his review of the church situation) his 'Propositions on the Aryan question in the church'. The German people, he still believed, had suffered much under the influence of the Jews. To champion their cause required 'real self-denial'. Yet champion their cause he did. Niemöller's rejection of the Aryan paragraph was absolute. Converted Jews must have access to every office in the Christian church. 'Contrary to what we may desire', he insisted, 'a fundamental stand is required of us, whether we find it agreeable or not.'

To shed the theological prejudices and presuppositions of one's family and forefathers is difficult. But Niemöller even managed to turn some of them to good effect, in defending his Jewish-Christian brethren. In 1935, on the tenth Sunday after Trinity, he preached again on the fate of the Jewish people. But he used the old theology to argue *against* any act of contemporary persecution. If God was in the process of judging the Jewish people, then that was enough. No one had the right to add his personal hatred to that judgement. 'There is no charter which would empower us to supplement God's curse with our hatred!'

'Even Cain received God's mark, that no one had the right to kill him', Niemöller preached. Jesus's command, 'Love your enemies', he added, 'leaves no room for exceptions.'

Niemöller's sermon of 1935 went even further in proclaiming his hostility to what was happening in Germany. If the Jews in crucifying Jesus had fallen from grace, the German people could easily suffer the same fate. It was far too simple to say that the Jews brought the Christ of God to the Cross, 'with an undertone of human and moral reproach, as though such a thing could not and dare not happen to a respectable people'. Niemöller, who had once been taken in by Hitler's profession of 'positive Christianity', now preached, 'quite harshly and sharply and bluntly that the Jewish people came to grief and was disgraced because of its positive Christianity!' Positive Christianity Niemöller now saw as the antithesis of the religion of Jesus. 'In the domain of religion', he explained, 'we consider anything to be *positive* which helps us to realize and stabilize our great aim of a united, strong and proud nation. Anything that does not serve that aim is of no interest to us; anything that opposes it must be eliminated.' But where did such beliefs leave Jesus Christ? Jesus preached on sin and forgiveness, repentance and grace. The crucified Saviour preached by the church sharply conflicted with the notion of Jesus as a moral hero devoted to the interests of the nation.

Niemöller's implication was clear: 'positive Christianity' was leading Germany astray. Two weeks later he returned to the same theme. The call for 'positive Christianity' was a call for 'a Christianity of life and action' which left to one side notions of sin, grace, faith, and justification. If the church would preach positive Christianity as the 'core of a national morality', then, Niemöller suggested, 'perhaps the words "state and church"', which do not properly harmonize today, would again sound somewhat like the old magic formula "throne and altar"', for which kings and priests alike had such a fondness in days gone by'. But, Niemöller concluded, such preaching was out of the question. The church could not pick and choose what it had to say, but could preach only Christ crucified, and the great doctrines derived from that.

In the same adroit way as Niemöller used the Jewish question to attack the so-called 'positive Christianity' of the National Socialists, so he used the example of the fate of the Jewish people to attack racialism itself. Did not the Jews of old insist 'We are of Abraham's seed and were never in bondage to any man', asked Niemöller. This same pride caused them to reject Jesus's call to repentance and faith. They saw no reason to repent. They were 'free, strong and proud men and belonged to a pure-blooded, race-conscious nation'. Again the implication of Niemöller's sermon was clear: the arrogance of 'pure-blooded, race-conscious' Germans was leading them to reject Jesus Christ.

In 1933, however, Niemöller needed to act decisively to defend not Jews in general but twenty-three Jewish Christian pastors threatened by the Aryan paragraph, along with those

Aryan pastors and church officials who had married 'non-Aryans'. Following the decision of the Prussian synod of 5 and 6 September that all these should be dismissed, the authorities asked pastors and their wives to submit evidence of Aryan descent. The Westphalian synod, with its small 'Gospel and Church' majority, urged refusal, and circulated every pastor saying this. And in Berlin three young pastors from the Mark, Eugen Weschke, Günther Jacob, and Herbert Goltzen, approached Niemöller and Gerhard Jacobi with the proposal that an emergency organization of pastors should be set up. At a meeting in Berlin sixty pastors immediately agreed to join such an organization.

When neither Fredrich von Bodelschwingh nor Bishop August Marahrens would accept the invitation to put themselves at the head of this emergency organization, Niemöller decided to take the lead. On 21 September he sent a circular letter to the 2,000 pastors throughout Germany whose addresses were on the mailing list of the Young Reformation Movement, inviting each of them to join a 'Pastors' Emergency League'.

His letter recounted some of the events of the previous months, beginning with the new constitution forced through by the majority at the recent Prussian synod and the dismissal of the General Superintendents the day after. He attacked the activities of the 'German Christians', who were refusing to allow unsympathetic congregations to use the central offices of the church and were harassing individual pastors. He added, sharply, that 'church "leaders" and authorities have, characteristically, capitulated to these endeavours'. There was, he wrote, 'a shameful faint-heartedness among many ministerial brethren'. Some pastors, 'although serious-minded men, have gone over even to the "German Christians", against their own better judgement and knowing this to be contrary to their ordination vow and a violation of their consciences'.

'*Because of this distress*', Niemöller continued, '*we have called into being an "Emergency League" of pastors, who have given one another their word in writing that they will be bound in their preaching to the Holy Scriptures and the Reformation confessions alone . . . and that they will, to the best of their ability, alleviate the distress of those brethren who have to suffer for this.*'

The aim, said Niemöller, was to set up such an organization in every church province, but bound to each other. 'Otherwise', he wrote, 'one province will be "cleaned up" after another.' It was essential, too, to mobilize the laity. Niemöller confessed himself to be 'well aware that this League will neither redeem the church nor shake the world'. But he insisted that any 'prudent retreat to the role of a mere spectator' amounted to a betrayal of those under stress, who desperately needed an assurance of brotherly solidarity. Niemöller was able to inform the pastors to whom he sent his letter that preliminary enquiries had already recruited about 1,300 pastors to the Emergency League – not counting members of the Westphalian synod, which had set up its own organization, and even though he had still to reach the whole membership of the Young Reformation Movement.

He ended his letter with the words, 'So let us act!' and then added the four pledges which each member would sign. These committed members to:

1. sole allegiance to the authority of the Holy Scriptures and the Reformation confessions as correctly interpreting the Scriptures;
2. a determination to protest against any violation of this confessional stance;
3. recognition of their responsibility to do everything possible for those persecuted because of this confessional stance;
4. a testimony that, with the application of the Aryan paragraph to the realm of the church, this confessional stance had already been violated.

By the end of September 2,300 pastors had signed the pledges. By the end of the year the membership of the Pastors' Emergency League was 6,000, and by 15 January 1934 the number had grown to 7,036 (out of a total of 18,000 German Protestant pastors). Niemöller had laid the foundation of the church's opposition to Hitler. On 20 October the leaders of the League met in Niemöller's Dahlem home and set up a central organization, the Council of Brethren, consisting of eight members. Small advisory groups of specialists were planned. The organization proved strong enough to survive Niemöller's arrest and imprisonment, and until the end of the Second World War managed to collect subscriptions and support persecuted pastors. Its initial act was to make a vigorous impact on the first national synod of the new Reich Church, held at Wittenberg on

27 September. By now Niemöller had learned the importance of taking the initiative, and not simply reacting to what his opponents did. On 24 September, in a boat on the Wannsee, he, Else Niemöller, and Pastor Fritz Müller, drew up an initial statement protesting against the Aryan paragraph and the ruthless suppression of minority opinion in the church's councils. The following day Müller, Jacobi, Dietrich Bonhoeffer, and Franz Hildebrandt joined Niemöller in elaborating and finalizing the document. Copies of the final draft arrived from the printer on the eve of the national synod, and Müller and Niemöller took them by car to Wittenberg, to be nailed to trees and distributed to delegates. Signed by twenty-two Berlin pastors in the name of the 2,000 who had already pledged themselves to the Pastors' Emergency League, the document protested against those who would fetter the preaching of the gospel, and declared, 'We shall not cease to work for the development of the German Protestant church in faithfulness to our ordination vows.'

The Wittenberg synod elected Ludwig Müller Reich bishop. The supposedly independent 'spiritual committee' which was to advise him, included (in its four members) Joachim Hossenfelder and Bishop Simon Schöffel. But the synod did not reaffirm the Aryan paragraph, even though it made no condemnation of those synods which had affirmed it.

This apparent concession was not due solely to Niemöller's vigorous campaign. The events in the German church were also causing concern abroad. Archbishop Erling Eidem of Sweden had publicly stated that if the national synod adopted the Aryan paragraph, he and his church would cut themselves off from the German Protestant church. The German foreign office took the unusual step of writing to Ludwig Müller on 22 September, advising the forthcoming synod not to adopt the paragraph, since there were other, less public means of achieving its aims.

When the synod was over, foreign churchmen kept up this pressure. On 23 October Bishop George Bell of Chichester wrote to Müller expressing his concern at the proposals to deprive 'non-Aryan' Christians of their offices. He asked the Reich bishop to outlaw such discrimination. And on 31 October, at the request of the American embassy, Hitler himself received the general secretary of the Federal Council of the Churches of Christ in America, the Revd Charles S. Macfarland. Macfarland reinforced

Archbishop's Eidem's views on the effects of the adoption of the Aryan paragraph. Its imposition, he asserted, would cut the German Protestant church off not only from churches in the United States but also from the whole world.

Bell's letter to Müller observed that, 'The suppression and silencing of men whose views conflict with the opinions of the group at present in power is a cause of great concern to all Christians who believe in upholding the freedom to preach God's word.' A determined effort was now being made to suppress the opinions of Niemöller himself. 'Since I founded the Pastors' Emergency League in September 1933', he said, 'I was aware that the Gestapo always had an agent of some kind at my services. Every step I took outside my house and every word I spoke was being reported.' On Saturday 11 November the Prussian church authorities notified him and two other leaders of the League (Pastors Kurt Scharf and Eitel-Friedrich von Rabenau) that they were suspended from office. This suspension was cancelled on the same day, apparently on the orders of the Reich Chancellery, but it was replaced the following Tuesday by notices of dismissal.

The intervening Sunday was the 450th anniversary of the birth of Martin Luther, whose 'heroic spirit' the 'German Christians' were now claiming as their own. Martin Niemöller welcomed this '1933 picture of Luther, which represents him as a fighter', as being 'in complete harmony with the present situation', since, said Niemöller, battle-lines were indeed being drawn up, between Christianity and 'German-Teutonic piety', between Christ and 'the neo-paganism of today'.

Many, he told his Dahlem congregation, were talking and writing about what they called the 'Luther spirit'. Behind all this talk and writing Niemöller detected a deep respect for the impressive human qualities of Luther, 'for his naïve unconcern, for his intrepid courage, for his tenacious steadfastness, for his straightforward and unflinching will, for his profound tenderness'. Behind all this too, Niemöller detected an unfulfilled desire: 'If only we had more of this Luther spirit', they were saying, 'the outlook for our nation and our church would be better! Let us cultivate this Luther spirit today, and tomorrow it will be seen that we are a step farther forward!' This, said Niemöller, was a pernicious error.

The struggle between Christianity and neo-paganism, Niemöller warned, could never be won with that spirit, for it substituted the human hero, Martin Luther, for the message God sent through him. It was as if the devil had been waiting for the 450th anniversary of Luther's birth in order to fill the minds of German Protestants with the delusion that they needed not the grace and forgiveness of God but the courage of Martin Luther. If so, Niemöller offered the paradox that the same Luther who put the candle of the gospel back into the candlestick would become the bushel under which the light is hid and finally extinguished.

Luther too had preached that salvation came not from any good works men or women did on earth, but solely from the goodness of God. Again, in 1933, that message was needed, said Niemöller, for once again the German nation was being told to seek salvation in works. 'One can even hear', said Niemöller 'that our whole nation would do the will of God if only it had purified its species and its race: deeds of the law, on which to base a claim to God's favour!' That too, Niemöller told his congregation, was the devil leading astray the German nation. And against that the real Luther would have protested.

This was certainly not the Luther preached by the 'German Christians'. A Nazi party circular, printed in the journal *Christliche Welt* in April 1932, had given permission for setting up a National Socialist church party, on the basis of 'positive Christianity in the spirit of Martin Luther'. This, the circular observed, meant the adoption of a warlike spirit and stringent laws to preserve the German race. It meant the rejection of Jewish-Marxism, along with humanitarianism, pacifism, and Christian cosmopolitanism.

'The church which celebrates the Reformation cannot leave our ancient Luther in peace', Dietrich Bonhoeffer lamented in the pulpit of the Kaiser Wilhelm Memorial Church in Berlin, 'for he is called in to support all the fearful practices which go on in our church today.' But others (such as Pastor Hesse of the committee of three that drew up the new church constitution in 1933) derived much pleasure from the absurd supposition that Reich bishop Müller, as Hitler's personal spiritual adviser, was drawing the Führer from Roman Catholicism to a careful reading of Luther.

Preaching on Reformation Sunday 1933, Niemöller deliberately set himself against this image of the Luther who supported nationalism and racism. 'There is absolutely no sense in talking of Luther and celebrating Luther's memory within the Protestant church', he insisted, 'if we stop at Luther's image and do not look at Him to whom Luther is pointing.' But that person, Niemöller reminded his congregation, was a Jew. 'Luther as a German seems to be nearer to us than the Jewish rabbi of Nazareth', said Niemöller. 'Luther with all his corners and edges seems less offensive to us than this Jesus.' But, he reminded his hearers, had not President Hindenburg told Reich bishop Müller, 'See that Christ is preached in Germany'. To say, as many did, 'If you are as much a nationalist . . . as our *Führer* desires, you are a Christian without knowing it', was to fail to preach Christ. But this nationalism, combined with Hitler's virulent racism, was precisely what some of the 'German Christians' were now proclaiming.

On 13 November over 20,000 'German Christians', mostly drawn from Brandenburg, came together for a mammoth demonstration at the Berlin Sports Palace. Joachim Hossenfelder presided, dressed in Nazi uniform. After the parade of flags, opening fanfare of trumpets, and the singing of 'Now thank we all our God', he announced that he had given orders to put the Aryan paragraph into effect in his diocese. He also announced the suspension of Niemöller, Scharf, and von Rabenau, whose activities, he said, were entirely foreign to the true spirit of Germany.

The main speaker of the evening was a senior Nazi official, Dr Reinhold Krause. Krause was leader of the Berlin 'German Christians' and a member of the Brandenburg church synod. The rally, he said, had been called 'to rekindle the fighting spirit of the movement and to place again in the forefront the original goals of the "German Christians"'. The ultimate aim was nothing less than the consummation of Luther's Reformation by the creation of a single German *Volkskirche*. This could be achieved, he said, only if everything that displayed a 'spirit foreign to our ears' were removed, 'be it every so ancient or apparently venerable.' From now on, for instance, 'holy places' should be sought not in Palestine, but in the Fatherland. Non-German elements should be eliminated from the worship of the church. This meant, said Krause, 'liberation from the Old Testament, with its Jewish money morality and its stories of cattle-dealers and pimps'. The New Testament, too, needed purging of its Jewish elements, especially the unheroic theology of the Rabbi Paul with his 'inferiority complex'. Even the crucifixion appeared in some respects unwholesome to Dr Krause. And just as Jewish elements needed purging from the Bible, so, argued Krause, they must be purged from the German church. 'If we Nazis are ashamed to buy a necktie from [a] Jew', he pronounced, 'we should be absolutely ashamed to take the deepest elements of our religion from the Jew.'

Krause's speech was again and again interrupted by applause. At the end of the meeting, resolutions were passed in support of his demands. Not only were the enactment of the Aryan paragraph and the setting up of a separate Jewish-Christian church demanded. The Sports Palace rally also resolved on the expulsion of all pastors who were unwilling to co-operate in fulfilling the Reformation by bringing about the new church in the spirit of National Socialism.

The rally was widely reported in the foreign as well as the German press. 'German Christian' leaders reacted enthusiastically. In the province of Saxony, for instance, Bishop Friedrich Peter in his diocesan newsletter for mid-November wrote that the German nation must now 'find the source of its strength in a positive Christianity, appropriate to our people, which was, is and shall be the basis of the National Socialist party and must also be the foundation of the Third Reich of Adolf Hitler'.

The leaders of the Pastors' Emergency League reacted differently. The day after the Sports Palace meeting Martin and Wilhelm Niemöller, along with Pastor Gerhard Jacobi, called on Reich bishop Müller, who had not stayed for most of the Sports Palace rally. Müller was not a good theologian. 'When I met him in Berlin in July 1933', wrote the Dean of Chichester, 'I got the impression of a man who, though undoubtedly sincerely religious, was without any theological acumen.' None the less, Müller was bright enough to see that Krause's views on the Bible were deeply objectionable. Krause's speech and the Sports Palace resolutions were bound to produce an outcry, both in the German churches and abroad. 'Ludwig Müller was very much terrified', Niemöller recalled. 'We put to him the ultimatum: you have to resign as president of the "German Christians" immediately, within twenty-four hours.' They also insisted that he dismiss those church officers responsible for the Sports Palace meeting, as well as those who had not protested against the resolutions. (MN/jb)

The following day Müller dismissed Krause from all his church posts. He resigned as president of the 'German Christians'. He issued a statement condemning Krause's attack on the Holy Scriptures, insisting that all congregations were bound by the Bible and the Reformation. The Aryan paragraph, he declared, was no longer in force. The demands made at the Sports Palace meeting, he declared, were 'nothing other than an intolerable attack on the church's beliefs.'

'That was the end of the "German Christians" practically', recalled Martin Niemöller, 'because they broke asunder in many parts.' (MN/jb) Even in Saxony Bishop Friedrich Peter changed their name to 'The People's Missionary Movement (German Christian)'. Some of their prominent theologians, including Karl Fezer and Gerhard Kittel, decided they could no longer publicly support a group which permitted such a blatant attack on the Holy Scriptures.

Müller did not, however, dismiss Hossenfelder (who, it was now being reported, had left the Sports Palace before Krause's speech). What is more, he ratified Hossenfelder's choice of another 'German Christian' to replace Reinhold Krause. Accordingly, the Pastors' Emergency League pressed on which its attack. On Saturday 18 November a crowded meeting in Westphalia demanded the right to preach the gospel as it was contained in the Scriptures and the Reformation confessions. The following day the 3,000 pastors who had already joined the Pastors' Emergency League read from their pulpits a defence of the gospel against the 'paganism' preached at the Sports Palace rally. 'We refuse to earn the reproach of being dumb dogs', the proclamation read. 'We owe it to our congregations and the church to resist the falsification of the gospel. We emphatically recognize the Holy Scripture of the Old and New Testaments as the unique test of our faith and life, and the confessions of our Reformation fathers as the explanation of Scripture.'

Seeing the dissension aroused by the 'German Christian' rally, the government, through official statements by the minister of the interior and by Wilhelm Kube, now began to distance itself from its former 'spiritual wing'. Bishop Schöffel resigned from the 'spiritual committee' on which he served with Hossen-felder. Hossenfelder also came under attack from church leaders in Bavaria, Württemberg, Hanover, Thüringia, Olden-burg, Hamburg, and Euten. Müller made an attempt to shore up the bishop's waning prestige by declaring, 'Hossenfelder and I are inseparable'; but the attempt was useless. Hossenfelder resigned first from the 'spiritual committee' and then, on 21 December, after another attack by the Pastors' Emergency League, from all his church offices, including the bishopric of Brandenburg.

During all this activity, Niemöller was also fighting to reverse his notice of suspension. Fortunately, he had the support of his congregation, whose church council included, he recalled, only two Nazis. 'I told them that I had been deposed as a pastor, but I was willing, if they agreed, to continue', he said. 'And they agreed.' (MN/jb) On the day of the Sports Palace meeting the three dismissed pastors had met in the home of Gerhard Jacobi and sent a telegram to the church authorities claiming that their dismissal was illegal. The following day representatives of some of the Lutheran bishops offered their support, as did Friedrich von Bodelschwingh. Niemöller, Scharf, and Rabenau continued to protest vigorously to the church authorities, including the harassed Ludwig Müller, and on 16 November Bodelschwingh even secured an interview with President Hindenburg – at which the president said he recognized Niemöller's 'military compe-tence and bravery'.

Such a reputation still carried weight. At the end of November the *Kölnische Zeitung* published a long open letter from a member of the Pastors' Emergency League, Pastor Heinrich Held of Essen, which, in the course of an attack on the rural administrator, Dr Krummacher, for supporting the 'German Christians', praised Niemöller as the leader in the struggle. The *Kölnische Zeitung* added a paragraph on Niemöller's war record, along with the observation that Pastor Gerhard Wilde of Sozenhagen – who had been suspended the previous Sunday and whose home had been raided by storm troopers – had been an officer in Flanders and had spent three years in a French prisoner-of-war camp. The newspaper declared that Niemöller and Wilde were men of the war generation now standing up as stoutly for their faith as they had for their Fatherland.

Niemöller longed for a united German nation quite as passionately as did the 'German Christians'. But he perceived that their doctrines, far from unifying the nation, were divisive. 'Today we like to talk optimistically of the new fellowship of the nation', he said as early as the fifth Sunday after Easter, 1933, 'but it is becoming more and more evident that even this new fellowship is constituted in such a way that at the same time it divides.' On this occasion he took up the Pauline command to love *all* men. It was, he preached, 'more important than ever to pray for all – that a Nazi storm trooper, shot and crippled, should pray for his enemies ... And *vice versa* that an official who has been dismissed because of his origin should pray for the men of the national government.'

Niemöller did not regard the doctrines of the church simply as some sort of moral underpinning of the ideals of the new German Reich. In consequence, he soon ceased 'to interpret the call for the church, which is today being heard on all sides, simply as a sign of reviving faith'. The call, in his view, must be followed by a willingness to listen, in the hope of hearing God's answer. 'But this much is clear', he added: 'God's answer will in every case prove irksome; it will in every case reduce our passions to naught; and then and only then will it be possible to decide whether this whole movement is a movement of faith towards God or whether it will turn away from Him in vexation.' The 'German Christian' movement, he believed, had turned away.

Yet he preferred as long as possible to give the new church authorities the benefit of the doubt. Those pressing for a widespread reconstruction of the Protestant church, he said, were 'animated by an honest purpose and by an enthusiasm which is contagious and irresistible'. He also, like many others, made a distinction between Adolf Hitler and some of the unpleasant things done by others in his name. Niemöller had sought a Führer too long to become easily disillusioned with Hitler. So, along with many others, he assumed that Hitler was not responsible for the behaviour of men like Ludwig Müller and August Jäger.

Hitler, too, seemed at last to be succeeding in giving Germany new honour in the world. At the League of Nations Hitler demanded equality of status for Germany, and when this was denied, announced that Germany had left that organization. Niemöller joined with several other leaders of the Pastors'

Emergency League in sending Hitler a telegram of delighted congratulations.

This scandalized both Dietrich Bonhoeffer, who had taken a post with a German congregation in London, and the recently ordained 'non-Aryan' Pastor Franz Hildebrandt. Because of this telegram, Hildebrandt turned down a post in the Pastors' Emergency League and decided to join Bonhoeffer in London instead. He wrote to Niemöller, observing, 'I find it impossible to understand how you can joyfully welcome the political move in Geneva when you yourselves refuse to adopt an unequivocal attitude toward a church which persistently denies us equality of status.'

Hildebrandt remained friends with Niemöller and in fact returned the following year to become his curate in Dahlem. But for a time there was a cleavage between this younger generation and the ex-submariner. Niemöller would have agreed with the sentiment of his old submarine colleague, Corvette Captain Max Valentiner, who had come to live in Niemöller's parish and whose children Niemöller baptized: 'A country that is not willing to take the most necessary precautions for its own defence will never have power in this world either morally or materially.' (ECMN) In opposing the 'German Christians', Niemöller did not cease to become a German. Their misunderstanding, he believed, lay in saying 'first we are Germans and secondly we are Christians too', whereas the proper stance of a German Protestant was to reverse the order, 'saying we are Christians and we are Germans too.' (MN/jb)

Not surprisingly, this stance could be misunderstood. As late as the end of April 1934 Dietrich Bonhoeffer could write in irritation that, 'Ingenious visionaries like Niemöller still go on thinking that they are the true National Socialists.' Bonhoeffer was at that time out of danger in London, and he had the intelligence to add that in the circumstances of Hitler's Germany such a stance might even be useful: 'it may indeed be Providence that has fostered their illusion, and this might even be in the interests of the church struggle.'

Bonhoeffer and Hildebrandt bombarded Niemöller with advice from London. After Hossenfelder resigned from the 'spiritual committee', some of the German bishops entered into fresh negotiations with Müller. Niemöller refused to take part.

The two pastors wrote him a nautical letter from London, fearing lest he was giving up the struggle. 'We should have liked to pick up the telephone again in order to fling ourselves on you in a brotherly way, to implore you with all the power of our youth not to hand over the navigation of the ship in this decisive moment to people who will certainly revert to an indecisive course and return the wheel to you only when it is too late.' Four days later they learned of a difference of opinion in the Council of Brethren and this time sent a telegram to Niemöller, expressing their dismay at the news that Jacobi had apparently left the Council and threatening that they would resign unless he were reinstated.

In spite of such messages, at the end of 1933 Niemöller – though still under notice of dismissal – had the right to feel some satisfaction at the success of the fight. 1933 had been a turbulent year. Looking back at the new men, new offices, new laws, and new ordinances that had appeared, Niemöller observed, 'In truth, our church has been thoroughly shaken out of its self-satisfied and meditative calm as never before since the days of the Reformation.' But on 8 December Ludwig Müller at last replied to Bishop George Bell's letter with the information that the Aryan paragraph had been set aside.

But, the Dean of Chichester observed, by now Ludwig Müller was being nicknamed 'lying' [Lügen] Müller. On 4 January 1934 he announced that the Aryan paragraph was in force again.

7. FACE TO FACE WITH HITLER

'THE FRONTS become clear, and that is all we want', Dietrich Bonhoeffer wrote from England at the beginning of 1934. 'Müller must be done away with and with him his bishops, and what seems most important of all – the new court-theologians.' Not content with re-enacting the Aryan paragraph, Reich bishop Ludwig Müller had now decided to stop any churchman even discussing his controversial behaviour in public. In the past month he had secretly concluded a treaty with the leader of the Hitler Youth Movement, Baldur von Schirach, virtually handing over complete control of the church's youth work to the Nazis. When this became public, Bishops Wurm and Meiser, as well as Niemöller's Pastors' Emergency League, joined in angry protest. Undeterred, on 4 January Müller appointed Pastor Zahn of Aachen Youth Pastor for the whole German Protestant church. Zahn immediately denounced the unrest in the church, adding the provocative observation that, 'The church knows that the future lies with the German who is a National Socialist.'

In an apparent concession to the leaders of the churches, whom he met for a day at Halle, Müller had promised soon to set up a new 'spiritual committee'. This conciliatory appearance was illusory. On 4 January, stating that 'the controversies about church politics are destroying the peace and holding back the unification of the church', Müller published the so-called 'Muzzling Decree' issued, as he put it, 'in responsible exercise of my office as Führer of the church'.

The Muzzling Decree declared:

1. The services of the church are for proclaiming the pure gospel, and for nothing else. Misuse of church services for controversies about church politics must cease. The loan or use of churches or other church premises for any sort of meeting concerned with church politics is forbidden.
2. Any officer of the church who circulates publications, especially pamphlets and circulars, directed against the church leadership or its constitution, or in any way publicly attacks them, departs from his legitimate duties.
3. Any church officer contravening paragraphs 1 and 2 will be

automatically suspended, and proceedings will be begun immediately to dismiss him.

To Niemöller the Muzzling Decree of 4 January 1934 threatened to introduce 'the rule of power and terrorism into the question of belief'. The Pastors' Emergency League reacted sharply against Müller's behaviour. On Sunday 7 July some 3,500 members read in their churches a declaration drawn up by Niemöller and Fritz Müller. Niemöller himself was preaching that morning in the Church of St Paul the Apostle, Berlin-Schönberg. After his sermon, on the theme of the darkness which hung over the German Protestant churches, he left the pulpit and, supported by four other pastors, read the declaration from the altar steps. Behind them were ranged the banners of the Church Youth Organization.

The declaration accused Müller of bringing the strife into the church. 'Since the July elections placed new church leaders over us', it read, 'strife, dissension, and disunity have prevailed in the churches. Worshippers feel themselves to be homeless and think of leaving the church. There is no legally set up "spiritual committee". Many church leaders have now declared that the national synod does not have the confidence of churchgoers.'

The declaration next attacked the 'German Christians', for attempting to make heretical doctrines the foundation of the church. In this confusion both the Scriptural foundations of Christianity, as well as the faith of the fathers of the Reformation were likely to be lost. 'Although many leaders of the non-Prussian churches, as well as very many pastors and innumerable laypersons have demanded that the teaching, life, and leadership of the churches be reformed according to the Reformation confessions', the declaration continued, 'the Reich bishop has failed to fulfil these demands.' In this way Müller had declared war on the church, leaving heretical church leaders unharmed but putting true Christians in danger. 'We protest before God and this congregation', said the declaration, 'against the Reich bishop's behaviour in threatening with force those who for the sake of their consciences and their congregations are unable to remain silent over the present plight of the church. We protest against his action in re-enacting those unconstitutional laws which he had himself revoked to preserve the peace of the church.'

The declaration shrewdly ended by quoting the Confession of

Augsburg, which had been drawn up in 1530 by Luther's henchman Melanchthon and had received the approval of Luther himself, before being presented to the Emperor Charles V. The quotation constituted an open attack on the new doctrines of the 'German Christians' and an avowal of disloyalty to those church leaders who endorsed such doctrines: 'Where bishops teach, maintain, or uphold what is contrary to the gospel, we have God's command to disobey them. No one should follow even a properly elected bishop when he is in error.' The only true attitude to the Reich bishop's decrees was to follow the command, 'Obey God rather than man.'

The leaders of the Pastors' Emergency League in Berlin kept up the pressure, as Müller attempted to fight back. Over 100 Berlin pastors had read the declaration. Huge meetings were arranged for the evenings of the following week. Müller forbade three of them. Crowds found three churches barred and guarded. But elsewhere, lay men and women were given forms to sign, pledging their loyalty to the Holy Scriptures and the Reformation confessions. In response, Müller suspended from office fifty pastors for reading the declaration of the League. Letters began to reach Niemöller detailing the harassment of some of these men and, ominously, the temporary imprisonment of others. (ZEKHN 62, Vol. 1031)

Niemöller was also disturbed that members of the Pastors' Emergency League in the dioceses of Bavaria and Württemberg had taken the advice of Bishops Meiser and Wurm and not read the declaration against the Muzzling Decree and Müller's behaviour. Meiser and Wurm, as well as some of the other church leaders, instead hoped to bring an end to the church conflicts by means of a personal appeal to Hitler.

The notion of a meeting between various church parties had been put to Hitler by the American clergyman Charles S. Macfarland, when the two men had met on 31 October 1933. Hitler had indicated his willingness to meet representatives of the parties, provided they requested such a meeting. Moreover, Müller's opponents believed that Hindenburg was growing alarmed at the Reich bishop's behaviour. On 12 January the President met Bodelschwingh and Graf Schwerin von Krosigk (the German finance minister), who were sufficiently persuasive for him to summon Müller and his assistant Heinrich Oberheid in order to express his concern at their behaviour. Hindenburg complained particularly at their failure to appoint a new 'spiritual committee' and the handing over of the church's youth organizations to Baldur von Schirach. The President then informed Hitler that he had lost confidence in Müller.

As a result, Hitler agreed to a meeting between the leaders of the various Protestant church parties, to be held on 24 January. This was a marked change from his earlier, impatient statement, after the outcry against the Muzzling Decree, that he had heard enough about the Protestant churches and wished to see neither Müller nor any other church leader. Müller's position was now obviously precarious. Hitler agreed to meet representatives of the 'German Christians' and their opponents. These included Bishops Wurm, Marahrens, and Meiser. The Pastors' Emergency League was represented by the far more determined Niemöller and Karl Koch, president of the Westphalian synod.

Because Hitler wished to be present at a funeral in Munich on 24 January, he postponed the meeting for one day. This enabled Niemöller to inject more resolve into the memorandum which Müller's opponents were to submit to Hindenburg. (Their indecisiveness was revealed when Karl Barth appeared among them to add weight to the opposition. When Barth abrasively attacked the 'German Christian' Karl Fezer at a meeting in St Michael's hospice, Bishop Meiser moaned that this was the end of the German Protestant church!) Even so, Niemöller was hopeful. The memorandum seemed certain to bring down Müller, especially now that Hitler knew of Hindenburg's opposition to the Reich bishop.

On the morning of the 25th, as Niemöller breakfasted before setting off to meet Wurm and the rest, he was telephoned by Walter Künneth of the Pastors' Emergency League. 'We have laid our mines', said Niemöller, lapsing into the imagery of a naval officer; 'we have sent our memorandum to the President. We have prepared our situation well.' Before the meeting of the church leaders and Hitler, Niemöller added, the Reich chancellor would be received by the President. At that preliminary meeting, Niemöller suggested, President Hindenburg would offer Chancellor Hitler ... Here Niemöller paused, and either his wife or his secretary suggested the words, 'extreme unction'. Niemöller repeated the joke down the telephone.

He then took a taxi to the hostel in the Wilhelmstrasse where his colleagues were staying. Although he noticed men who obviously seemed to be Gestapo spies in the hall, he found Müller's opponents in good spirit, firmly believing that Hitler would dismiss the Reich bishop. The church leaders went by foot to the nearby Chancellery. They passed Göring in the hall, as they were led into Hitler's office. Behind Hitler stood Müller. The minister of the interior, Wilhelm Frick, introduced the visitors to the Reich Chancellor.

The proceedings, however, were opened neither by Hitler nor by any of the church leaders, but by Göring, who joined them to read a telegram from the secret police. It contained an elaborated, but substantially accurate account of Niemöller's earlier telephone conversation with Walter Künneth.

The church leaders later assumed that the conversation had been recorded. Because no such record has ever been found (though written notes of the conversation were kept by the secret police), it is impossible to ascertain precisely what Göring told the meeting. But his words caused complete dismay among Müller's opponents. According to Göring's own account, they 'were so terrified that they literally collapsed, to the point of becoming dumb and invisible'.

According to Bishop Wurm's account, Göring reported that Niemöller had said, 'The Reich president will give the Reich chancellor the necessary directions for the solution of the church conflict. The ministry of the interior seems favourable to us. Hindenburg will give Hitler extreme unction. At the very worst we can take the leap into a Free Church.'

Niemöller later recalled that for a moment he too was 'struck dumb'. He explained that amongst the company, he was a mere parish pastor. 'I stood in the back row, naturally. I had to make my way through all the bishops in front of me, because I knew Hitler would refer to this telephone conversation.' And Hitler was enraged. (MN/jb)

'Do you believe', Hitler asked, 'that with such outrageous backstairs politics you can drive a wedge between the Reich President and me and so endanger the basis of the Reich?' (Extract from 'Allgemeine Evangelisch-Lutherische Kirchenzeitung', 23 February 1934, in ZEKHN 62, Vol. 1002) Hitler began to speak of his expectations of the churches, Niemöller recalled. Everyone was making life difficult for him, he complained, as was Pastor Niemöller. 'I was very frightened', Niemöller said later. 'I thought, what do I answer to all his complaints and accusations? He was still speaking, speaking, speaking. I thought, dear God, let him stop.'

At that moment Hitler heard a motor car turning in the half-circle outside the Chancellery. Niemöller remembered that the Reich chancellor, by whose authority he had been completely overawed till that moment, then said, 'Every time I leave this Chancellery in my car, I am aware that someone might take a revolver and shoot at me.' At those words, Niemöller recalled, 'I felt absolutely liberated. That was my salvation. I knew this man was more anxious than I was. I felt, "You have given yourself away. If he has more anxieties than I have, then I have the courage to face him." His authority was absolutely negated when I felt that he was more governed by fear than me.' (MN/jb) Niemöller was now standing in the front row of the church leaders, fourth from the right. According to Bishop Wurm's account, he tried to explain that the struggle of the Pastors' Emergency League for the authentic faith of the church was not directed *against* the Third Reich but that it, too, was *for the sake* of the Reich. Hitler retorted sharply that the clergy should leave the care of the Third Reich to him and, as Niemöller recalled, the pastors should concern themselves with getting people to heaven and looking after the church.

This was Hitler's final word to the meeting, but Göring added the further accusation that the Pastors' Emergency League had foreign connections. The other church leaders had by now regained some sort of composure, and they hastened to try to calm tempers. Wurm's group insisted that isolated expressions of political discontent did not mean that the pastors as a whole were against the Third Reich. They still urged that Müller had not the qualities needed in a Reich bishop, adding that his conduct had made him look ridiculous. Their own concern was purely to prevent any admixture of false doctrines to the churches' teaching. The 'German Christians' denied that they taught any heresy. The whole struggle, they said, was simply concerned with church government, not with doctrine. And Müller himself, once again secure in his position, announced that he was going to invite the leaders for further discussions about the formation of a new 'spiritual committee'.

As the pastors prepared to leave, Niemöller wondered whether Hitler, following the usual habit of shaking hands with everyone, would actually shake hands with him. He had determined, if possible, to give the Führer one more short word, about his remarks on the sole duty of the church being to bring people to heaven, in a way that showed that he did not feel inferior to Hitler. He now felt, he recalled, 'quite tranquil'.

Hitler did shake hands with Martin Niemöller, and Niemöller said to him, 'A moment ago, Herr Reich Chancellor, you told us that you would take care of the German people. But as Christians and men of the church, we too have a responsibility for the German people, laid upon us by God. Neither you nor anyone else can take that away from us.' As Niemöller later remembered, 'Hitler didn't say a single word any more. He just touched my hand, took his hand away and went on.' (MN/jb)

The church leaders left the Chancellery. When Niemöller arrived home, Else Niemöller was anxiously waiting for him at the door. 'Is he a great man?' she asked. 'He is a great coward', Niemöller replied. But he added that in the days to come Hitler would certainly take his revenge. (MN/jb) That evening members of the Gestapo went through their home, taking away files of the Pastors' Emergency League. A few days later a bomb exploded inside the house, setting part of the roof on fire. The police arrived – although no one had called them. No one was arrested for the outrage. On 28 January Niemöller was again deprived of his office and taken to the headquarters of the secret police. He was released on the same day, but required to report every day.

Göring's tactics had not only confirmed Müller in his office but also sorely split the opposition. After the meeting, all but Karl Koch accused Niemöller of ill-conceived rashness. Hitler had insisted that it was absurd to dismiss Müller after so short a time as Reich bishop. Göring's report of Niemöller's conversation with Künneth made the notion unthinkable. 'You will understand that even if I had wanted to separate myself from the Reich bishop', Hitler had told them, 'I could not do so now.' The following day Bishops Schöffel and Marahrens, with Jakob Kessler, president of the church of the Palatinate, sought a meeting with Müller. On

27 January he met them, and obtained their support in return for a promise to set up the 'spiritual committee' and keep political power out of church affairs. The heads of all the non-Prussian Protestant churches capitulated to him, confessing their 'unconditional loyalty to the Reich and to the Führer'.

Niemöller refused to capitulate. On 16 February he circulated the members of the Pastors' Emergency League with his account of the meeting with Hitler. But the capitulation of others severely weakened the League itself. 1,200 members from Meiser's Bavarian diocese and 350 members from Marahren's diocese of Hanover resigned. In Wurm's Württemberg diocese the League folded up. From a total of over 7,000 at the beginning of 1934, the League's membership declined to around 5,250.

By now the conflict in the German churches was exciting even more interest abroad. *The Times* began reporting seriously on the events from the Sports Palace affair onwards. Niemöller recognized the importance of the free foreign press, and he obtained and carefully annotated the account in the *Manchester Guardian Weekly* of what had happened on that occasion. (ZEKHN 62, Vol. 1002) Alarmed at Müller's increased power, Bishop Bell of Chichester now prompted Archbishop Eiden of Sweden to pay a personal visit to Hitler. The meeting only revealed the extent of Hitler's commitment to Müller, for the moment Eiden mentioned the Reich bishop, the Reich Chancellor flew into a rage. On 23 February Müller set up a new 'spiritual committee' without allowing its members to be elected. This committee was totally under his control. On 7 March he set up a foreign office for the Reich church, under the control of Bishop Theodor Heckel. Any attempt to communicate with a foreign church, he decreed, must now pass through Heckel's office. Heckel's attitude to Martin Niemöller is well illustrated by his attempt to force Niemöller's father (who, of course, was a staunch member of the Pastors' Emergency League) to retire on the grounds of age. Heinrich Niemöller asked Heckel how old he was, and learning that the bishop was forty, retorted, 'Then you are much too old!'

Once again the parish council of Dahlem refused to recognize the legality of Niemöller's own dismissal, on the grounds that a pastor cannot be dismissed without the congregation's consent. Niemöller continued to preach and minister as before – save that now he was under no illusions as to the attitude of Adolf Hitler to the church. On the fourth Sunday before Easter he preached on the parable of the weeds among the wheat, using a text from St Luke's gospel in which Jesus's disciple Peter promised loyalty to his master even unto death. 'He who is not ready to suffer, he who calls himself a Christian only because he thereby hopes to gain something good for his race and his nation, is blown away like chaff by the wind of this time', Niemöller declared. The 'German Christians', though discredited as a body by the Sports Palace affair, were none the less still strong, and Niemöller warned his congregation against them. 'If today an attempt were made to base the morals and morality of our nation on something other than Christianity', he preached, on Palm Sunday, 'it would be very difficult in view of our Christian past; but the possibility cannot be disputed.' Even in his pastoral work he remained uncompromisingly anti-Nazi. Von Ribbentrop was a leading National Socialist politician who lived in the fashionable Berlin suburb of Dahlem. He was no churchgoer, but no 'German Christian' either. He asked Niemöller to baptize his youngest daughter, and the pastor called on the Ribbentrop household, along with his wife Else. When Ribbentrop boastingly pointed to a chair which Adolf Hitler had sat in, Niemöller stiffened. When Frau Ribbentrop tactlessly began to speak of the 'German Christians', Niemöller became even more reserved. The daughter was never baptized. And later, when Ribbentrop desired to join the church in preparation for his work as ambassador to Great Britain, arguing that 'The English will expect it of me', Niemöller insisted that this was an utterly insufficient reason to allow anyone to be confirmed.

He also fought to get back his legal status as a pastor of Dahlem. His method was ingenious. He urged his congregation *not* to pay him, so that he could take them to court. The Berlin court eventually found for Niemöller, thus invalidating his dismissal. Müller attempted to oust him by appointing a 'special commissioner' for Dahlem, Pastor Scharfenberg of Köpenick; but Niemöller continued to preach to a packed church, and Scharfenberg never appeared.

The telephone-tapping episode had genuinely distressed Niemöller, since his activity harmed others in the struggle. (MN/jb) But he was appalled at the concessions of some of the church leadership afterwards. Wurm, Meiser, and Marahrens had announced that they now took up 'a united stand behind the Reich bishop, declaring themselves willing to enforce his policies and decrees in the sense desired by him'. They promised to hinder all opposition to him in the churches and do everything to consolidate his position. Müller had immediately made this declaration public, before proceeding to take savage reprisals against members of the Pastors' Emergency League, suspending or dismissing some and sending others to concentration camps for a spell. Bishop Meiser himself realized the enormous power he and his colleagues had given to the Reich bishop, and he wrote to him after signing the declaration to say that this did not mean he approved of the Muzzling Decree or had abandoned the Pastors' Emergency League. But the damage had been done.

His confidence in the church leadership eroded, Niemöller at this perilous moment placed all his hopes, in the struggle against power-politics in the church, in the local congregation. Here pastors could seek the support of lay men and women, in their fight against arbitrary action by the authorities. This was the theme of an article he published on 20 February 1934 in the journal of the Young Reformation Movement. 'This is a time for us to be obedient to such possibilities as God offers us', his article ended. 'And that is enough.'

In fact Niemöller was already at work creating new possibilities of opposing the Nazi tyranny over the churches. By adding lay support to the Pastors' Emergency League, Niemöller and his allies were in effect creating a new church structure within German Protestantism. Soon they were organizing free synods, in opposition to those controlled by Müller. Since these synods aimed at reinforcing the traditional confessions of the Reformation against the new doctrines of the 'German Christians', the new organization came to be known officially as 'the Confessing church'. The Confessing church, as Niemöller put it, became 'a fluctuation within the whole structure of the German Protestant church'. (MN/jb) To become a member an individual Christian had to obtain a red membership card. Some members supported the Confessing church with enthusiasm and determination. Others fluctuated in their support. Some, such as Professor D. Balla of Marburg, who habitually lectured on the Old Testament dressed as one of Hitler's Brownshirts, joined by mistake. Balla did not spot that he was out of place in the Pastors' Emergency

League till April 1934, when he resigned (see Niemöller's reply of 27 August 1934, ZEKHN 62, Vol. 1001).

The Confessing church membership in Rhineland-Westphalia alone soon amounted to 800 thousand. Niemöller sometimes despaired, temporarily, over its vacillations, but the Confessing church undoubtedly presented the sole coherent opposition to Hitler's religious (and therefore racial) policies within Germany. It also did offer considerable support to leaders of the struggle such as Niemöller. But in Hitler's Germany no support, however coherent and considerable, could now keep Niemöller out of a concentration camp.

8. BATTLE FOR THE CHURCH

IN THE middle of the German church struggle, Eden Theological Seminary, Missouri, made Gerhard Jacobi and Martin Niemöller honorary doctors of divinity. The president of the Seminary, S. D. Press, wrote to Niemöller, on 11 February 1936, 'It has fallen on you under peculiarly trying conditions to preserve the liberty of the Christian Gospel.... you still stand firmly for the complete freedom of the Gospel at the present critical moment, and by the grace of God you will continue this loyal stand for the sake of the Gospel because you cannot do otherwise.'

Niemöller was deeply touched, not solely because of the honour but also because, as he wrote to Press on 17 April, the award showed that 'the centrepoint of the struggle in which we find ourselves is understood by you and our fellow believers in North America, and that in fraternal alliance you will sustain us in this struggle'. His letter revealed that he had no sanguine hopes that the way ahead would be easy. 'We often think here', he added, 'that we have much much further to go, before the Protestant church in Germany finds itself once again, in its entirety, true to the proper sources of its life. We pray to God that he will not leave us weary on the way, and we thank from our hearts our brethren throughout the world for their help and prayers.' (ZEKHN 62, Vol. 1021)

The danger under which Niemöller and his colleagues lived was physical as well as spiritual. Thomas Mann recorded in his diary, horrified, an account of a young communist in Hitler's Germany, his jaw shattered by the pistol butt of an SA officer, forced to scream verses in honour of the Führer. Increasingly, Niemöller received reports of similar acts of brutality to members of the Confessing church – and not only pastors. On 15 September 1936, for instance, Pastor Petersen of Berlin wrote to him about Fräulein Erna Schneider, a member of the Confessing church, denounced by the police and confined for nine weeks 'in a kind of prison or concentration camp'. But pastors were particularly at risk. On 3 August Niemöller wrote that 'anyone studying theology runs a great risk, for we Confessing pastors all live a totally uncertain existence'. At any moment laws could be passed depriving them of office. 'None of us has a guaranteed permanent position or place to live in.' (Ibid.)

At risk with these men were their wives and families. On Sunday 11 August 1935, seven years after all the rest (so to speak), Else bore their youngest son, in the pastor's house in Dahlem. Niemöller's father baptized the boy, and 'little' Martin as he came to be known appears photographed amongst the many children of the prolific Dahlem pastors in the parish newsletter. The elder children and wives of these men shared their husbands' anxieties. Pastor Wilhelm Stählin, a doughty member of the Confessing church who after World War II became Bishop of Oldenburg, confessed in his memoirs that he followed certain Nazi regulations (such as placing the swastika in his church) against his conscience, for fear of what might happen to his family.

The risks faced by Martin and Else Niemöller and their children were, of course, far greater than those faced by the Stählin family. Some of Niemöller's friends (including a number of Nazi officers) wished to smuggle him out of the country into Sweden, but he refused. Often at this time he would quote some lines of Theodor Storm:

> One man may ask, 'What comes of it?'
> Another, 'What is right?'
> And that is what distinguishes
> The vassal from the knight.

From his pulpit he condemned the violence now being used within the province of the church itself. As early as June 1934 he was protesting in his Dahlem church against those in neighbouring churches who left the service offensively and noisily during the reading of the Old Testament and would later insult the pastor in the street. Niemöller's conclusion was that 'we must radically and systematically change our ideas concerning the relation of the fellowship of Jesus to the world – to the world within the nation and the world within the church'. On an earlier occasion he reminded his congregation that once 'we were accustomed to view the church and the nation as one ... Today we are faced with an entirely different situation: church and nation, nation and church can, and indeed dare no longer be regarded as one.'

Sermons such as this one, preached scarcely a year after the start of a regime supposedly based on positive Christianity, reached a wider audience on publication. Small wonder if the regime tried to restrict the number of copies printed. (Sending some of Niemöller's sermons to Landgerichtsrat Klara Abel on 10 December 1936, Niemöller's parish secretary commented, 'unfortunately no more sermons have been printed'. (ZEKHN 62, Vol. 1021)

What precisely was the essence of this struggle in which the Hitler regime sought to suppress the opinions of one of Germany's national heroes? In 1934, seeking complete relaxation from contemporary events and also, as he put it, 'to audit my own progress', during a holiday in a remote woodland spot on the shores of the Baltic, Niemöller wrote *From U-Boat to Pulpit*. He described it as 'a much belated piece of Great War literature', written after repeated requests by many of his friends and acquaintances. It revealed Martin Niemöller as a supremely patriotic German, one of those who, in his words, 'found their true selves during the Great War and who, in that Mighty Furnace of God, reverted back to the elementary and simple basic truths of humanity, which, after the end of the War, impelled them to seek a new life'.

From U-Boat to Pulpit proved an immense success, adding to the fame of its author in his own country and abroad. It was published in an edition of over 90 thousand copies, and Niemöller's private papers are full of requests for copies of the book and photographs of himself. In turning to the Christian ministry for his new profession, Martin Niemöller had in no way rejected the patriotism of his wartime service. Looking back in 1934, he could only quote Psalm 118: 'O give thanks unto the Lord for he is good; for his mercy endureth for ever!' The book ends with his ordination on 29 June 1924 and the baptism of his son Heinz Hermann. 'The journey from submarine to pulpit was completed', he wrote, 'and my service for my people and native country, in my new profession, was beginning.' Ten years later this Christian patriot was regarded by many who held political power in Germany as an untrustworthy and dangerous enemy. What had gone wrong?

'Peaceful coexistence between church and state', as Niemöller explained forty years later, had been 'developed and consolidated ever since the end of Bismarck's Kulturkampf in the 1880s.' The churches in Germany evinced little desire for democracy. But from 1933 Germany was ruled by a new sort of dictator, 'not just a political dictator, but a man who wished to dictate everything'. So for Niemöller the question suddenly arose of the limits of state authority, of the limits of obedience, and of the relevance of the apostolic rule, 'We must obey God rather than men.'

The churches, Niemöller conceded, had not in the past dealt with this question entirely satisfactorily. Whereas the Bible said, 'You shall not kill', since the time of Constantine, whenever the state said, 'You shall kill', the churches had not said no. Now, under Hitler, the earthly powers said, 'You shall hate the Jew and the stranger', whereas Jesus had said, 'You shall love your neighbour, even if he is your enemy.' Thus, Niemöller concluded, 'in the late Summer of 1933 the "church struggle" began'.

He added that from outside the struggle was seen as a minority in the church competing with the majority for public recognition as the true church. Indeed, although the question of Jews remained, so far as their position in the church as converts was concerned, the struggle was won. The German Protestant churches threw out the Aryan paragraph. They protected their Jewish officers and pastors as best they could – sometimes embarrassed by them, but ultimately insisting on regarding them as Christian brethren. Because so few converts had in fact taken office in the churches, the problem of, for example, finding 'non-Aryan' pastors security abroad was comparatively easy. But this very question raised acutely such apparently abstruse theological problems as what is the meaning of baptism, what are the true foundations of Christianity, and where does true authority lie.

This at times gave the opposition to Hitler the character of a theological quarrel. But because, as it turned out, Hitler was willing to kill his enemies, these were quarrels about matters of life and death. Forced to ask what really constitutes a Christian church, these men and women were eventually obliged to set up a church that was, in Niemöller's words, 'an enemy of the state, because she not only refused to acknowledge the totalitarian claims of the state but openly challenged them'. This was an uncertain road for German Protestants. 'A Protestant Christian who is an enemy to the State, and likewise a Protestant State which is an enemy to the Church are contradictions in themselves', Niemöller said in his Dahlem pulpit in 1935. But this was Hitler's Germany. After the fateful meeting in Hitler's study on 25 January 1934, Karl Koch had observed, 'Now, brother Niemöller, we have to appeal to a higher authority.' So in 1935 Niemöller continued his sermon with the words, 'But if the state command us to do wrong, "We must obey God rather than men".'

As a student Niemöller had once asked his friend Professor Wehrung what was the essential meaning of the expression, 'the Church'. Wehrung had replied, 'Why worry about it? Is it so important?' Now people were asking Niemöller for an answer. On 6 February 1936 the publishing firm of Christian Kaiser in Munich even asked him to write a book explaining both what the church is and what it is not. 'You have the freshness and the feeling that pleases the young', wrote Christian Kaiser's editor. 'You know what young people of today listen to, and what moves them. You also know what the gospel in the church has to say to them all . . .' He concluded, 'Truly, I could not think of a better author for such a book than you.' (ZEKHN 62, Vol. 1021)

In fact, virtually every public action of Niemöller's between 1933 and 1937 posed the question of the role of the church in a tyrannous and pagan regime. In an article published in September 1936, he considered three possible ways in which the church could respond to the Hitler state. It could remain a *Volks-kirche* – Niemöller's former ideal – but in that case, it seemed, the church would now become completely subservient to the state. The second possibility was to become a Free Church. But even in this case, the state could still refuse to tolerate any independence. Should that happen, Niemöller concluded, the only remaining possibility was a church of martyrs and the catacombs. He was by that time certain (as he had told Frau Buddenbrook of Heiden in a letter of 28 June) that since Müller and Jäger had destroyed the proper church authorities in Prussia in 1933, the only true church leadership in the Province had been that provided by the Prussian Council of Brethren – 'as', he added, 'Marahrens, Meiser and Wurm recognize.' (Ibid.)

These three bishops had, Niemöller believed, taken far too long to reach that conclusion. They were, in his opinion, far too readily seduced by the state church. Indeed, the only time they fully co-operated with him in opposing the Reich church authorities was in 1934, when their own positions were seriously threatened.

Early in that year Ludwig Müller decided to incorporate Marahrens' diocese into his own projected 'Reich church'. Marahrens indignantly refused to sign the deed of incorporation, and when he appealed for support to his pastors, three-quarters of them remained loyal. Meiser similarly succeeded in resisting Müller's attempt to incorporate the diocese of Bavaria into the proposed Reich church. Wurm in 1934 had even more reason to dislike Müller's rule, since it was announced on 16 April that he was no longer fit to be bishop, having lost the confidence of his diocese. Wurm was, in fact, extremely popular throughout Württemberg, and when Müller and Jäger arrived to unseat him, made strenuous and successful efforts to resist them. Their high-handed behaviour made Wurm, Meiser, and Marahrens for a time ready to co-operate with those who were trying to set up an alternative, free government for the German churches.

In January delegates from 167 Calvinist churches had already held a free synod, at Barmen in Westphalia. Their aim (in the words of Karl Barth) was to work out not 'how one could get rid of the "German Christian" nonsense, but how it was possible to form a front against the error that had devastated the Protestant church for centuries'. Barth defined this error as the notion that alongside God's revelation 'man also has a legitimate authority of his own, over the message and the form of the church'.

The Calvinist delegates adopted Barth's 'Declaration' reiterating the notion that the church was founded on Holy Scripture alone, as interpreted by the Reformed confessions. It could not, therefore, be interfered with either by a church Führer or the demands of an all-embracing state. Barth was convinced that his 'Declaration' had said everything 'in terms which serious Lutherans would be able to accept without surrendering anything on their side'. He was right. On 19 February a second free synod, attended by delegates from 30 of the 33 Rhineland church synods, and including Lutherans, adopted the 'Declaration'.

The movement for free synods was spreading. On 5 March, representatives of the Pastors' Emergency League, meeting in Niemöller's parish hall, discussed whether to boycott the provincial synod headed by Müller. Two days later a free synod for Berlin and Brandenburg met at Dahlem. There four hundred and forty delegates from seventy or so churches ratified Barth's 'Declaration'.

The opposition to Müller was becoming much more like a church of lay men and women, and not simply a group of pastors trying to defend themselves and their brethren. To Dietrich Bonhoeffer, who was present at the synod in Berlin, it seemed that he might now be able to persuade his English friend, Bishop George Bell, to make some ecumenical statement in support of Niemöller, Jacobi, and the opposition. He wrote to Bell that at the free synod he had met 'Niemöller, Jacobi, and some friends from the Rhineland' and that the free synod itself was a sign of 'real progress and success'. He asked Bell to speak out on behalf of his friends. He wished, he wrote, that Bell could be present at a meeting of the Pastors' Emergency League. 'It is always, in spite of all gravity of the present moments, a real uplift to one's faith and courage.' Bell was soon persuaded to speak out.

Meanwhile the free synod movement continued to spread throughout Germany. On 16 March one was held in Dortmund. There Lutheran representatives from Westphalia elected Karl Koch as president, as well as a Council of Brethren to act as its co-ordinating body. This synod voted to associate itself fraternally with the faith of the free synod of the Rhineland, which had met a month earlier.

When the fifth free synod of 1934 assembled in Ulm cathedral on 22 April, delegates were available from virtually the whole country. Ulm was Bishop Wurm's own cathedral. Meiser brought diocesan representatives, still indignant over Müller and Jäger. The free synods of the Rhineland, of Westphalia, and of Berlin-Brandenburg sent delegates, as did many of the congregations throughout Germany that had been led by recent events to reaffirm the traditional confessions of the church.

Emboldened by this countrywide support, the free synod of Ulm not only set up its own Council of Brethren (almost all of whom had been involved in the work of the Pastors' Emergency League). It also took an unprecedented step, by claiming before 'the whole of Christendom' that it was 'the constitutional Protestant church of Germany'.

This declaration, signed by Niemöller among the other leaders at Ulm, reveals his new appreciation of the importance of international Christian opinion. In August a meeting of the Universal Christian Council for Life and Work was scheduled to meet at Fanø in Denmark. Bishop Heckel was clearly unlikely to allow anyone of Niemöller's party to be invited. It might, however, be possible to use Bonhoeffer's friendship with George Bell in order to circumvent Heckel and have members of the church's opposition invited as full representatives of German Protestantism. At Ulm the delegates to the free synod not only set themselves up as the true representatives of German Protestantism, in opposition to Müller, Heckel, Jäger, and those who wanted a state church in harmony with the Nazi ideology. They also took this step specifically in an ecumenical context – 'before the whole of Christendom'.

To consider appealing to international opinion marked a remarkable *volte-face* in a man who six months earlier had congratulated Hitler for withdrawing from the League of Nations. In the post-war humiliation of Germany after the Treaty of Versailles, very many German Protestants saw the nascent ecumenical movement as part of the whole international campaign against their own country. Ecumenical activity, Paul Althaus asserted, was unpatriotic. In 1920 the Protestant church leaders, refusing an invitation to join the Faith and Order movement of the world Christian churches, explained that, 'In view of the enormous amount of lies and allegations which were launched against our Fatherland and our church during the world war by representatives of enemy countries, it would be a lie for members of a Protestant Germany at the present time to meet with representatives of these churches to discuss questions of Christianity, as though the deep abyss which separates us simply did not exist.' The church leaders continued, 'Any full relationship with church authorities of enemy countries is at present impossible, after these bodies still accuse our Fatherland of dishonour and have threatened to sit in judgement with enemy judges over our leader and heroes, and have taken part in the demand, which is against all divine or earthly law, to condemn in a most shameful way the German Kaiser, who always proved himself from his innermost conviction to be a fine guardian of the Protestant church.'

Bonhoeffer, who had become a pacifist during his stay in Union Theological Seminary, New York, was a notable exception in rejecting such views. They were entirely acceptable to an ex-U-boat commander such as Niemöller. Now he and some of his colleagues were beginning to change. And on 10 May this change of heart was rewarded by a letter sent by Bishop George Bell to the representatives of every church belonging to the Council for Life and Work, expressing his anxieties about the German church. 'The chief cause of anxiety', wrote Bell, 'is the assumption by the Reichsbishop in the name of the principle of leadership of autocratic powers unqualified by constitutional or traditional restraints which are without precedent in the history of the church.'

Bell added, 'The exercise of these autocratic powers by the Church government appears incompatible with the Christian principle of seeking in brotherly fellowship to receive the guidance of the Holy Spirit. It has had disastrous results on the internal unity of the church; and the disciplinary measures which have been taken by the Church government against Ministers of the Gospel on account of their loyalty to the fundamental principles of Christian truth have made a painful impression on Christian opinion abroad, already disturbed by the introduction of racial distinctions in the universal fellowship of the Christian Church.'

Bell had come out entirely on the side of Niemöller in his challenge to Müller's policies and the introduction of the Aryan paragraph into the German church. Before international Christian opinion could be further exploited, Niemöller attended the fifth and greatest of the free synods of the church struggle, that held at Barmen in Westphalia, which began on Tuesday 29 May.

On 2 May Bishops Meiser and Wurm, Karl Koch, Martin Niemöller, Gerhard Jacobi, and six other representatives of the free synod churches, met in Berlin and sent a sharp protest to the minister of the interior about the unacceptable use of power politics in the church and about the true, confessional basis of Christianity. This unity among the church leadership was unusual and impressive. But of far greater significance, in the long run, was a suggestion made by the young Pastor Karl Immer at this meeting. Immer was pastor of the Gemarke church in Barmen, where the coming free synod was to be held. A courageous opponent of the Nazis, he was arrested by the Gestapo in August 1937. (Six days later he suffered a stroke, and was released on humanitarian grounds, after which he never fully recovered his strength.) On 2 May 1934 Immer proposed the setting up of a sub-committee of three persons to prepare a theological statement for submission to the delegates who would be present at Barmen. The three theologians chosen were Karl Barth and two Lutheran theologians, Hans Asmussen and Thomas Breit.

In the end, the bulk of the work was done by Karl Barth. By his own account, 'The Lutheran church slept and the Reformed church kept awake.' The three men met in the Basler Hof Hotel, Frankfurt, and drew up a preliminary draft of six statements to be presented to the synod. After lunch, according to Barth, Asmussen and Breit took a three hour siesta. 'I revised the text of the six statements, fortified by strong coffee and one or two Brazilian cigars.' As a result, by that evening, the final text had been prepared. Barth, who was never averse to boasting, said later, 'I don't want to boast, but it was really my text.'

This was the remarkable document adopted by 139 church delegates at the synod of Barmen, in the Gemarke church of Pastor Karl Immer. Karl Koch presided. Meiser and Wurm were delegates. Even Marahrens, though not an official delegate, was present and was shrewdly asked to conduct the opening devotions. By the time the synod ended on 31 May, it had adopted Barth's theses as its own confession of faith.

This was a major theological achievement, especially in view of the fact that the synod included delegates drawn from different groups of the Reformation. No one supposed that the synod of its own power could achieve anything like a total reconciliation of Calvinists and Lutherans! Members of each group were to understand the declaration in the light of their own traditions. But everyone agreed that the supremely important part of the declaration was thesis 1, which utterly rejected the doctrines of the 'German Christian' movement. The first thesis of Barmen insisted that the Word of God is Jesus Christ, that this Word is found in the Holy Scriptures, and that for the purposes of constituting the church, it is found nowhere else. In short, as far as the church's struggle under Hitler was concerned, Barmen decisively rejected the notion that God had specially revealed himself through the German nation, through German blood, through a superior race, or even through Adolf Hitler.

Niemöller dated the creation of the Confessing church from Barmen. 'We had confessing congregations in the Rhineland, in Westphalia, in Brandenburg, in Berlin before then, but you needed a greater group under one general denominator', he said. 'This began with the Confessing church in May 1934 in Barmen. What was then needed was to continue to promote the Barmen Declaration to all those people who didn't want to be "German Christians" and wanted to work together as members of the Confessing church or congregation.' (MN/jb) He himself had played little overt part in the proceedings of the synod. But the astonishing achievement of creating a Confessing church within little more than six months was substantially his. The Confessing church was a direct development of the Pastors' Emergency League. As Karl Barth correctly put it, 'In the struggle against the Christianity *à la mode* of 1933, under Martin Niemöller's direction first the so-called Pastors' Emergency League came into being and then, on a broader basis, the Confessing Church.'

The achievement is all the more remarkable in view of the sometimes vicious harassment with which the League had continually to contend. Müller had also been shrewd enough to try to split the church's opposition to him by offers of apparent conciliation. On 24 March, for instance, he had published his own Good Friday sermon announcing that the 'spiritual committee' was to grant an amnesty. Now the 'committee' would consult with the authorities in each local church to discover which suspended pastors could be reinstated. Müller, however, made it clear that he was planning to distinguish between those pastors deprived for what he called 'political' differences and those deprived merely for 'ecclesiastical' differences. Only the latter would be pardoned. Moreover, his sermon made it completely clear that none of the new Nazi elements in the nation's faith were to be disowned. Not only the crucifixion (the ostensible topic of his sermon), but also the Great War and the coming to power of Adolf Hitler revealed, Müller claimed, God's purposes in history. In short, what Karl Barth dubbed 'the "German Christian" nonsense' must also be accepted by those co-operating with the amnesty. Müller's tactical sense did not extend, either, to perceiving that totalitarian methods in church affairs were also deeply offensive to the clergy he had deprived. Instead of renouncing these methods, he insisted that before the Nazis came to power the church had lost its dynamism and buoyancy. It had become remote from the world of real men, who were now injecting new life into it. But, said Müller, this could not always be accomplished solely by 'churchly' means.

The Council of Brethren of the Pastors' Emergency League issued a declaration 'firmly rejecting an amnesty which has so little to do with real forgiveness that it is made dependent on unconditional submission'.

After Barmen the National Socialist theologians fought back, particularly Gerhard Kittel. A group of such pastors and professors in Tübingen had drawn up twelve articles asserting that National Socialism represented God's call to the nation and Adolf Hitler its God-given leader. Kittel now announced his support for these articles – a stance which explicitly attacked Barmen. As the chief author of the Barmen declaration, Karl Barth publicly disputed with Kittel. In a series of open letters published between them, Barth argued that Kittel had confused the divine mystery of 'creation' with a human theory about 'race, blood, soil, people, state, etc.'

Martin Niemöller would often poke fun at his own lack of theological expertise. But in truth, he was well aware of the theological importance of what was being debated. Moreover, Kittel's attack was specifically addressed to the Council of Brethren. On 22 June he sent Niemöller a circular which put the blame for the upheavals in the German Protestant churches on Niemöller's party, and on the false doctrines which *they* were teaching.

Kittel's circular condemned as false two beliefs:

1. that there ever was in any place or time a proclamation of the gospel which was not related to the historical moment, 'as if nothing had happened';
2. that there ever could be a proclamation of the gospel that was not generally co-determined – in its approach and in its total pattern – by God's hour, ordained for the gospel on behalf of the world and nation and mankind.

Since the proclamation of the gospel was co-determined by its historical context, Kittel argued that it needed to be preached 'every day anew'.

God's ordained hour for Kittel was, of course, the hour of Adolf Hitler. Kittel's theology had immense political consequences – though, ironically, those accused of preaching politics by Reich bishop Müller were the Christians on Niemöller's side. It was they, Kittel wrote, who, by refusing to recognize the necessary amalgamation of the traditional gospel with the demands of the hour, were bringing about 'the confusion in people's minds, the devastation of the church, the destruction of parishes'. Their error, he added, would also bring about the destruction of what they supposed they were defending, namely, the church's stance on Holy Scripture and the old confessions.

Six days later Niemöller sent his answer, utterly rejecting Kittel's proposed new gospel. 'Your phrase with the passage "every day anew" at least is so erroneous that I could never sign it', he wrote. And 'In connection with this, I hold the last sentence of your condemnation, with the word "generally" and with the phrase "world *and* nation *and* mankind", to be essentially wrong.' (ZEKHN 62, Vol. 1009)

The words are Niemöller's, but the theology was Karl Barth's. Barth protested against 'hyphenated Christianity', Christianity joined with a further supposed source of God's truth – and therefore co-determined by something else (such as the German nation and its 'historic hour'). 'Our protest', he wrote in 1933, 'must be directed fundamentally against the fact (which is the source of all individual errors) that, besides the Holy Scriptures as the unique source of revelation, the "German Christians" affirm the German nationhood, its history and its contemporary political situation as a second source of revelation, and thereby betray themselves to be believers in "another God".'

This was the substance of Niemöller's sharp rejection of Kittel's attacks upon Barmen. At this time Karl Barth's fierceness against what he saw to be the errors of Hitler's court-theologians made it difficult for him to make or keep many friends in the German Protestant churches. But he soon came to see the strength of Niemöller, as well as his supreme skill in organizing the opposition in the church struggle against Hitler. Niemöller, for his part, came increasingly to rely on Barth's theological judgements. 'I met and grew to know him as a member of the Council of Brethren', Niemöller recalled. 'Later I visited him several times in Basel. We very seldom confessed our love for each other, but he was very near to my heart. I was never close to him as a theologian, but he kept and brought me on the right way.' Niemöller then quoted the first sentence of the Barmen declaration, formulated by Barth: 'Jesus Christ, as witnessed to us in Holy Scripture, is the one word of God to which we have to listen, trust and obey in life and death.' Niemöller added, 'I can only say that this has become my whole dogma of theology.' (MN/jb)

Convinced that the opponents of the Pastors' Emergency League had effectively rejected the Christian gospel and embraced paganism, Niemöller wrote to members of the League after the free synod of Ulm, claiming the right of the confessing movement 'to speak in the name of the church'. At Barmen that right was reaffirmed. The synods declared that those churches and congregations that accepted the Barmen declaration 'are the legitimate German Protestant church: they are assembled as the Confessing Synod of the German Protestant church'. The forthcoming meeting at Fanø of the Universal Christian Council for Life and Work gave Niemöller and his ally Karl Koch the chance to persuade Christians outside Germany to recognize this claim.

In spite of the unchristian behaviour of the German authorities, this task was by no means an easy one. Many educated men and women in Britain, for instance, openly wished for a Hitler in Britain in the 1930s. In November 1933 the journal *Theology* carried an article asserting that 'there can be no real denying that the Hitler régime offers to the Protestant church opportunities that have not been hers hitherto at any period since the war'. It was possible to find, in England as elsewhere, Christians willing to defend Hitler's anti-Semitic legislation. In 1933 Arthur Cayley Headlam, the distinguished Bishop of Gloucester and fellow of All Souls College, Oxford, condemned the violence with which German Jews were being attacked in 1933. But, he said, 'some words of warning were necessary'. Many Jews, he declared, were responsible for the violence of the Russian communists. Many Jews had helped to inspire the violence of the socialist communities. The Jews, he concluded, 'are not an altogether pleasant element in German, and in particular in Berlin life'.

Bishop George Bell of Chichester shared no such views. Before the rise of Hitler he had begun to take an interest in German church affairs. Now he was close to Dietrich Bonhoeffer and extremely well informed. As secretary of the Church of England Council of Foreign Relations (of which body, however, Headlam was chairman), he now produced, in May 1934, a survey on the affairs of the continental churches which gave a detailed account of what had happened to the German Protestant churches since the coming to power of Hitler. This account described 'the struggle of the Christian Churches in Germany to preserve their independence in the face of exorbitant demands on the part of the State' as 'probably . . . the most significant event in the history of the Christian Church since . . . the beginning of this century'.

On 7 June Bell managed to persuade the representatives of the Anglican clergy, meeting in Convocation at Canterbury, to pass a resolution calling attention 'to the warnings given in the recent declaration of the Confessional Synod of the German Evangelical Church at Barmen against certain tendencies regarding revelation, race and the state by which the Christian faith is imperilled'.

Bell thus managed to persuade the Church of England, in its first official reference to the German church struggle, tacitly to acknowledge the claims of Barmen to speak for the whole German Protestant church. Through him, Martin Niemöller and Karl Koch now hoped to have delegates from the Confessing church invited to the Fanø conference as representatives of the legitimate German church. After a meeting with the two men in Berlin on 19 June, Dietrich Bonhoeffer conveyed their hopes to Bell. Bonhoeffer also wrote to the Genevan secretary of the council, H. L. Henriod, to press the claims of the Confessing church. Henriod replied expressing his deep sympathy with the situation of the Confessing church, but refused to act other than through Bishop Heckel's office in Germany. Eventually, George Bell managed to elicit a personal invitation to Fanø for Karl Koch (which added that the presence of Bodelschwingh, too, would be welcome). In the end, neither man was allowed to go to the conference. Only Bonhoeffer was there to represent the confessing movement. Yet the matter did not end there. The Universal Christian Council elected both Bonhoeffer and the absent Karl Koch to be consultative members. And in a resolution carried on 30 August the Council assured 'its brethren in the Confessing synod of the German Protestant church of its prayers and heartfelt sympathy in their witness to the principles of the gospel, and of its resolve to maintain close fellowship with them'.

International support for the Confessing church, however

much the German authorities might try to ignore it, was increasingly welcome. Niemöller told his congregation that Barmen, far from making matters easier for Christians in Germany, was highly likely to stir up even more hatred for them. 'I do not stand here as a prophet, dear brethren', he said, 'or I should perhaps be obliged to paint a dark picture of the future, showing distress and tribulation coming upon the fellowship of Christ, showing lukewarmness and defection in our ranks, with only a few of our number managing to save their bare life and their bare faith.' Müller responded to the challenge to his authority in the Confessing church by persuading the national synod, meeting on 9 August in Berlin, to enact an oath of loyalty to the Führer which would be compulsory for all pastors. The Council of Brethren refused to recognize either the legality of the oath or that the national synod represented the legitimate Protestant church.

On 23 September Müller had arranged to have himself consecrated Reich bishop (though he had been using the title for many months) in the cathedral of Berlin. 'The storm has come', Niemöller told his congregation on that day. But, he reminded them, this was because Christ himself was with them in the ship. As Luther himself had warned, 'If Christ enters the ship, the weather will not long remain calm, but a storm and tempest will arise.' After his sermon, Niemöller read a declaration asserting that Müller and his aides had lost any claim to obedience, since they had taken up a hybrid 'Nordic-Christian' religion, leaving the Confessing church as the one rightful Protestant church of Germany.

The storm arose in the dioceses of Württemberg and Bavaria. Neither Wurm nor Meiser (nor any bishop not appointed by Müller himself) had attended the consecration of the Reich bishop on 23 September. August Jäger had already forced Wurm to go on leave, and the bishop had spent three days under house arrest. Ruthlessly determined to take over control of Wurm's diocese, Müller next issued a decree altering the diocesan constitution and replacing its synod with a new 'German Christian' one. On 6 October Wurm was again placed under house arrest and four days later the new synod called on him to retire immediately. Two days later August Jäger issued a decree dismissing from office Bishop Meiser of Bavaria. 'Violence is now being used in the province of the church itself', declared Niemöller.

The Confessing church instantly moved to defend the two bishops, denouncing the actions of Müller and Jäger, in a manifesto to be read from church pulpits, as an attack on the integrity of the church. Niemöller preached openly and powerfully. 'Last Sunday we held a service of intercession for the persecuted Protestants in Württemberg', he reminded his congregation. 'In the interval things have not become a whit different or even better. The lawful bishop of the state has been deposed by an unlawful and unchristian synod. He and his fellow workers have been deprived, with the aid of the secular authority, of their personal liberty, and have been forbidden to act in an official capacity. The oppression which lies over the community of the faithful continues in undiminished form.'

Now, Niemöller continued, reports were being received 'of the violent attack of the anti-Christian forces on the Bavarian church'. There too, he declared, 'a reign of terror' was being set up, while the public was being misled by lies and half truths. The bishop of Bavaria had been deposed and robbed of his freedom. All this, he said, was in the name of 'that so-called "union" which is destroying a church already united in creed and constitution'. As in Württemberg, this second attack upon the church had been carried out, Niemöller noted, 'with the assistance of the temporal power, against the unanimous will of the Protestant community'. He had no hesitation in comparing what Müller and Jäger had done to a new Gethsemane, when 'the power of darkness' attacked Jesus Christ himself. 'It is dreadful and infuriating to see how a few unprincipled men who call themselves "church government" are destroying the church and persecuting the fellowship of Jesus.'

On this Sunday Niemöller did not rest content with attacking Müller and Jäger alone. In addition, he spoke of the failure of his hopes in the new Reich, thus implicitly attacking the whole Hitler regime. 'What hopes we had for the work of the Protestant church in our newly united nation! As the young men of Emmaus said, "We trusted that it had been He that should have redeemed Israel".' Now there was only 'the bitterness of disappointed hope'. It was, said Niemöller, 'the old story: men with swords and staves, the secret betrayal and the treacherous kiss, calumny and false witnesses, temporal and ecclesiastical judgement and the cross!'

In this atmosphere the Confessing church held another synod, on 19 October. This time the delegates came together in Niemöller's own parish hall in Dahlem. The synod, which lasted over two days, accused Müller and Jäger of attempting to introduce a kind of 'papacy' into the German Protestant church. Again the repudiation of the Scriptural and confessional basis of the church was denounced, as was the introduction of the Führer principle into church affairs. Martin Niemöller was particularly vehement against the new paganism of the 'German Christians'. Afterwards a member, claiming to speak for many (*Eine für Viele*), wrote to congratulate him. 'In the Dahlem Synod you did what had to be done.' 'The "German Christians"', Niemöller's correspondent continued, 'have no knowledge of the heavenly. They are completely bound up with this world.' All their bandying of Biblical words was mere 'tactical juggling'. (ZEKHN 62, Vol. 1021)

This Dahlem synod took a further extremely important step. It set up on behalf of the Confessing church a small executive committee to conduct its affairs. This was a direct result of the behaviour of the Reich church authorities in Württemberg and Bavaria. 'The rape of the south German churches', the synod declared, 'has removed our last hope that order can be restored to the church by working from within.' A state of emergency now existed. The constitution of the Protestant church in Germany had collapsed. 'The men who have taken over the leadership of the Reich church have behaved in a manner that cuts them off from the Christian church.' As a result, the synod appointed the Council of Brethren to lead and represent the German Protestant church, as a federation of confessionally bound churches. 'We call upon Christian congregations, pastors, and elders to accept no instructions from the previous Reich church government and its authorities', the declaration concluded. 'We call upon them to abide by the instructions of the Confessing synod of the German Protestant church and of its recognized organs.'

The new 'Council of the German church' comprised Karl Koch as president, Hans Asmussen as its theological adviser, Thomas Breit, representing the Lutherans, Karl Barth, representing the Calvinists, Martin Niemöller, representing the churches of the old Prussian union, and Eberhard Fiedler, as their legal adviser. These six men were now the executive arm of the Council of Brethren, whose membership was extended to twenty-two.

On 25 September Niemöller published an article on the aims of the Confessing church. 'The Confessing church is nothing to do with a new or an old dogmatic, nor a Lutheran or Calvinist matter, nor to do with schism or separation, so long as we are not expelled', he wrote. It was supremely to do with 'calling Christianity back to the sources of its strength', in opposition to 'a new and different gospel, authorized and taught under a false flag'.

For a moment it seemed as if those who promulgated this false teaching had suffered a setback. In suspending Bishops Wurm and Meiser, Ludwig Müller and August Jäger had certainly overreached themselves. Both suspended bishops were extremely popular. (Ten thousand Bavarians demonstrated in the Adolf Hitler Platz in Nuremberg in favour of Meiser.) And the dismissals had been carried out with vulgar displays of authoritarianism of a kind scarcely ever before seen in the Protestant churches. Even some of the 'German Christians' objected. Müller's own deputy, Dr Fritz Engelke, resigned. Otto Zänker, whom Müller had made Bishop of Silesia, announced that he and 850 Silesian pastors were joining the Confessing church. Finally, Jäger resigned (on the pretext that his work was done).

Müller's position was all the weaker since Hitler clearly perceived that he had failed to unite the Protestant church. At the end of October Hitler ordered the release of Wurm and Meiser from house arrest. He summoned the two bishops and Marahrens to an audience, and told them he was no longer interested in church affairs – a clear indication that he was tired of supporting his unsuccessful Reich bishop. A week later the three bishops, with the addition of Otto Zänker, publicly called on Müller to resign.

The southern bishops had been assured by Hitler that henceforth the German Protestant church would be governed constitutionally. They were optimistic because Jäger had been forced to resign, it seemed at Hitler's insistence. Their optimism was dangerous. Hitler's change of heart did not extend to the dismissal of the Reich bishop. It arose far more from annoyance at the extent of the opposition Müller's policies were causing in areas that Hitler regarded as particularly pro-Nazi. He was especially anxious at this time not to encourage the kind of criticism in other countries that Bishop ˙Bell was stirring up in Britain. But he had been in no way converted by the attitude of the Confessing church. Far from allowing freedom in the church again, the minister of the interior at the beginning of November forbade the public discussion or even reporting of the problems of the church.

Yet, to Barth and Niemöller's consternation, some of the Council of Brethren set up at Dahlem seemed to be toying with the idea that they should not only get rid of the Reich bishop but even replace him. Marahrens was particularly keen to temper Barth's intransigent line, in order to make the gulf between the Confessing church and the state authorities less impassable. (In November he went so far as to describe Barth as 'the greatest danger to the German Protestant church'.) Bodelschwingh was weakening. Even Karl Koch and Karl Lücking felt that some kind of compromise was possible. Under pressure from the south German bishops, at an overnight meeting on 20/21 November in St Michael's hospice, Berlin, the 'Council' set up at Dahlem was replaced by a 'Provisional Church Government'. On 22 November, Marahrens became head of this new body.

'In those nocturnal tumults in St Michael's hospice', Barth wrote to Martin Niemöller, 'without further synods, Dahlem was invalidated, and while Barmen was "intact" and "unassailable", it was only a document.' The cohesion of the church's opposition to Hitler was breaking up. Barth, Niemöller, Karl Immer, and Hermann Albert Hesse (who had been one of the three to negotiate the first church constitution with the Third Reich) resigned from the Council of Brethren in anger.

This split had, in fact, been foreshadowed at Barmen. Niemöller, Hesse, and Pastor Horst Michael of Berlin had handed a motion to the president Koch suggesting that the Reich church government was no longer fit to administer the constitution of the German Protestant church and that, in consequence, 'the synod and the churches represented by it refuse to co-operate with the present church government in any reform of the constitution'. Bodelschwingh had at this point felt constrained to make a personal statement concerning a report (in the *Basler Nachrichten*) that he had been asked to serve on the legal committee of the Reich church government. Such an approach *had* been made. Rather than reject it entirely, Bodelschwingh had said he would in no way work with the Reich church government unless assured of complete freedom in that work and *unless the south German churches were agreeable.* He added that he did not think such a motion as that put down by Niemöller, Hesse, and Michael ought to be passed as binding on the leaders of the south German churches. Now, under pressure from 'the pernicious Bodelschwingh' (as Barth called him) and these south German bishops, Dahlem was being demolished. On the day Marahrens agreed to head the new Provisional Church Government, Barth wrote to Niemöller, 'We based our cause on God and not on success.'

Niemöller confessed that during the days of the Barmen synod, he had been filled with wonder that churches, pastors, and laymen from such different traditions had been at one. Within four months, Marahrens, Wurm, Meiser, and Bodelschwingh had destroyed that unity. In the eyes of Niemöller, it was an act of betrayal. It was also precisely what the state authorities wanted. Niemöller's colleague, Eberhard Röhricht, had a friend in the Office of Cultural Peace who learned that Heinrich Himmler refused to ban the Barmen synod because he did not wish to see the delegates united under opposition and believed that left alone they had a good chance of splitting up.

The task of rallying the Confessing church in these circumstances now fell largely to Martin Niemöller, who was shortly to be without the personal help of Barth. Barth had already decided not to take the newly prescribed oath of loyalty to Adolf Hitler, which made the loss of his professorial chair at Bonn inevitable. Indeed, even before he received notice of dismissal, the rector of the university announced the name of his successor, a 'German Christian'. At the beginning of March 1935 he was banned totally from speaking in public, and his last address (in defiance of the ban) was a sermon against idolatry (with which he connected the new Nazi religion) at the second free Calvinist synod held at Siegen on 26 March. By July he had accepted a chair at the university of Basel and was no longer in Germany. Niemöller was left to carry on the fight.

Church order, Niemöller wrote to Pastor Berger of Breslau on

28 February 1935, had been destroyed. To put it right, 'the proper foundation' was 'that of the Confessing church'. (ZEKHN 62, Vol. 1002) Soon it was clear that the overtures to state led by Marahrens (who, it was rumoured, hoped to replace Müller himself) were meeting with little success in changing the official Nazi ideology. Although Müller had lost Hitler's support, he was not dismissed. And in February, alarmed at the resurgence of pagan ideas, the Provisional Church Government decided to issue a manifesto warning parents especially against the spread of such notions in schools.

In March the Prussian Confessing Synod issued its own manifesto, warning against 'the deadly danger' of 'a new religion', which made idols of blood, race, nation, honour, eternal Germany, and so on. 'The state receives its sovereignty from God', the manifesto asserted, 'who also limits human authority'. Niemöller read it before a large congregation in Dahlem parish hall, and then said each Christian must make plain where he or she stood. The whole congregation then took the pledge of loyalty to the Confessing church.

The state authorities soon took reprisals. First, the minister of the interior announced the reduction by one fifth of church taxes in Prussia. Next 700 Prussian pastors were either imprisoned or put under house arrest for reading the manifesto. Those who had not read the manifesto the previous Sunday were warned by the police to ignore it. On Sunday 17 March groups of police made certain that pastors under house arrest did stay at home. In Berlin, Jacobi was prevented from going out. His place was taken at church by a colleague who courageously read the manifesto and was himself arrested. Niemöller was not planning to preach that Sunday. None the less, he too was arrested and taken to police headquarters in Alexanderplatz. (He was allowed to take some books with him and telephone home.) Jacobi was also arrested.

All the arrested pastors were released within two days, but to Niemöller's anger, the behaviour of the authorities had persuaded even Karl Koch to seek some sort of truce. The result was that on Sunday 24 March the manifesto was read again by all the Prussian members of the Pastors' Emergency League, with the addition of a preamble in which it was stated that President Koch had explained to the minister of the interior that 'the manifesto was directed only at the new heathen religion and the threatened danger contained in it for both nation and state'.

Niemöller took the opportunity of preaching, to his congregation and to the secret police now sitting amongst them, a powerful sermon against the new pagansim. 'We see more and more clearly', he said, 'how there is being propagated a new heathenism, which wishes to have nothing to do with the Saviour, who was crucified for us, while the church which acknowledges that Saviour as its only Lord is exposed to reproval as an enemy of the state.'

The virtual disappearance of Ludwig Müller, far from resulting in a reduction of the 'Nordic' propaganda of the Third Reich, had been followed by the appearance of far more virulent forms of this teaching. Dr Artur Dinter was now active again, with his belief in the racial hierarchy which put Jews at the bottom of humanity and Germans at the top. Dinter taught that Jesus had been a Godlike Aryan. He despised Müller for capitulating to Wilhelm and Martin Niemöller and Gerhard Jacobi after the Sports Palace rally. Dinter described Müller as 'the arch-reactionary Yahweh-priest, whose heart drops down into his trousers at the report of the Sports Palace demonstration'. Now Niemöller pointedly asked from his Dahlem pulpit why 'a Dr Dinter and others should be allowed to harangue the people and canvass for their anti-Christian views, while we are condemned to silence in public'.

Increasingly, Niemöller's sermons referred to pastors arrested by the police. As he wrote to Superintendent Buth of Griefenberg (after energetic complaints by the Confessing church had secured the release of a young Pomeranian pastor), this practice clearly displayed 'the undergirding of the illegitimate church government by the state'. (ZEKHN 62, Vol. 1021) Now the arrests were multiplying. Niemöller and the Confessing church were determined that the victims should not be forgotten. From his pulpit on Passion Sunday, 1935 Niemöller said, 'Today all the bells of the German Protestant churches are silent, and at the same time in every divine service intercession is being made for the five Protestant pastors from Hessen and Saxony who have been taken away from their congregations and put in concentration camps in spite of the remonstrances of the Provisional Church Government to the authorities concerned.' If one suffers,

Niemöller insisted, the whole church suffers. He spoke of a Frankfurt pastor, arrested nearly three weeks previously for refusing the instructions of his 'illegal' bishop to leave his congregation. The pastor's mother, said Niemöller, was in hospital suffering from cancer. His father had suffered a stroke on hearing the news of his son's arrest.

The fall of Müller in no way led to an end to state interference in the affairs of the church. On the contrary, on 19 July 1935 it was announced that one of Hitler's cabinet members, Hanns Kerrl, had been appointed to the newly created post of Reich minister for church affairs. Kerrl was an anti-Semitic lawyer who had been Reich commissar for the Prussian ministry of justice. Kerrl saw his task as bringing peace to the divided Protestant church. But to achieve this he felt it necessary to take into his own hands both the financial control of the churches and the right to settle legal disputes within them. Although his ostensible task was to bring peace to a troubled church, he was by no means averse to seeing pastors imprisoned. And, as it turned out, the Gestapo were on occasion quite willing to hamper, harass and imprison pastors without reference to the new Reich minister for church affairs.

Martin Niemöller had no doubt that Kerrl's office was yet another illegitimate attempt by the state to interfere in the affairs of the church. He was also extremely anxious over the prevaricating attitude of Christians in the camp of Meiser, Wurm, and Marahrens. At the end of July he expressed these fears in a circular letter. 'In recent months we have been waiting for the decisive success of our church administration and for official recognition by the state of the Confessing church', he wrote. 'But we have received only one disappointment after another.' It was faithlessness 'to put our trust in men rather than God'. No doubt many were tired and despondent, but 'we must ask our brethren to examine their hearts to see if they are ready for the future struggle'.

Kerrl's initial attempts to interfere in the Prussian church met with failure. His direction that by 23 August all pastors in the Confessing church must deal only with his new financial department was ignored. He failed to prevent a meeting of the Prussian synod of the Confessing church in Berlin-Steglitz at the end of September, even though he went so far as to release some imprisoned pastors as a peace-offer.

He did, however, make his influence powerfully felt at the synod, by sending a representative, Dr Julius Stahn, who warned the delegates of the unpleasant consequences that would follow if they displeased the authorities by passing contentious resolutions. 'Learn to hold your tongues', Stahn insolently told the delegates, 'and in so doing you will insult no one'.

A good number of faint-hearted delegates wished to keep the conference as uncontroversial as possible. To them Niemöller was now an embarrassment. Meiser and Marahrens were particularly anxious lest he bring up the Jewish question again. On 15 September the so-called Nuremberg Laws ('for the protection of German blood and German honour') ushered in a new phase of anti-Semitic activity in the Reich. Marahrens and Meiser desperately tried to persuade Koch, as president of the forthcoming synod, to keep the question off the agenda. 'I await with considerable trepidation the coming Prussian synod, if such things as the Jewish question are to be broached', said Meiser. 'I would like to raise my voice against a self-inflicted martyrdom.' Niemöller and his allies insisted on debating the subject. But the synod considerably toned down what should have been a protest against racism. Its final resolution did assert that everyone, including Jews, should be offered salvation in Jesus Christ and it deplored the fact that some congregations were forbidding the baptism of Jews. Niemöller, for his part, deplored the fact that no real word of 'Christian brotherhood' had been spoken. It was not enough to say merely that 'Jews should be baptized', and to him it was painful that the synod had confined itself to that. 'We shall be obliged to say more', he told the delegates, 'and it will be that our mouths will only be really opened, when we have to undergo suffering ourselves.'

Kerrl had won a partial victory. The Confessing church was splitting up. On 24 September he and Adolf Hitler signed a decree which 'empowered the Reich minister for church affairs to issue ordinances with binding legal force, for the purpose of restoring orderly conditions in the German Protestant church and the regional Protestant churches'. On 14 October he set up a Reich church committee, with the task of setting up smaller committees that would bring peace to the whole church. He shrewdly managed to persuade the widely respected Wilhelm Zoellner to chair the new body.

In July forty-nine members of the Pastors' Emergency League had signed Niemöller's circular calling for 'a clear, uncompromising answer of "No" to every temptation to try to solve the church's problem in a way which contradicts the decisions of Barmen and Dahlem'. Barmen, said the circular, defined the church's confessional stance, Dahlem its order and organization. 'If it comes to the point', the circular concluded, 'may God help us to be able to speak this "No" gladly and in unity.' But there was no unity. In October Kerrl visited Marahrens to say that he proposed to disband the Council of Brethren, unless it agreed to disband itself. Church leaders, said Kerrl, were invited to co-operate now with the new Reich church committee. On 14 November Marahrens told Niemöller and Fritz Müller of his intention of backing down before Kerrl and co-operating with the new ministry. That same day fifteen members of the Council of Brethren ('the faithful opposition', as Niemöller called them in his diary) met in Niemöller's home and resolved that 'collaboration with the Reich church committee is incompatible with membership of the Confessing church'.

Convinced that he had split the leadership of the Confessing church, Kerrl now took a further repressive step. On 30 November the Council of Brethren was given notice that henceforth anything they wished to distribute must be approved by police headquarters in Berlin. Niemöller read the order from his pulpit, with the comment that it would 'reduce the church to a state of absolute slavery at the mercy of a high-handed state'. The Reich minister for church affairs, he said, was 'trying to compel the church to tolerate racial heresy and poison itself with such doctrines'.

On 2 December Kerrl declared illegal the organizations of the Confessing church. Two days later the Confessing synod of Berlin-Brandenburg met as planned in the parish hall at Dahlem. Gerhard Jacobi chaired the meeting. Niemöller welcomed the delegates in the name of the Council of Brethren. When secret police arrived, he welcomed them and asked them to take the seats that had been reserved on their behalf. They drove away again. After a two-hour discussion, the 180 delegates (in the presence of 500 guest observers) unanimously resolved that Kerrl's decree of 2 December violated the freedom and the inner life of the church. To submit to it would mean giving up obedience to the church's Lord. That evening Niemöller received a police order forbidding him to speak anywhere in the Reich.

Niemöller was being increasingly isolated by Kerrl. And although Fritz Müller in Dahlem stood staunchly by him, the parish itself was divided. Eberhard Röhricht went along with them still, but only with reservations. Elsewhere pastors were openly expressing their doubts about the wisdom of Niemöller's refusal to compromise with Kerrl. 'What in fact is left?' asked Heinz Brunotte of Hanover on 10 December. 'Is there really anything more than a small circle in the old Prussian union that has reached a dead end as a result of Niemöller's tactics?'

The seriousness of the attempt to ban Niemöller was revealed in January 1936, when he issued a pamphlet with the title *The State Church is Here!* This pamphlet, though published under Niemöller's name, had in fact been written by the deposed General-Superintendent Otto Dibelius. It consisted of a biting attack on Kerrl's willingness to impose his views on the church by means of the Gestapo. It deplored the attacks on the church by members of the Hitler Youth and SS. A politicized church, Dibelius argued, cannot be free. He attacked those who co-operated with Kerrl in setting up such a church, which was bound to impose the views of the 'German Christians' on the Protestant church. A state church, Dibelius concluded, already exists, designed to serve the political authorities, not to preach the gospel. Many copies of the pamphlet were printed. Most were seized by the police, who even entered pastors' homes to confiscate them.

The following month the split in the Confessing church became even more dangerous. At a national synod held at Bad Oeynhausen between 17 and 22 February, Meiser, Wurm, and Marahrens were determined to carry the majority with them in agreeing to collaborate with the Reich church committee. As a result, Niemöller, Martin Albertz, and Hans Böhm took the extreme step of setting up a second provisional church administration, in opposition to those who now seemed to be abandoning the hard-won claim that the Confessing church, and that alone, truly represented the Protestant churches of Germany. None of this deterred Marahrens. He had been assured, along with Meiser

1. Heinrich Niemöller and his family beside the Christmas tree. Martin sits at the table, left.

2. Martin Niemöller and Hermann Bremer as naval cadets.

3. The U-boat captain in World War I.

4. Niemöller and the crew of UC67, Kiel, November 1918.

5. Martin and Else Niemöller, with their children Jochen and Martin, c.1930.

6. Dora Schultz and three of Niemöller's grandchildren.

7. Martin Niemöller talks with an American soldier after his release; Tyrol, May 1945.

8. Niemöller and Bishop George Bell of Chichester greet each other on 28 October 1945 in the Marienkirche, Berlin.

9. Martin Niemöller with his wife Else during a press conference of the Federal Council of Churches of Christ in America, 1947.

10. Martin Niemöller with Bishops Otto Dibelius and Hanns Lilje at a meeting of the World Council of Churches in Chichester, July 1949.

11. With Metropolitan Boris, on his return from Russia in 1952.

12. Martin Niemöller and Karl Barth.

13. The last picture of Martin with his wife Else before her death in an accident, 7 August 1961.

14. Martin and Sybil Niemöller, with Sybil's son Marc, 1979.

15. Martin Niemöller, Linus Pauling, and Sybil Niemöller in the garden of their home in Wiesbaden, 3 July 1983.

and Wurm, that the Reich church committee would set up no sub-committees in the dioceses of Hanover, Bavaria, or Württemberg. He now, however, resigned as president of the Provisional church government to head a committee appointed by Kerrl to administer the Protestant church of Hanover. To this committee Kerrl even appointed a 'German Christian'.

Niemöller did not conceal his bitterness over Marahrens and over those who had collaborated with him. On 6 April he wrote to Bodelschwingh that he was appalled to see 'a man like Marahrens putting a "German Christian" on the governing body of his church'. Niemöller added, 'In accordance with the cunning plan of Messrs Kerrl and Zoellner, these men Marahrens and Meiser have now happily smashed to pieces the Confessing church, in order to preserve their own lives. No blessing will come from this betrayal. Alas that one must now connect the name of Bodelschwingh with this course.' (ZEKHN 62, Vol. 1020)

As Bonhoeffer had written to Martin Niemöller on 12 August 1935, the German church needed 'a fundamentally different interpretation than hitherto of Matthew 22.21' (where Jesus is reported as saying, 'Render unto Caesar the things that are Caesar's, and unto God the things that are God's'). For Niemöller, the stance of the German state authorities on church affairs was utterly unacceptable. 'The relation between the state and us which is denoted by the words "authority" and "obedience" will not satisfy us in the long run', he told his parishioners. 'We should like a direct personal connection of trust and love.' On 15 November he protested in a sermon that it was no longer possible to decide what things belonged to God and what belonged to Caesar, since Caesar was now claiming all. Niemöller, along with the vast majority of German Protestants, remained still intensely patriotic. When, in August 1936, the Council of Brethren made yet another attempt to protest against attacks on Christianity in the Third Reich and the dissemination of pagan ideas, by issuing a manifesto (this time written by Karl Koch and Fritz Müller) to be read in all churches, Niemöller was perfectly willing to read the passage that stated, 'We are prepared to sacrifice all our worldly goods and our blood for the state and our German people.' What the pastors were not willing to do – as the manifesto continued – was 'to have it said of us before God's judgement seat: "When the gospel of Jesus was attacked in Germany, you were silent and, without resisting, left your children to an alien spirit." '

Niemöller now had no doubt that the conflict would worsen, in spite of the apparent calm produced by the capitulation of church leaders to Kerrl. On 4 June he published an open letter on the situation of the church, which observed, in nautical language: 'We have at the moment comparative peace, like a ship in the middle of a typhoon: it is only a question of time before the storm breaks out again, with greater force.' He quoted the prophet Isaiah: 'Strengthen the weak hands; make firm the feeble knees.' On 9 June he was encouraging a correspondent with a quotation from St Paul: 'Though our outward body perish, our inner man is renewed day by day.' (ZEKHN 62, Vol. 1021)

Niemöller's belief that the battle would become fiercer was no doubt inspired in part by the fact that the Confessing church had just made its sharpest attack on Hitler's policies, by delivering in secret a memorandum to Hitler himself. Drawn up in its final form by Niemöller, Hans Asmussen, and a courageous young pastor from Lübeck, Wilhelm Jannasch (who delivered it to the Reich chancellery), the memorandum declared that the attacks on the church were now harsher than at any time since 1918 and had the backing, it seemed, of important state officials. Pastors were subject to imprisonment for expressing dissenting views. Some were even in concentration camps. National Socialist organizations such as the Hitler Youth now worked in direct opposition to the churches. Paganism was disseminated in the press and on the radio. The Aryan race was absurdly glorified, though the Bible taught that all men were sinners. And Christians were being forced to hate Jews, whereas Christ demanded that they should love their neighbour.

In July the contents of this memorandum were leaked to the foreign press. The 'culprit' was deemed to be Dr Friedrich Weissler, a 'non-Aryan' lawyer now working as legal adviser to the Confessing church. Weissler was dismissed, and on 19 February 1937 died in Sachsenhausen concentration camp as a result of Gestapo brutality.

Privately and in public, Niemöller continued as before to denounce anti-Semitism. To correspondents he recommended books and articles about the value of the Old Testament (e.g. to

Sister Käthe Beck, 9 December 1935: ZEKHN 62, Vol. 1021).
When parishioners who wished to get married in St Anne's
church asked him *not* to read an Old Testament passage during
the service, they were firmly reproved. In his pulpit he reminded
his parishioners that Jesus Christ was a Jew, and that the Sports
Palace meeting would have condemned *him* too, would have
taught the German nation 'to join in the shout "Away with the
Jews; we do not want Him to reign over us! – His blood be upon
us and our children."' When 'German Christians' mocked the
God of the Old Testament as 'Jah, the demon of the wilderness',
Niemöller observed that 'the words which once led our nation to
the living God are one after the other being filled up with debris a
yard high'.

He used the opportunity of the Harvest Festival celebrations to
attack Nazi teaching on German 'blood' and 'soil'. It was not
good enough, he said, to speak of our 'native soil' and our
'nationality' with a 'renewed reverence', as if 'all the men and
women of German blood and German soil could here find a
supreme religious experience, shared by us all and independent of
all narrow dogmas and doctrines, and beyond all the bounds of
confessionalism that separate us from one another'. These
Germanic elements in the national character were, like all things,
subject to sin and death. 'We cannot, as creatures condemned to
death in the midst of a creation condemned to death, honestly
give praise and thanks, without remembering that there is a death
knell at the end,' said Niemöller. On 22 November he elaborated
this theme with the startling observation that 'those who say we
live on for ever in the life of the German nation are merely
attempting to deny the solemn fact of death and covering it up
with a pious lie!'

By now, as his private correspondence reveals, Niemöller was
well aware of the great risks he was running. Hans Ehrenberg, a
'non-Aryan' pastor who, after suffering in Sachsenhausen,
escaped to safety in Britain, wrote that when Englishmen asked
'Who amongst you has really been able to resist Hitler?' there
was one consoling answer: 'Niemöller, who was a submarine
commander in the last war, has managed it.' But in 1936, though
still resisting, Niemöller no longer expected to succeed in
protecting the Jews of Germany – not even those who had become
Christian. He urged them to escape while they could. On 29 July

1936 Corvette Captain Walter Schmidt-Henrici wrote from Erfurt asking advice about his son, who was studying theology, 'for he is not purely Aryan'. Captain Schmidt-Henrici explained, 'I myself am pure Aryan, but my wife's parents were not Aryan, and as young children became Christians. My wife was baptized as a small child and brought up as a Christian.' Niemöller advised him to try to get his son out of the country and into Switzerland, for, he said, 'the future of the Confessing church in Germany is cloudy, and theological education in Germany is dubious'. (ZEKHN 62, Vol. 1021)

Theological education was in fact increasingly subject to 'German Christian' doctrines and the determined interference of the state authorities. For this reason, as early as June 1934 Niemöller and Karl Koch had suggested to the Council of Brethren that Dietrich Bonhoeffer should be invited to direct an independent preachers' seminary on their behalf. Niemöller and Jacobi both had to fight hard to get Bonhoeffer accepted as a suitable director of such a seminary, but their views prevailed. It was a risky venture and in the end was closed down by the Nazis. After Kerrl's accession to power, Bonhoeffer wrote unhappily that 'everything we do here is now illegal and contrary to the law of the state'. Yet he and Niemöller took courage from each other. On 3 December 1936 Bonhoeffer wrote to Martin, 'Despite the seriousness of the situation we are very happy and confident. For the rest we act in accordance with Mathias Claudius's wonderful hymn:

> I pray that God may grant
> The little that I want;
> For if he doth the sparrows feed,
> Will he not fill my daily need?'

By now the initial suspicion shown by Bonhoeffer had disappeared, and on occasion he was even willing to defer to Niemöller's judgement against his own. During the 1936 Olympic games, Jacobi, Asmussen, Dibelius, Iwand, and Niemöller decided to use St Paul's church in Berlin as the venue for a series of lectures on the situation of the German Protestant church, as a counter to the way in which Hitler was using the games to bolster up his own image abroad. Bonhoeffer thought the whole venture a waste of time, but out of deference to his friends, agreed to take part. While in Berlin, however, he did copy out from a shop window near St Paul's church some verses to send to Niemöller which revealed the true viciousness of their adversaries. They read:

> After the Olympiad
> We'll beat the Confessing church to pulp;
> Then we'll throw out the Jews,
> And that will be the end of the Confessing church.
>
> *(Nach der Olympiade*
> *Hauen wir die BK zu Marmelade;*
> *Dann schmeissen wir die Juden raus,*
> *Dann ist die BK aus.)*

Niemöller's activity during the Olympic games of 1936 again reveals his new appreciation of the importance of international opinion. He and Hans Asmussen even contemplated going to a meeting of the Universal Christian Council for Life and Work, held at Chamby in August. (This time Bonhoeffer's view that they would only waste their time prevailed.) Niemöller was increasingly keen to meet foreign Christians visiting Germany, to give them his version of what was happening to the German churches. At the end of August he had a long discussion on the subject with Professor John Brown Mason of Colorado Women's College, USA. And early in 1937 he met for the first time Bishop George Bell of Chichester. 'He was like a man on fire', wrote Bell, 'but smiling and friendly all the time – and a man of very great faith. He was not just a fighter, though he was that too. He was warm-hearted and humorous, and full of the spirit of friendship. He said that faith was greater than organisation, and that there had been too much interest in organisation everywhere.'

1936 had been a tough year for Niemöller. To the widow of Pastor Karl Lange of Neustätten he wrote on 11 September that 'This year the struggle for the church amazed us all by becoming harder.' (ZEKHN 62, Vol. 1021) But 1937 was to be worse. On New Year's Day Niemöller attacked the proscriptions on preaching the gospel, the destruction of theological colleges, and the imprisonment of pastors. The previous August he had reminded his congregation of St Paul's words (in the letter to the Philippians, 1: 27, 29) about the privilege of suffering for the sake of the gospel. When St Paul wrote those words, said Niemöller, he was in prison. In August 1936 he observed that many Confessing pastors were imprisoned behind the walls of their churches, forbidden to speak outside. Now, in January 1937, nine Confessing pastors in Lübeck were put under house arrest. These men were by no means extremists. One of them, Bruno Meyer of the church of St Aegidien, had as junior colleague Wilhelm Jannasch, who had delivered the fatal memorandum of protest to Hitler. Bruno Meyer had noted in his diary that he and Jannasch 'were completely agreed' in opposing the 'German Christians'. Pastor Meyer added, 'If only he were not so fearfully headstrong and incautious!'

Now the cautious (albeit uncompromising) Meyer was silenced, along with eight of his Lübeck colleagues. Niemöller denounced what had happened from his pulpit on 30 January. The church was in chains, he declared, unable to preach the gospel of Jesus Christ. 'The one word Lübeck speaks too plainly for its importance to be missed: Lübeck, the town in Germany where the preaching of the biblical gospel is forbidden by the police; Lübeck, the town in the German Fatherland where all the Protestant preachers have been forcibly prevented by the police from bearing witness to the Lord Jesus Christ as the one Saviour and Redeemer.' It was no exaggeration. What had happened to the nine well-loved pastors in Lübeck had revealed the hollowness of Kerrl's protestations of friendship for the churches. It also destroyed his policy. The Confessing church in Lübeck had been very much inclined to follow the lead of Marahrens in co-operating with the Reich church committee, and indeed had written to Niemöller telling him so. But the nine pastors found themselves unable to accept the 'German Christian' polemics of their bishop, Erwin Balzer. Zoellner therefore decided to visit them to try to work out some accommodation between the silenced pastors and the bishop. The Gestapo refused to allow it. On 12 February 1937 Zoellner and his committee resigned.

Niemöller was now the focus of the whole opposition to the domination of the church by the National Socialist state. On 10 March 1937 Gerhard Jacobi wrote saying that only he could avert a catastrophe. 'I hope you still have good relationships', said the letter. 'All mine have been destroyed.' (ZEKHN 62, Vol. 1021)

The time for 'good relationships' had in truth long passed. Without sacrificing his principles, Niemöller had hitherto done his best not to provoke the authorities. The original draft of his pamphlet on the meaning of the Confessing church had, for instance, included a passage describing what ought to have happened at the notorious Sports Palace Rally. Surely a Christian should have leaped onto the platform and cried, 'Do not believe what you are being told here about the superiority of Nordic man! That is all nothing but dreams and fairy tales! The word of God teaches that all men (from Adam to Adolf Hitler) are, without exception, sinners.' In the published version, Niemöller prudently omitted the words 'from Adam to Adolf Hitler'. (Bp. 10. 17)

Since that time, however, the interference by the state in church affairs had become increasingly vicious. Niemöller by April 1937 was publicly praying for and naming colleagues of the Confessing church under arrest or in concentration camps. And he openly associated himself with known enemies of Kerrl's religious policies.

At the end of April, for instance, he paid a visit to Clemens August von Galen, the Roman Catholic Bishop of Münster. The previous month, Pope Pius XI had decided to take action over the repeated violation of the Concordat signed by the papacy and Hitler in 1933. An encyclical to the Catholic bishops of Germany, *Mit brennender Sorge*, was secretly smuggled into the country and on Palm Sunday was read in every Catholic pulpit.

'With burning concern and mounting consternation', said the Pope, 'we have been observing for some time now the cross carried by the church in Germany and the increasingly difficult situation of those men and women who have kept the faith and remained true to her in thought and deed.' He then condemned those who made 'race, nation and state' the supreme norm of all values. 'The culmination of revelation in the gospel of Jesus Christ is final and binding for ever.' The encyclical proceeded to condemn interference in the church's youth work and schools. It infuriated Hitler, who ordered all copies to be seized and closed down Catholic printing presses in reprisal.

Galen in particular refused to be intimidated. As early as 1935 he had been outspoken in his criticism of the new paganism of Germany. In spite of attacks from Kerrl's ministry, he refused to keep silent. On 21 December 1936 he had sent a protest to the Westphalian president, complaining of a decree threatening with instant dismissal any Catholic secondary school teacher who read in Sunday schools the pastoral letters of the bishops. Now, in spite of Hitler's anger over *Mit brennender Sorge*, Galen refused to let the matter drop. In early summer, 1937, he preached for nearly two hours, listing violations of the Concordat. Sisters of Mercy had been expelled from schools and hospitals, he complained. Catholic teachers had been thrown out of church schools. Many church organizations had been dissolved, and their property confiscated. The right of church authorities to visit schools had been vetoed. 'All this, and much else that is in contradiction to the Concordat, is known to all of us', Galen concluded. 'The Pope knows it too! Should I therefore remain silent?'

Niemöller publicly praised his stand. In a sermon in Bielefeld on 18 June he explained that, at a time when the very foundations of Christianity were being disputed, 'new gulfs open up and also new links are forged.' He went on: 'I truly believe I could join in common prayer with a man like the Bishop of Münster, whereas I find it inconceivable that I could ever go the Lord's Supper with a "German Christian" bishop.' Great changes were coming about, he said. 'At any rate, for me the gulf between the Protestant church and the "German Christians" is deeper and wider than that between us and our Catholic fellow-believers.' Here Niemöller was working out in practice the theme of part of a book which he and Otto Dibelius had edited and published in March. The book urged Germany to return to the true God. Niemöller's section of the book was based on Jesus's words, 'He that is not with me is against me.' By now Niemöller had little time for the cautious. He had virtually abandoned caution himself. When the secret police tapped a telephone conversation in which he spoke disparagingly of Bodelschwingh, Kerrl was jubilant, threatening to publicize the speech and discredit Niemöller. Otto Dibelius could scarcely restrain Niemöller from telephoning Kerrl to demand instant publication, to show the world the Gestapo's methods.

As well as acknowledging his solidarity with Roman Catholics in the struggle for the gospel, Niemöller also sought to make contact with the budding ecumenical movement outside Germany. He and four other members of the Confessing church had decided to take part in a 'Life and Work' conference in Oxford later that summer. The Reich church committee had no intention of allowing this, and on 14 May the passports of the five men were confiscated.

Three days later Niemöller preached that those who were demanding a national church and the end of loyalty to the Reformation confessions were in truth concealing their intention to do away altogether with both the Christian churches and the Christian faith. And as for those who now claimed the right to rule over the church, the Lord Jesus ordained none of them, he said. All that the Holy Scriptures demand, he asserted, is that Christians humbly repeat the word of God.

During all this, Niemöller was still faithfully serving his congregation as a pastor. The last confirmation he ever conducted at Dahlem took place at Easter. Niemöller was photographed proudly leading his confirmands from the church after the service, his Bible in his hand. Hans Ehrenberg too held a confirmation service on that day. As he later noted, he and Martin Niemöller were to be arrested, also on the same day, later in 1937.

In February Hitler had ordered new church elections for membership of the national synod. On Sunday 6 June Niemöller read a statement from the Provisional Church Government and the Council of Brethren asking what precisely 'free elections' could mean. So many pastors had been arrested or forbidden to speak, so many election leaflets had been confiscated, so many houses had been searched, that the church was in no way living in freedom. Niemöller had instituted week-day services of intercession, when the names of arrested pastors were read out. In the following week, the Confessing church fought hard against the repression in the church, organizing 'services of renewal' and taking collections for theological students.

The persecuted were still seeking Niemöller's help. On 15 June a Lutheran law student from Berlin named Ernst Walter wrote to him explaining that because his grandmother on his father's side had Jewish blood, his own hopes of becoming a judge had been dashed. (ZEKHN 62, Vol. 1021) There was little Niemöller could do to help. On the same day his friend Jacobi and two other Berlin pastors were arrested on a charge of incitement to disobey the law. On 19 June Niemöller took five minutes to read the list of those pastors who were either forbidden to speak, ejected from their parishes or under arrest. He mentioned especially Pastors Wilhelm Busch and Heinrich Held of Essen, who had been imprisoned merely for defending themselves against attack (a right supposedly guaranteed by the Führer himself) and Pastor Wilhelm Niesel who, along with seven other members of the Prussian Council of Brethren, had been arrested merely for announcing the names of people who had seceded from the church. Niemöller commented on these arrests with the ominous question, 'Does the Führer's word still hold good?' And he quoted a slogan first used four years ago: 'The gospel must remain *the gospel*; the church must remain *the church*; the creed must remain *the creed*; Protestant Christianity must remain *Protestant Christianity*.' He added, 'We must not – for heaven's sake – make a German gospel out of the gospel; we must not – for heaven's sake – make a German church out of Christ's church; we must not – for God's sake – make *German* Christians out of Protestant Christians.'

Hans Asmussen had gone into hiding. On 19 June his wife was questioned for four hours by the police at the Alexanderplatz because she refused to give any information about her husband's whereabouts. 'They would like to put the rest of the members of the Prussian Council of Brethren under lock and key', Niemöller said. Of the twenty-five leaders, twenty had been taken away by the police. 'I still had two weeks time until I was imprisoned myself', Niemöller recalled. 'They didn't want me immediately, and I had two weeks to look for twenty persons who were willing and able to replace the ones who had been imprisoned. That was the severest and hardest piece of work I had to do, to find people to fill up the ranks. But I thought, "Ah, God has left me something to do, as long as I am a free man and can travel around."' (MN/jb)

On Friday 25 June Niemöller celebrated Holy Communion and was incensed to discover three members of the Gestapo present, 'whose duty it was', he complained, 'to inform upon the community of Jesus in their praying, in their singing, and in their teaching'. Niemöller professed himself appalled that these young men, 'who certainly were once baptized in the name of Jesus and who certainly have pledged their faith to the Saviour', were now laying traps for his flock. He was equally incensed at a newspaper report that Asmussen had taken flight to escape lawful arrest. He announced that he had written to the Reich minister of justice: 'Pastor Asmussen will naturally be at your service as soon as a writ of subpoena is served against him or a warrant issued for his arrest.' The minister replied that he had sent a copy of Niemöller's letter to the secret police.

In his sermon on Sunday 27 June Niemöller referred to the attempt to arrest Asmussen. Asmussen had fled, he explained, on the advice of the Prussian Council of Brethren. But he was ready to give himself up if the authorities issued a proper summons. 'We have no more thought of using our own powers to escape the arm of the authorities than had the apostles of old,' said Niemöller. 'No more are we ready to keep silence at man's behest, when God commands us to speak. For it is, and must remain the case, that we must obey God rather than man.'

The subject of Niemöller's sermon was the Rabbi Gamaliel who (according to Acts 5) had persuaded the Jewish Sanhedrin to show tolerance to the teaching of St Peter and his fellow-Christians. As a result, the apostles were released from custody. No doubt, said Niemöller, one would wish for such a pious and intelligent man to plead for tolerance now. But, he pointed out, the troubles of the apostles did not come to an end. The Sanhedrin 'accepted Gamaliel's advice as regards freedom of conscience, and released the prisoners – though not without beating them and renewing the embargo on their speech', he said. And in the very next chapter of Acts there breaks out the 'lightning flash' of persecution.

Neutrality was impossible in Germany, said Niemöller. Persecution had begun.

I think, for instance, how on Wednesday the secret police penetrated the closed church of Friedrich Werder and arrested at the altar eight members of the Council of Brethren.... I think how yesterday at Saarbrücken six women and a trusted man of the Protestant community were arrested because they had circulated an election leaflet of the Confessing church.... And we recall today how the pulpit of St Anne's church remains empty, because our pastor and brother Müller, with forty-seven other Christian brothers and sisters of our Protestant church, has been taken into custody.

There was more suffering ahead, said Niemöller. 'It may still be a long road until we are truly glad ... like the apostles, who were counted worthy to suffer shame for Jesus's name.'

Niemöller never preached again in Dahlem church until after the death of Adolf Hitler. He was extremely surprised to have escaped imprisonment during the wave of arrests a fortnight earlier. (MN/jb) On Monday 28 June he visited his brother

Wilhelm in Bielefeld, and preached in St James's church. The following day he was in Wiesbaden, where he made no less than three speeches on the 'spiritual bolshevism' that he saw infecting Germany. He called on an old school friend, Ernst Königs, who had been ordained and become a staunch supporter of the Confessing church. From there he went to Bethel, 'to battle' with Bodelschwingh, Wurm, and Meiser, who had assembled there. 'I attended the bishops' meeting', Niemöller recalled. 'They couldn't throw me out. I thought they needed strengthening. Then I took a fast train and arrived in Berlin during the night.'

'You had to restrain your anxiety with all your power in 1937', Niemöller added, 'You couldn't avoid anxiety, but you had to overcome it.' In Berlin he took the unprecedented step of asking Franz Hindebrandt to take the next morning's confirmation classes. 'I told my friend Hildebrandt I was absolutely done for. I wanted to sleep and have a good morning's rest.' As he took breakfast with Else on the morning of 1 July, the secret police arrived and arrested him.

9. HITLER'S PERSONAL PRISONER

NIEMÖLLER HAD been arrested five times previously and kept in prison for a day or so. This time, he recalled, 'they brought me to the secret police headquarters in Alexanderplatz. I was not interrogated in any way, but brought to Moabit prison. It was to be a short thing, but this short thing lasted for eight years!' (MN/jb) The same day the secret police returned to Niemöller's home, where several pastors were comforting his family. Determined to find evidence of his illegal activity, the police ransacked the house throughout the whole day, refusing to let anyone leave. They took away documents and papers belonging to the Confessing church. From a wall safe they took 30,000 marks that had been earmarked for the Pastors' Emergency League. They also took all Niemöller's diaries for the years 1933 to 1937. (ZEKHN 62, Vol. 425/2449a)

Otto Dibelius took the imprisoned pastor's place in the Dahlem pulpit the following Sunday. He preached on the set reading for the day, which was an account of the sufferings of St Paul. The church was swarming with secret police, conspicuous by their refusal to take any active part in the worship. Although Dibelius mentioned Niemöller only in his final prayer, this was enough to have Dibelius arrested ten days layer. At his commital proceedings, the judge observed, 'You refer to the apostle Paul all the time, but in fact you always mean Niemöller.' Other pastors were ready to take Dibelius's place. On subsequent Sundays in Dahlem Niemöller's brother Wilhelm attacked the Nazi press for describing the imprisoned pastor as a traitor to his country. Others expressed their solidarity in different ways. Dietrich Bonhoeffer published his *Cost of Discipleship* that year with the dedication, 'To Martin Niemöller in brotherly gratitude: a book he himself could have written better than its author.' And the women of the Dahlem parish choir came to sing hymns outside Else Niemöller's window on the evening of her husband's arrest.

In Moabit Niemöller occupied a cell with one window, a table, stool, and wooden bed, which hooked up on the wall when not in use. He was warned not to let it down during the day. The prison doctor, however, turned out to be a 'non-Aryan', and soon changed this rule, so that Martin could, if he wished, sleep at any time. 'I was not pleased with being cut off in this way', he later recalled, 'and suddenly not knowing any more what was happening with the church.' (MN/jb) In one of his letters home he ruefully quoted Jesus's last words to St Peter: 'Another will come and carry you where you do not wish to go.' Without his strong leadership, the Pastors' Emergency League inevitably lost its thrust in the church struggle; but Niemöller was delighted to discover that it still continued supporting dismissed pastors until the end of the Second World War. (MN/jb)

On the day after Niemöller's arrest Bishop George Bell wrote in protest to Rudolf Hess. Hess sent a four-page reply, in the course of which he reminded Bell of the ever-present dangers of Bolshevism and told him that the Niemöller affair was a problem for Germany and no one else. He asked Bell what he would think if Germans wrote to Britain about parsons who had been dismissed. 'Pastor Niemöller', he observed, 'like any other citizen, will be dealt with by the courts.' (Bp. 10. 23f.) But the authorities were especially concerned that the courts should not acquit Niemöller. They were particularly annoyed at the acquittal of Dibelius in August. Niemöller remained in Moabit for seven months, while his case was prepared.

Else was allowed to see him every ten days, always in the presence of a gaoler. Sometimes she brought one of their children. On the first of these visits, she was so shocked at his condition that she forcefully complained, and his food ration was increased. Gradually he reconciled himself to the solitary cell. 'I have at length in four and a half weeks been able to accustom myself to my loneliness', he wrote on 2 August. 'At first it was not at all easy, but since I have had a Bible and a hymnal to make the most of my time, it is astonishing how quickly it goes. At first I had some worry in remembering the "claustrophobia" of the days when I was an ensign and a lieutenant before the war. But now I learn patience.' Every day, he said, he learned a few hymns and read the Scriptures thoughtfully and calmly. 'I am certain that God's way is righteous, wherever it may lead.' And he added, 'My wife is well and brave.' (Bp. 10. 30f.) He thought a great deal of his naval days, and this crept into the language of his letters. 'Somehow', he wrote after six months in gaol, 'the ship of the church has freed herself and is floating again. The paint is peeling, the masts are broken, she is a sorry sight. But the Lord Jesus still stands at the helm, and the ship is afloat.' He was also busy answering his numerous correspondents, though the prison officials eventually limited his outgoing mail to twelve postcards a day. Undaunted, Niemöller continued to write to his brother Wilhelm, expressing his heartfelt thanks that Wilhelm was both caring for Martin's family as best he could, as well as keeping up the fight for the gospel. He wrote to Ernst Königs, happy that his old schoolfellow remained firmly on the side of right. He busied himself with his lawyers. He took twenty minutes' exercise a day. And above all he wrote to his beloved Else, separated from him now but still close to him in faith as well as love. 'So often have I said to a bridal couple what now I quote to you and me: "allied with you in faith and devotion"', he wrote on 2 July. His anxieties arose only, he said, from fear for his family and his parish. 'My cares all come from outside, not from inside me', he told Else in a letter of 12 August, 'for if I could think of you and the congregation without worrying, then – in spite of my two-and-a-half square metres of cell – I would be a happy child of my Father in heaven.'

Fortunately, Else was not left to struggle on alone in the Dahlem household. On moving into Cecilienallee, she had been confronted with fourteen rooms, all needing cleaning and dusting, on top of the problems of looking after six children (seven when 'little' Martin appeared on the scene) and fulfilling her long-held ambition to help her husband in a parish. The Niemöllers engaged a maid. When she left after three years, they persuaded a petite blonde Berlin widow, Dorothea Bertha Schulz, who was working in the parish with the intention of becoming a deaconess, to help out for a time. The Niemöller children persuaded her to stay. Dora, as everyone called her, became another member of the family and an invaluable help to Else. Martin's letters to Else from Moabit frequently sent his love and affection to Dora. With Dora's help, Else kept up her courage and strength. 'My wife is healthy and brave', Martin wrote to Ernst Königs on 2 August. 'We are both thankful to share the same faith.'

His allies were campaigning for his release. Each Sunday, to the authorities' annoyance, churches throughout Germany prayed for him. A huge service of intercession was arranged for Sunday 8

August in the largest of Dahlem's two churches. As the congregation arrived, they found the church cordoned off by the police. Representatives had come from all the Brandenburg churches and were unwilling to return home without a protest. Finding the second Dahlem church also closed by the police, the congregation began a protest march. The police arrested 250 persons, including Franz Hildebrandt. But the protests could not be stopped. On Reformation Day the churches of the Confessing movement were crowded for the reading of a manifesto which declared that 'The church of Christ is today being oppressed. Belief in Christianity is reviled. Those who profess Christ's name are faced with many acts of persecution and many hardships. A new political religion is being expounded, so that there may no longer be a place for the teaching of the Bible.'

In Moabit Niemöller missed Else enormously. 'You know you have my love', he told her in a letter of 17 November, 'but let me expressly assure you of it once more.' It was rumoured that there might be a Christmas amnesty for all imprisoned pastors and churchmen. Niemöller longed to spend Christmas with his family. 'My yearning is great', he wrote to Else on 6 December; 'deepest deepest greetings, my love.' Four days later he wrote, 'In my thoughts I take you in my arms, dear dear wife.' It was not to be. Many were released for Christmas 1937, but Niemöller stayed in Moabit. Dietrich Bonhoeffer made sure his family all got Christmas presents – a practice he continued each year until he himself was under arrest. (In spite of his own many anxieties, Bonhoeffer also took care to write each year on Else's birthday, and to send her Easter greetings.)

On Martin Niemöller's forty-sixth birthday, Moabit prison was inundated with 3,000 letters and birthday cards. He was in good spirits. After all, he wrote, he had survived the Red Scare of 1918, 'and after such a scene one no longer fears every ghost, but first of all feels what is under the white sheet!' And although he missed his wife, he refused to let even this depress him. On 12 February 1938 he wrote her a poem:

> Ah little Else, sweet little Else, would God I were with you
> But such deep waters are flowing between us both.
> *(Ach Elslein, liebes Elslein, wollt Gott, ich wär bei Dir!*
> *So fliessen tiefe Wasser wohl zwischen Dir und mir!)*

'Yet', he added, 'they cannot separate us.'

Dietrich Bonhoeffer continued to remind Else of the greatness of her husband's example. At the beginning of Holy Week 1938 he wrote that 'the thoughts of many people, and especially of many young theologians who look to your husband for inspiration . . . go out to you and your children'. He added, 'people keep asking about your husband wherever one goes'.

Niemöller was increasingly spoken of abroad as well as inside Germany. In 1937 James Moffat of Union Theological Seminary, New York, introduced a translation of some of Niemöller's sermons to 'explain how he is to be found among the ministers of the Lutheran church who are rallying a core of their faithful fellow-countrymen against the insidious new paganism which in the name of patriotism is undermining loyalty to the Christian gospel'. Moffat observed that although Niemöller fought against the allies during the war, 'he will win from many of them in this country a deep sympathy with his efforts to win the greater War against dark powers of worldliness in political and even ecclesiastical life'. In England too George Bell was tireless in keeping Niemöller's name before the public. In a letter to *The Times* Bell insisted that Niemöller was not an agitator against the state. 'The truth is that he is a preacher of the Gospel of God and that he preaches the Gospel without flinching', wrote Bell. The question was not the fate of Niemöller alone, but a question of the whole attitude of the German state to Christianity and Christian ethics.

German opinion was at this time extremely sensitive to foreign criticism. After reading Bell's letter, Dr Reinhard Becker wrote to him from Germany defending the actions of the regime.

You suppose that Christianity is oppressed in Germany and that there is a rule by force and secret trial. Though this is not the case, the German State cannot be expected to tolerate incessant attacks, open or veiled, by ministers of the Christian faith upon its very foundations. There are recalcitrant pastors who seem to be unaware of the fact that they would have been shot, hanged or burned long ago if it had not been for the gigantic and successful struggle of Adolf Hitler to safeguard civilization in this country against the horrors of Communism. Therefore by attacking National Socialism, they are striking at themselves.

Becker continued, 'I do not ignore [the fact that] it is difficult for an Englishman to think of National Socialists other than as bullies. But we bullies have clothed and fed our neighbours rendered destitute by the insane Versailles Dictation. We have made Germany a finer, cleaner, healtheir, better, and happier country.' This was a sentiment that Niemöller himself might once have shared before he saw through the propaganda of Adolf Hitler. Dr Becker ended his letter by observing that 'If it is heathen to have one's lads bright-eyed, vigorous, clean, eager, disciplined and full of admiration for what is manly, strong, noble and beautiful, I stand for paganism. But I know this is the very ideal of a young Christian gentleman.' (Bp. 10. 26f.)

Unfortunately Bell's colleague, Bishop Headlam of Gloucester, was willing to lend his support to views dangerously similar to these. The Dean of Chichester devoted the whole of the fourth survey of the affairs of the continental church sponsored by the Church of England Council of Foreign Relations to the worsening situation in Germany. Headlam, as chairman of the Council, added a preface suggesting that the survey was one-sided and unbalanced. 'The idea seems to prevail among many people that the Confessional Church has a monopoly of true religion', he wrote. 'This is not true.' He quoted Dr D. Cajus Fabricius (whom he described as a 'learned and respected German theologian' as well as 'a whole-hearted supporter of the Führer) on Hitler's extraordinary Christian virtues. He insisted that 'there is no persecution of religion' in Germany 'but only a correction of political activity on the part of Christian clergy'. The arrest of Niemöller, far from changing Bishop Headlam's mind, only confirmed his views. 'These pastors are deliberately irritating the government in Germany', Headlam wrote to *The Times*, 'and they cannot complain if, as a result of that, they are arrested.' He thought it foolish to encourage them. In September Nathaniel Micklem of Mansfield College, Oxford, tried to reason with Headlam. Micklem had visited Germany in April, still hoping that delegates would be allowed to attend the 'Life and Work' conference in Oxford. Now he wrote to Headlam pointing out that, 'In a totalitarian State, everything is political which is declared by the party in power to be such, but in our English and more limited sense of "political", Niemöller has committed no wrong.' But Headlam refused to be convinced.

The Nazi authorities were naturally delighted to find such a supporter in Britain. Headlam's views were given wide currency in the Reich. Ribbentrop was instructed to cultivate him; and the Nazi agent Friedrich von der Ropp began to cultivate Dr A. J. Macdonald, Headlam's right-hand man on the Church of England Council for Foreign Relations. Shortly after Niemöller's arrest, Macdonald wrote to *The Times* to say that although he had the greatest respect for the pastor as a Christian minister and spiritual teacher, Niemöller grew fanatical about the relationship between church and state. If he had contravened the regulations of the German 'Home Office', he would no doubt be dealt with like other such offenders. 'We in this country have also to obey police instructions of this kind', said Macdonald. But of course conditions were different in a totalitarian state. 'I was put in prison for "misusing the pulpit for political reasons" ', Niemöller later ruefully recalled, 'which meant whatever the judges or the court decided was misuse.' (MN/jb)

George Bell strove in England to counteract the opinions of Headlam and Macdonald, and to make his own views felt in Germany. To the very great annoyance of Bishop Theodor Heckel, he managed to persuade the Oxford conference on 'Life and Work', from which Niemöller and his colleagues had been excluded, to condemn what was going on in Germany. In a message of August 1937 the conference stated, 'We are greatly moved by the afflictions of many pastors and laymen who have stood firm from the first in the Confessional Church for the sovereignty of Christ and for the freedom of the Church of Christ to preach His Gospel.' The message was not well received by the Nazi authorities. On 11 October 1937 the *Völkischer Beobachter* commented: 'A Christian conference which undertakes to lay down the law and pass judgement upon the church, people and state, has forfeited the right to appeal to the gospel. It serves not the faith, but politics, and is building a world church alongside the Vatican in Rome.' The German authorities were still extremely sensitive about Niemöller.

In view of the Nazi reaction to outside pressure over Niemöller, no one could be certain that such pressure did not do more harm than good. In January 1938 it was announced that Niemöller would, at last, be put on trial early in the following month. George Bell wrote privately that 'we should be very slow to make an agitation now about the fact of a trial', since it was important to try to shield the court from any kind of political pressure, British or Nazi. But there was strong international pressure to ensure if possible that foreign observers would be present in court. Dr Henry Smith Leiper, for instance, who was executive secretary of the department of relations with churches abroad of the Federal Council of Church of Christ in America, sent a telegram to Bell from New York on 4 February: 'Consider presence at Niemöller trial of prominent representation of Church important.' Among the three suggested observers, Leiper included Bishop Bell's dean, A. S. Duncan-Jones. (Bp. 10.39) In the event Duncan-Jones and Dr W. G. Moore of Oxford went to Berlin in the hope of observing the trial, but neither was allow in. Duncan-Jones was well known to the German authorities as a friend of the Confessing church. On a previous visit to Germany he had talked privately, in a bugged room, to two Confessing church leaders. Both were subsequently arrested. The secret police repeated to them the contents of their conversation with the dean.

Niemöller was charged with breaking the law which forbade the announcement from the pulpit of the names of those who had renounced their church membership. He was accused of defaming leading state personalities and state measures. He had, it was alleged, 'caused unrest among the people' by urging 'rebellion against the laws and ordinances of the state'. As Bell and others feared, the indictment concluded by stating that his views were the regular fare of the hostile foreign press. Three weeks before the date of the trial, an additional charge was added, alleging that in the course of his duties as a pastor Niemöller had published material discussing affairs of state in a manner likely to cause a breach of the peace.

On 7 February the trial opened in secret. The ministry of justice had refused to issue press tickets. Around 200 persons were outside the Moabit courtroom doors by 6 a.m., hoping to be let into the trial. Very few managed to obtain tickets, and most of these (including Frau Niemöller) were removed once the charges had been read. Amongst the few allowed to stay were Dr Hans Böhm of the Confessing church and Niemöller's relative, Dr Max Diestel. They were expelled on the second day.

As Martin Niemöller walked anxiously along the tunnel leading into the courtroom, an extraordinary event tok place. He heard a voice repeating a verse from the book of Proverbs: 'The name of the Lord is a strong tower: the righteous runneth into it and is safe.' The voice was that of the guard leading Niemöller into court. This man had discovered a point along the tunnel where words whispered into the wall could be heard by the prisoner. Secretly he was comforting Niemöller.

The trial was chaos. Niemöller and his defence lawyers, who were led by Dr Horst Holstein, had decided to emphasize the pastor's patriotism and personal loyalty to the state. Niemöller recounted not only his war service but also his service in the *Freikorps*. He told the court that he had no personal political animosity to the National Socialists, for whom he had voted in 1924 and in whose favour he had preached in 1933. Distinguished Germans testified to his character, including Lieutenant-General Oskar von Watter, commander of the Wehrmacht at the time of its co-operation with the *Freikorps* after the Kapp *Putsch*. Admiral Otto Schulze testified that Niemöller served as a U-boat commander and submariner with 'tenacious energy and tireless readiness for action'. The defence had even persuaded one of Göring's sisters to witness to the pastor's patriotism.

When the prosecution attempted to counter this testimony by suggesting that both Niemöller and his defence counsel were in touch with foreigners, the defence counsel withdrew in anger. The court appointed another lawyer, with whom Niemöller refused to co-operate. For ten days the trial was adjourned. When it reopened, Niemöller insisted that he had no quarrel with his lawyers, and Holstein and his colleagues were reinstated. Holstein described Niemöller as 'a completely unpolitical man, whose activity has been exclusively determined by the word of God'. Niemöller even admitted that he found Jews unsympathetic – although, however difficult some might find this, he was obliged to acknowledge that Jesus Christ had been a Jew. He insisted that obedience to God's word was prior to any other obligation. But he concluded his defence speech with the declaration that he understood his oath of allegiance to the Kaiser not as simply binding him to the old imperial house but as also carrying the obligation to turn aside from anything that might shame the *Volk* and the Fatherland.

By the end of the week the charges against Niemöller had been reduced to dealing solely with his activities in the pulpit. Legislation about what clergymen could say in the pulpit arose from two enactments. The first was a virtual dead letter, deriving from Bismarck's attempt to stifle Roman Catholics without making them martyrs or openly disloyal to his regime. This law allowed an offender to be confined for up to two years in a 'fortress', i.e. not a prison. Article 20 of the German penal code allowed fortress confinement only for those whose motives in erring had been honourable and who had done nothing harmful to the German people. The second law relating to the pulpit had been passed by Hitler. It forbade the reading out of the names of those in prison.

Judgement was postponed until Wednesday 2 March. On that morning Niemöller, dressed in a dark suit and wearing a wing-collar and black tie, entered court smiling and joked with his counsel before the judges entered. Else and their daughter Brigitte had been allowed into the proceedings, as were another 200 of Niemöller's supporters. Niemöller was virtually acquitted. In a fifteen-page report, the judges found that he had acted entirely honourably, though he had, in fact, violated the pulpit clause. He was sentenced to seven months' confinement in a fortress, and a fine of 2,000 marks. Since he had already served eight months' solitary confinement in Moabit, the term of confinement was remitted, along with 500 marks of the fine. All Niemöller had to do was pay 1,500 marks (or alternatively serve three months in gaol).

That evening in St Anne's church, Dahlem, Fritz Müller happily told the congregation that their pastor had done nothing dishonourable. As Duncan-Jones reported, 'the judgment of the court was in effect an acquittal, which left Niemöller's honour unstained'. In America Thomas Mann wrote, 'Let us not forget that a National Socialist People's Tribunal is a rather crude institution. There is small concern for justice; trials are brief. Yet even such a tribunal could not bring itself to condemn Martin Niemöller.'

Else Niemöller had packed their trunks for a holiday on her husband's 'acquittal'. According to strict regulations Niemöller should have been able to go home that same afternoon. It did not happen. As Martin Niemöller learned later, 'when Hitler got the news of this sentence, he became furious and called his whole cabinet together that afternoon. In this cabinet he wanted a resolution that Pastor Niemöller should be brought to a concentration camp. Not one of his cabinet ministers gave his consent. And so in his fury he declared, "This man is my personal prisoner, and that is the end of it."' (MN/jb) Late that night two Gestapo officers drove Niemöller to Sachsenhausen concentration camp, north of Berlin.

Yet Niemöller remained extremely grateful for his acquittal, especially to Dr Schwarz, the judge he deemed chiefly responsible for it. A judge of so independent a spirit soon fell foul to the Nazi authorities and was himself interned in a prisoner-of-war camp. After World War II, Niemöller was able in a small way to repay Schwarz. An American of Canon City, Colorado, Mr G. S. Bilheimer, read in the *New York Times* a suggestion by Niemöller that one way of helping Germans was to write to their families, sending supplies of food and clothing. Bilheimer wrote to Niemöller asking for the names of six families, and Niemöller included in these names that of Dr Schwarz. On 6 September 1947 the German pastor wrote a letter to Bilheimer which reveals why he remained so grateful to the judge. 'It has been a great joy to learn that you are taking care of Dr Schwarz in Berlin', Niemöller wrote. 'He was one of my judges in 1938, and I am very much indebted to him as it happened, thanks to his personal influence, that I was sentenced not to prison, but to fortress, which enabled my family afterwards to stay in our rectory in Berlin, and I could stand the eight years of imprisonment and concentration-camp rather undisturbed, knowing that my family at least had a place where to live.' The pastor had continued to take an interest in the Schwarz family, and he added that shortly after her husband's release, Mrs Schwarz was run over by an autocar in Berlin. The judge, he said, was suffering sorely from Mrs Schwarz's condition. (ZEKHN 62, vol. 499/2485a)

In 1938 none of this alleviated Else Niemöller's anxiety for her husband. On 9 March a German professor wrote to George Bell that he had met Else who wanted him to thank the bishop for his help and kindness. The professor reported that Niemöller 'is not badly treated, even better than many in his situation in so far that Mrs Niemöller can see him every four weeks. But he is absolutely isolated in his cell, and loneliness and hopelessness are telling on him, strong as his nerves and his character and his faith may be.' (Bp. 10. 127f.) After the war Niemöller told Franz Hildebrandt that his years in solitary confinement (four in all) had indeed been 'frightful and nerve-racking'. (ZEKHN 62, vol. 394/2422a)

10. IN SACHSENHAUSEN AND DACHAU

AS SOON as Niemöller arrived at Sachsenhausen he was deprived of all his personal possessions. In the morning the camp commandant informed him that he was there as the Führer's personal prisoner. Niemöller asked to be given back his Bible and his wedding ring, and the camp commandant complied. Hans Ehrenberg, who was also in Sachsenhausen at this time, described Niemöller's condition in solitary confinement, 'that is, in a single cell in the small auxiliary prison which was for us "beyond the wall". I wasn't more than two hundred yards from you', recalled Ehrenberg, 'yet I was not allowed to see you. Prisoners in solitary confinement are not allowed to speak to anyone; even the boilermen are sternly prohibited from conversing with them.' The only human sounds which Niemöller could hear, Ehrenberg reported, 'were the cries of the tortured' in nearby cells and the moans of the wretched prisoners who in the yard outside Niemöller's cell were given 'the twenty-five lashes which the Commandant "legally" inflicted for the offences they were alleged to have committed'. Ehrenberg, whose job in Sachsenhausen was to carry away corpses, remembered twice removing dead bodies from cells only a few yards away from Niemöller's own.

Niemöller was forced to exercise alone and eat alone. Even so, he managed to make some slight contact with his fellow-prisoners, in a characteristic fashion. On the second morning after his arrival in Sachsenhausen, he heard prisoners exercising outside his cell. Standing on his stool, which itself was perched on the cell table, he was able to see out of the high window. Fifteen prisoners were walking round and round on the grass. The following day, and every day after that, Niemöller would quietly read to them from his recently returned Bible – sometimes from the Old Testament, sometimes from the New. Yet his condition gave Else much cause for concern. On the first occasion she was allowed to see him, they met at the police headquarters in Alexanderplatz, where Niemöller had been brought under an armed guard. He told her to take a holiday, since he believed there was no possibility of his release. He said, too, that his Bible and hymn book had been returned to him. But although he seemed in good spirits, Else doubted his prospects of resistance in the long run.

Strenuous efforts were being made to secure his release – so many that on 25 March Hanns Kerrl gave instructions that no more petitions for Niemöller were to be forwarded to his office, since the matter had nothing to do with him. Kerrl did his best to prevent any reprisals against Niemöller's family, holding that they must continue to occupy the Dahlem home. Although Niemöller was suspended from duty, Kerrl's office insisted that his family was eligible to receive eighty per cent of his salary. A year later a new law was promulgated allowing pastors to be dismissed without the necessary consent of their congregations. Niemöller was put on half pay.

In truth there was not the slightest possibility that Hitler would allow Niemöller to be released. In May 1938, when all surviving submariners were expected to attend the dedication of the Kiel U-boat memorial, Hitler refused permission for Niemöller to leave Sachsenhausen for the occasion. On the occasion of the Führer's birthday in 1939 Else Niemöller wrote to him saying that this coincided with her wedding anniversary: could her husband be released? Hitler replied that to release him would endanger the state, for Niemöller would once again start organizing pastors in opposition to National Socialism. As the golden wedding of Heinrich Niemöller approached it was actually Göring who advised the family once again to ask for Martin's release. Hitler again turned down the request.

In his letter to Heinrich and Paula Niemöller on their golden wedding, Martin compared himself to St John exiled on the island of Patmos. 'The longer I stay here on my Patmos, the more doubtful becomes the prospect that I shall ever return to a life of freedom and activity, and the more all things of second and third rate value disappear into oblivion', he wrote, 'although they from time to time painfully reassert themselves, when it is as in Luther's hymn: "Let them take body, goods, honour, child and wife . . .".' (Bp. 10. 238)

International pressure was equally ineffective in securing Niemöller's release, even though it was supported in powerful quarters. Telegrams of protest at his continued imprisonment after the acquittal of March 1938 were sent to Hitler, Kerrl, and the Reich minister of justice by the Primate of Sweden, the Greek

Orthodox Archbishop of Thyateira, the Archbishop of Canterbury, and the chairman of the foreign affairs department of the Federal Council of the Churches of Christ in America. Six British admirals, in a letter to *The Times*, wrote that 'we wish to place on record our respect for a former valiant foe who distinguished himself in the service of his country and who is now suffering from no less a cause than that of our common Christian faith.'

Did such protests do any good? The British ambassador in Berlin, Sir Nevile Henderson, thought not. He noted that whenever anyone mentioned Niemöller, Hitler invariably flew into a rage. And he told the British foreign secretary that 'if we had not made such an outcry in England about Niemöller, he might never have been sent to a concentration camp at all'. Martin and Else Niemöller both disagreed. At moments of deep depression in Sachsenhausen, Martin greatly feared that the world would forget about him. At the end of February 1939, Else smuggled a message to George Bell (for now she feared to write herself) saying that her husband was 'well in body but very depressed'. The message continued: 'He feels that he is alone – deserted by his brethren. His sense of honour as an officer is outraged, and he asked, "Why do they allow it?" Further, he talked much of his death, as if he felt it was near, and kept telling his wife what to do for the family's future.' (Bp. 10. 165f.) Else herself felt the need for the support of friends, outside as well as inside Germany. Martin Niemöller later recalled that her strongest support came from Archbishop Berggrav of Norway. (MN/jb) On 15 February 1939 Berggrav had tried to visit Niemöller in Sachsenhausen. He failed, but saw Else instead, and reported to George Bell: 'When Mrs Niemöller talks with her husband, she uses the phrase "Uncle George." She was VERY VERY thankful for your letters. She said, "such luck that Uncle George writes letters that the Gestapo cannot read. But please ask him if he might only sign "George" or "Bell" and never use the dangerous word "Chichester". His letters means so much to me. Give him my love.'

International opinion in fact almost certainly saved Martin Niemöller's life. In 1947, during the Nuremberg trials, the American prosecutor Robert M. Kempner produced a secret document from the Rosenberg papers indicating that in 1938 Goebbels had wished to have Niemöller liquidated. Alfred

Rosenberg had objected, not on human grounds, but for fear of foreign opinion.

Because of the contact with George Bell which Else Niemöller so much treasured, we are able, through the messages she smuggled out to him, to trace the state of her husband's health and spirits in Sachsenhausen. He was initially extremely badly fed there, until, it is said, his daughter Hertha learned this from Else and told her schoolfellows, who then wrote in protest to Hitler. In July 1938 Bell learned that Else herself had suffered a breakdown after seeing Martin, whose health was causing great anxiety. Although he learned in June (through Wilhelm Niemöller's wife) that Martin was 'well but lonely', he none the less took the trouble in September to write both to Hess and to Ribbentrop to say that the prisoner should be moved out of solitary confinement into the camp sanatorium. This did not happen, and Niemöller remained depressed. In June 1939, however, Else was able to report that 'His health seems much improved. In every way he was better than on the previous visit.' The warder, she added, had described him as 'the personal prisoner of the Führer'. Her next message reported that Niemöller 'did not look bad but he was a little apathetic, indifferent'. She had pleased him by saying, 'Uncle George gives his love to you.' In that month, too, she told Bell that Niemöller's salary had been stopped and the family moved out of their Dahlem home. (Bp. 10. 120, 140, 165, 168 and 183f.)

In fact the medical orderly at Sachsenhausen, as Hans Ehrenberg reported, examined Niemöller weekly and declared, 'He is a man of iron.' It was Else's health that in the end gave way. George Bell could do little, but the Niemöller family were assured of his sympathy. Just before Christmas 1938 he wrote to Else: 'I thought of you both all December 15 and wondered whether you were together; and a friend of ours may possibly be paying a visit to give you remembrance. This is especially to give you and your husband and children a very special Christmas greeting, with the prayer that peace may be yours and that the New Year may give you greater and particular merits. We do not say much but we think and feel and hope a great deal; and we pray.' (ZEKHN 62, Vol. 393/2442)

1939 brought not peace but war between Britain and Germany. Just before war was declared, Bell learned from

Niemöller's wife of her husband's longing 'to be released as soon as possible'. Martin also asked 'his friends abroad not to forget him'. (Bp. 10. 246) In September Niemöller wrote to Admiral Raeder, offering, as a reserve officer, to serve his country 'in any capacity'. Goebbels took the letter as nothing more than a move by Niemöller to save his own skin, and contemptuously rejected it. Raeder refused to reply, but Field Marshal Keitel, using Niemöller's title of Lieutenant Commander (Rtd), wrote to say there was no intention of recalling him for active service in the navy.

Niemöller's action in offering to serve Hitler's Germany in 1939 was later to provoke much ill-feeling towards him. Six years later he himself wrote a long letter to George Bell explaining why he had done this. 'We Christians in Germany were aware of the fact that we had a people and a mother country that we loved', Niemöller explained. In September 1939 there seemed open to him only two possibilities. '1) Should Hitler win the war, Germany would be lost as Hitler was the murderer of her soul long before he became a mass-slaughterer of huge proportions. 2) Should Hitler lose the war, Germany would be lost because the other powers would tread us down completely and would not treat us as they did in 1918.' Both possibilities were horrifying to him. 'In this dilemma', he went on, 'there seemed to me, as for thousands of other Germans who loved their country, no other hope, considering the war had actually broken out, but that through a new government we might come to a negotiated peace.' His letter ended: 'I could see no other way for myself either as a Christian or a German.' (Bp. 10. 335) Other factors too were present in his mind, as he later recalled. For one, his lawyers had advised him to make the application. For another, he was deeply conscious that his family was at war. 'My two sons were already soldiers, and the third one was going to be a soldier, had to become a soldier. And I, the father of three soldiers, was sitting behind the bars of the concentration camp. When my sons are facing the enemies of our nation and trying to make the best of it, can I really sit here doing nothing in my cell? And that becomes an insupportable, an intolerable situation.' (MN/jb)

After the outbreak of war, Niemöller was no longer allowed to leave Sachsenhausen even to visit his wife in the police headquarters in Berlin. Else now had to visit him in Sachsenhausen. Hitler relented only once in his determination to keep Niemöller confined. Hienrich Niemöller had been allowed to visit his son for half-an-hour in 1940. In March the following year the old man was clearly dying, and Martin, heavily guarded, was allowed to visit him. One member of the Gestapo was even stationed behind a screen in the old man's bedroom, as he talked for the last time on earth with his son. The old man told one of their cigar jokes. 'Give the man a cigar', he said to Paula, indicating the officer, adding that she mustn't give him one of their best ones!

In their determination to discredit Niemöller, the Nazis were quite willing to release to the world's press the details of his attempt to enlist. In November 1939 a circular of the international press service in Geneva announced that he had offered his services in the German navy and been rejected. Shortly after his father's death, rumours began to circulate that Niemöller had become a Roman Catholic. The tone of many of his letters at this time (all of which were read by Nazi censors) was clearly inclining that way. Some of his staunchly Protestant friends grew extremely anxious to discount the rumours. Bonhoeffer asked Else whether the news was true, and passed on a message from her that even Bishop von Galen believed Niemöller would remain a Protestant. In fact, the rumours were true. Niemöller (as he told Franz Hindebrandt) was seriously thinking of becoming a Catholic. (ZEKHN 62, Vol. 394/2442a) In the hope of hastening the process, the authorities decided to take him out of solitary confinement and expose him to the daily influence of three Roman Catholic priests. In July 1941 he and these three priests were taken by car from Sachsenhausen to Dachau concentration camp in southern Germany.

The move enormously improved Niemöller's pattern of life. In Sachsenhausen he had managed to make some sort of contact with other prisoners. His fellow Berlin pastor Heinrich Grüber scratched messages to him in the gravel paths. 'I was forced to walk alone', Niemöller said. 'But I had no supervision save that of a man in a tower twenty yards away. He could see what I did but not hear what I said. I looked up once and saw, through the bars of his cell window, Ernst Königs, my fellow pastor and friend, with whom I'd walked to school every morning.' (MN/jb) Yet they could not speak to each other now.

In Sachsenhausen he had tried not to let his spirit be broken. 'I am content', he once wrote, 'and thankful to let myself be carried along by that which I have preached.' But the transfer to Dachau was a great release. Although he was alone in his cell by night, during the day he was in the company of the three priests. And although in the end he did not become a Catholic, he grew to respect his fellow-prisoners and relish their conversation.

In Dachau too Niemöller struck up a remarkable friendship with a captured enemy of his country, a British colonel named Richard Stevens. Stevens had been arrested as a conspirator against Germany in supposedly neutral Venlo in Holland. Brought to Sachsenhausen, for two years he was kept in solitary confinement, often chained to a wall, before being transferred to Dachau. He had known Germany as a student before World War I, as a soldier between 1914 and 1918, as a staff officer on duty between the wars, and finally as a prisoner. Militarily erect, with a clipped moustache, Stevens spoke excellent German. After World War II he told the Oxford diocesan conference that if, as a result of his treatment in a concentration camp, 'I hated the Germans or at least remained wholly indifferent to their fate, it might, I think, in the circumstances be understandable.'

Instead the British colonel and the former U-boat commander conceived an enormous affection and admiration for each other. Long after the war they continued to correspond. Richard Stevens's wife Moja once wrote, 'Martin gave him so much strength and comfort in prison.' Stevens himself told a German pastor in March 1946, 'Martin and I were for many years together in Sachsenhausen and Dachau, and I should be most grateful to you, should you see him, if you would give him my most heartfelt greetings. One day, I hope very much to see again the man for whom I acquired so deep and lasting an affection, but meanwhile if these few greetings could reach him, I should indeed be pleased.' Stevens looked back on his time in Dachau with so much nostalgia that he sometimes signed his letters to Niemöller not 'Dick' but 'Fuchs', the code-name given to him by his German captors. (ZEKHN 62, Vol. 414/2445e)

Once the war was over Stevens sought out Niemöller's friend Bishop Bell as soon as he could. 'He spoke much of you', Bell wrote to Niemöller in March 1946, 'and much of what your presence meant to him at Dachau.' (Bp. 10. 356) Richard

Stevens was in fact one of the few Protestant 'special prisoners' in the camp. Martin's Catholic friends now included four priests. Three of them, as Bavarians, received regular food parcels from the diocese of Munich, which they would divide up amongst their fellow-prisoners. As Stevens recalled, they appointed a young village priest as quartermaster and he would say: 'Ah ha! der Dick – der Dick Stevens – last time he got an egg, a pat of butter and a cigar. This time he can only have a bun and a cigarette.' The priests would hoard little delicacies for special occasions such as birthdays.

On Niemöller's fiftieth birthday Stevens was listening on a clandestine radio to a service from London. The following morning, standing next to Niemöller in a shower in Dachau, he said, 'I have direct news and greetings from your friend the Bishop of Chichester. Last night they had a service in St Martin-in-the-Fields, on the occasion of your fiftieth birthday: the service was conducted by the Archbishop of Canterbury, and your friend the Bishop of Chichester preached the sermon.' Niemöller's comment was, 'So, the very first man who congratulated me when I was fifty on the 14th January, was George Bell.'

In 1943 the Catholic priests in Dachau were permitted to consecrate a cell for their acts of worship. The seven 'special' Protestant prisoners were not permitted to worship, and just before Christmas 1944 were told that they should not even be allowed to sing carols. The seventy-two-year-old Dutch ex-minister of war, Dr J. C. van Dijk, protested. For four years he had been in Dachau without any proper act of worship. Surprisingly, the guards relented, and Niemöller was ordered to conduct a Christmas service. 'There were seven of us', Niemöller recalled: 'a British colonel, a Dutch minister of war, two Norwegian ship-owners, a Jugoslav diplomatist and a Macedonian journalist, and me, the Lutheran pastor from Germany. When I realized what a task I should have to fulfil, I felt embarrassed and even desperate; for how should I – the German – find the right way to the hearts of this congregation, to men who hated Germany and Germans and who could not do otherwise?' Then something even more remarkable happened.

At noontime before Christmas Eve [Niemöller recorded] somebody knocked at my door, the cell was opened, and in came the Dutch minister of war with his Gestapo guard. 'Good morning, pastor', he said,

'I am just dropping in to ask you something. My comrades and I myself want to celebrate Holy Supper with you tonight after your sermon. You may be astonished, but we could not help asking you.' In this way it happened that in the evening I preached my sermon: 'Glory be to God in heaven and peace on earth to all men of good-will!' And peace there was, when we knelt down, seven people of different nations, divided by hatred and war, but now united and bound together by the love of God and by the grace of Jesus Christ. The small cell widened, walls and wires disappeared, we felt liberated and, in a flash, we saw God's promise fulfilled: 'Peace on earth'.

After that Niemöller and the six others were allowed to worship together once every four weeks. The Catholic priests lent them their consecrated cell, as a gesture of Christian solidarity. In his first letter to Franz Hildebrandt after the end of the war, Niemöller wrote, 'For the rest of my life I shall never forget our celebration of the Lord's Supper on Christmas Eve and Maundy Thursday.' (ZEKHN 62, Vol. 976/3027 and Vol. 394/2442a)

But not everything gave cause for rejoicing. Else's health was failing. On 23 May 1942 Dietrich Bonhoeffer wrote anxiously to George Bell, 'Mrs Martin has been ill for a few weeks, so we have no news about her husband.' By June she was in hospital and their nineteen-year-old son Heinz Hermann was seriously ill. One of the defence lawyers at Niemöller's trial wrote asking Hitler to give permission for Niemöller to look after his family. 'The Führer has refused an alleviation of the custody of Pastor Niemöller' was the reply.

Happily, Dora Schulz was still loyally and devotedly helping to care for Else and those Niemöller children who were still at home. Other friends rallied round. One of these Martin Niemöller never met. Albert Lempp was the owner of the Munich publishing company Christian Kaiser Verlag and the publisher of Karl Barth. Even after Barth had been expelled from Germany, Lempp still boldly supported him. (In 1936 he published a Festschrift in Barth's honour which would have been called 'The Freedom of the Fettered', had not the German censors objected to the title, as well as some of the contents.) Lempp solved the problem that Else in Berlin was 350 miles from Dachau by offering her part of his home on the Munich side of the Starnberger Lake. He died in 1943, but his widow Maria continued the arrangement. Else, the children and the faithful

Dora lived in three cramped rooms. But at least Else was able to visit Martin again.

Here, in rapid succession, two unexpected blows struck the family. Suddenly, on 30 December 1944 after an illness lasting barely two days, the Niemöllers' youngest daughter Jutta died of diphtheria. Martin Niemöller had been extremely close to Jutta, as he was indeed to all his children. Lying in Moabit prison on 10 November 1937, just before the girl's ninth birthday, he wrote to Else, 'I think so much of that hour when the child came, and we were both alone together.' Now an SS guard came to tell him brutally and brusquely that Jutta was dead.

The second blow fell two months later. On 28 February 1945 the Niemöllers' eldest son was killed in battle, north of Stargard in Pomerania. He had been born on 16 July 1922 and, Niemöller wrote, 'was named, after my deceased friend Emsmann, Hans Jochen, while we, his parents, hoped and prayed that he would grow up to be as straight and fine a German as was this late submarine commander of the Great War.' This time Else came to tell the news to Martin herself, bringing her young children with her to give them all some strength. But the guards refused to let the children into the camp, and they could only wave to their father from outside.

Niemöller was by now an extraordinary symbol of the resistance to Hitler. Pastor Paul Schneider, who was also arrested in 1937, kept Niemöller's picture in his Buchenwald cell until his death two years later. Niemöller, wrote Karl Barth, had come to embody 'the German Protestant church, with its distinctive approach and for all its limitations, as an opponent of National Socialism.' His example was a source of strength to others who were suffering in the struggle. To his British friends Hans Ehrenberg said, 'one Niemöller has created countless unknown Niemöllers'. From Tegel prison on 18 May 1944 Dietrich Bonhoeffer wrote, 'Please harbour no regrets about me. Martin has had nearly seven years of it, and that is a very different matter.'

Abroad too his name symbolized resistance. As early as January 1938 one of his British supporters (Mrs Dorothy Buxton) wrote to George Bell, saying 'I suppose there can be no doubt that, if only the German authorities would realise how much the name of Dr Niemöller means to the world outside Germany, they might

hold back from any extreme act of barbarity, in regard to him.'
(Bp. 10. 36) Bell himself, in a BBC broadcast, declared that 'His
name symbolizes the tragic struggle of thousands of martyrs and
his silence in a lonely cell speaks eloquently to us.' The dean of
Chichester, Duncan-Jones, added a further chapter to *From U-
Boat to Pulpit* and brought it out in Britain under a new title: *From
U-Boat to Concentration Camp.* (On 2 June 1945 he wrote to
Niemöller, 'I had the temerity to write a continuation of your
book ... at a time when you could not do it yourself. I think it
was of use for English speaking people, and I hope you will not
disapprove of it too strongly when eventually it comes to your
notice.') (ZEKHN 62, Vol. 394/2442a)

Some of Hitler's opponents took the legend of Martin
Niemöller to heights of absurdity at this time. 'Personally, I
would give almost anything if I could have the privilege some
happy day of walking into that German concentration camp,
straight up to Martin Niemöller, and saying, "My brother in
Christ, the Nazi evil is no more. With God's help we destroyed it.
Come back, Martin Niemöller, to your old pulpit, and preach
with no let or hindrance,"' wrote Norman Vincent Peale in
1942. He continued: 'To behold that saint, white of hair,
emaciated of body, as a result of his suffering, as he would climb
the pulpit stair, in a great free Germany, and to think that I in
even a small way had helped to make it possible, would give me
the deepest joy I can imagine.' Norman Vincent Peale was
introducing a book called *I was in Hell with Niemoeller* by Leo W.
Stein. The book was a complete fabrication, as was the author's
name. 'Stein' claimed to have suffered with Niemöller both in
Moabit and Sachsenhausen. He set down long alleged conversations and tales of Niemöller's heroism. He even gave an account
of an imaginary interview between Niemöller and Adolf Hitler.
'Hitler completely lost control of himself', 'Stein' quoted
Niemöller as saying. 'Then, I turned in order to leave the room.
He screamed after me, "Pastor Niemöller, you will either have to
come to terms, or you shall die – you shall die, as everyone shall
die who is in my way." I heard his fists hammering on the desk as
I left the room.'

'Stein's' account of this meeting had appeared in the American
magazine *Liberty* on 20 September 1941 and by the middle of
December the journal *Christian Century* was attacking it as 'A

Niemöller Hoax'. Ehrenberg (who *had* been in Sachsenhausen
with Niemöller) and Hildebrandt (who knew the truth about
Niemöller's one and only meeting with Hitler) were both
shocked at 'Stein's' fabrications. (Bp. 10. 269) Yet it was
scarcely possible, in the heightened emotions of the time, not to
seek in Niemöller a hero of almost mythical proportions. Martin
himself was aware of the danger. An English clergyman in Bell's
diocese, for example, wrote a poem about him in 1938:

> You, Martin, our brother, partaker in tribulation,
> In Kingdom and in patience, which are in Christ,
> Because of your witness and the Word of God
> Are in their culture's camp of concentration
> That is called Dachau . . .
>
> Train us to think and do the right by numbers
> That when the inevitable barrage descends
> Our obstinate wills may function to the last.

The poem was moving enough and sincere. Its author, the Revd
Lawrence Wilson, gave it to Bishop Bell and eventually it reached
Niemöller. After the war Martin sent his thanks. 'But', he added,
'I feel induced to say that I bow humbly in front of that symbol,
which you have raised and which is not I but this Martin
Niemöller which I ought to have been.' (ZEKHN 62, Vol.
398/2442e)

Niemöller never wished others to overestimate his courage
during the church struggle, or the dangers he had faced. Thirty
years later he said that those years had not been a time of either
superhuman or human heroes. He believed that his 'salvation'
had come paradoxically from Hitler himself. No one knew
precisely how Hitler's 'personal' prisoner ought to be treated. But
'because everyone was afraid to put the question or to bring my
name to the knowledge or the conscience of Adolf Hitler,
therefore no one knew how to treat me.' (MN/jb) And no one
dared let anything too drastic happen to him.

In 1945, however, this comparative immunity disappeared. As
the war began to draw to an end, Dachau concentration camp
began to fill up with distinguished 'special prisoners' of the Reich.
These included distinguished foreign statesmen, such as the
former president of France, Léon Blum (along with his wife), the
former chancellor of Austria, Dr Kurt von Schuschnigg (along

with his wife and their little daughter Maria-Dolores whom everyone affectionately called 'Sissie'), and the former prime minister of Hungary, Nikolaus von Kallay. In addition to these men and women, a number of enemy officers captured by the Germans were brought to Dachau. Among these were the Italian General Sante Garibaldi and a British intelligence officer, Captain S. Payne Best, who had been apprehended with Colonel Dick Stevens at Venlo. The full complement of 150 'special prisoners' was made up by German civilians and officers who in one way or another had fallen foul of the Hitler regime. These included members of the Stauffenberg family, Baron Fabian von Schlabrendorff, a distinguished lawyer named Josef Müller, and the former president of the Reich Bank, Hjalmar Schacht. Among the important group of German officers now in Dachau were General Alexander von Falkenhausen, the former C. in C. of Belgium and northern France, General Georg Thomas, and Colonel Bogilav von Bonin, who had served with Rommel in Africa and under General Guderian at Hitler's GHQ – all of them now enemies of the Third Reich.

It was inconceivable that Hitler would allow all these to live. Payne Best brought news of the execution of those closely involved in the July 1944 plot against Hitler's life. These included Dietrich Bonhoeffer. Nevertheless Niemöller tried to comfort the new arrivals in Dachau by suggesting that they might, after all, be allowed to stay there until the war was over. Yet even he was amazed when Hjalmar Schacht drew him aside for a quiet talk and then, instead of discussing their danger and the possibilities of escape, discoursed for over an hour on the importance of the gold standard.

Niemöller's hopes of remaining in comparative safety in Dachau proved false. On 20 April, for the last time, Else Niemöller came to talk to her husband in the concentration camp. In a letter to Franz Hildebrandt of 20 September that same year, Niemöller described what happened next. 'Four days later I was in a convoy of about 150 "special prisoners" who had been gathered together in Dachau, from where we were transported first of all to a camp *en route* for Innsbruck, and a few days later across the Brenner Pass to Pustertal and the South Tyrol. We found ourselves on the country road outside Villabassa, without shelter on a day of pouring rain which soon turned to snow.'

With the party, Niemöller added, was a German 'death squad'. (ZEKHN 62, Vol. 394/2422a)

Men of the stamp of Falkenhausen, Sante Garibaldi, and Martin Niemöller had, however, no intention of being killed by a group of Nazi criminals. When the demoralized guards took to the bottle before going to sleep, Payne Best surreptitiously ransacked their orders and found that they did indeed intend to kill at least some of the prisoners. He managed to spot on the list the names of Schuschnigg, Blum, Schacht, Müller, Falkenhausen, Thomas, and Niemöller.

Garibaldi began to make plans to seek the assistance of Italian partisans, while the German officers worked out how they might make contact with regular soldiers, who might offer protection against the hated SS. Niemöller had discovered that Colonel von Bonin was armed and ready to fight. So was Niemöller. His letter to Franz Hildebrandt continues:

as soon as I learned that the SS had been ordered to bump us all off, I plucked up my courage and approached the storm trooper who was leading the convoy. I informed him that we had weapons and would defend ourselves. That visibly took the wind out of his sails, and he said that he had no evil intentions against us. Towards evening that day we came upon a German divisional HQ, and some of the officers amongst us found that they were acquainted with officers there. Immediately they telephoned the German HQ. After a horrible night, during which two of us were posted on guard behind every SS man, German officers and soldiers came, put the execution squad in a truck and sent them on their way, guarded by machine guns. The Germans brought us to a hotel in Bergen, where we were very well fussed over and fed and looked after. That lasted three days, when one morning an American company arrived, disarmed the Germans and took us into their care. (Ibid.)

Niemöller was now safe – but annoyingly, not yet free. Since the American HQ was in Naples, the 'special prisoners' were flown there, which made his homecoming all the more delayed. However, he was put up in a decent hotel. He and Dick Stevens explored Pompeii together. He was delighted to meet one of his former Dahlem parishioners, Richard Pauly, whom Niemöller had confirmed (along with Richard's sister Irene) in 1936. Pauly had left Nazi Germany for the United States and was serving as a first lieutenant in the American army. The German pastor also found a congenial companion in the Revd David L. Ostergren,

American army chaplain with the unit based on Naples. Ostergren took to Niemöller too. On 31 August, after Niemöller had finally reached home, David Ostergren wrote to him, 'You can be sure that I miss that fine fellowship that you and I had together during your stay in Naples. The visits we had together at meal times and the walks we had morning and evening have left indelible memories in my mind. I shall never forget that simple child-like faith of yours. You have suffered terribly before coming here and yet your complete confidence in God had not been dimmed . . . I have the highest regard for you.' (ZEKHN 62, Vol. 525/2507)

Yet the undoubtedly delightful company of Richard Pauly, Dick Stevens, and David Ostergren was no substitute for that of his wife, their younger children, and Dora. Niemöller was detained for six irksome weeks in Southern Italy. His anxieties increased when an American journalist from Rome told him that his son Jan had been captured by the Russians and had broadcast from Moscow. Niemöller was under siege from the press. He was asked to give advice to Eisenhower's high command and flew to Field-Marshal Alexander's HQ at Caserta to do so. (He recommended that political parties should not, initially, be set up in Germany. Instead each Burgermeister should be elected locally, in areas small enough to foster 'a spirit of democracy, and so that people would really know the people they had elected'.) (MN/jb) Alexander gave him a splendid lunch. But during all this time he was longing to be home.

At length the German 'special prisoners' were reunited and flown to France, to spend a couple of days in an internment camp near Versailles. Thence they flew to Frankfurt, where the greater part were set free. Niemöller, however, was taken to an interrogation centre in Wiesbaden. It was now mid-June. On 27 December 1937, after half a year in Moabit prison, he had comforted Else with the words, 'Now live well, dear one. One day we'll have struggled through these things and it will be time to feast.' That was seven-and-a-half years ago, and the occupying powers were now proposing to keep him in Wiesbaden. 'I'd had enough,' Niemöller told Hildebrandt, 'and I went on hunger strike.' This forced the authorities' hand. Four days later he was free, with the papers needed to cross Germany. In Frankfurt, carrying only a briefcase (for most of his possessions had been left behind in Naples), he met Hans Asmussen, and they travelled towards Bavaria in a borrowed car.

Even now the journey was slow and difficult. Near the Danube they were stopped by three American soldiers – all of them perhaps slightly the worse for drink – who examined their papers. Spotting that he was in the presence of a 'national hero', the sergeant said, with obvious sincerity, 'I'd like to kiss you!' Instead he shook Niemöller's hand and waved the car on. Niemöller arrived at Maria Lempp's house on the Starnberger Lake, where Else and the rest were staying, early on 24 June. 'In the morning at six o'clock', he told Hildebrandt, 'I stood under my wife's window and found her with Hertha, Martin and Dora.' (ZEKHN 62, Vol. 394/2422a)

11. GUILT AND REPENTANCE

IN HIS diary for October 1939 Ulrich von Hassell, the former German ambassador to Italy who was now active in the conservative opposition to Hitler, contrasted the extremely light treatment of those who attacked or even killed Jews with the Nazi treatment of Martin Niemöller. Yet in December 1941 when another conspirator against the German Führer suggested that if Hitler could be brought down the right person to replace him as chancellor might be Niemöller, von Hassell had doubts. 'I am convinced that the man whom Trott has proposed has some unsuitable characteristics,' he noted. 'He is somewhat unbending, non-political, and not a good strategist. Aside from all this, I think that, after the first effect had worn off, he would not be a successful symbol. On the contrary, he might even create opposition.'

It was a prescient observation. Niemöller had some astute political instincts. It is doubtful whether any strategist could have succeeded in the face of Hitler (von Hassell's own strategies did not succeed in unseating the Führer). But von Hassell was right in supposing that Niemöller could create opposition. In concentration camp he was a silent symbol onto which anyone could project his own picture of the 'good' German. Once let out Niemöller became, as before, a man of uncompromising and sometimes unpopular opinions.

The free press of the world eagerly sought those opinions, and on 5 June 1945 Niemöller gave a press conference in Naples. He took the opportunity of defending his own nation. Asked about the brutality and atrocities of Hitler's concentration camps which had so appalled the liberators of Germany, he replied, 'No honest man or woman in Germany feels responsible for these things. Good Germans took Nazism as a new religion. These people are shocked by the revelations which have shown that Nazism was not idealism, but a means to the performance of criminal acts.' He insisted that even he was unaware of much that went on and had been 'shocked and horrified' to learn of it on his release. 'I never imagined such things could possibly happen', he told the journalists, 'and I saw ten times as much as people outside the camps. I was not ill-treated. I saw isolated acts of brutality, but I took them to be isolated. Now I see them in a different light.'

As well as refusing to exaggerate his own sufferings, Niemöller spoke of his attempt to enlist for active service in 1939. 'In war a German feels bound to join the ranks without question', he said, adding, 'Three of my sons were called up. I could not hold back. I wrote from the concentration camp to Admiral Raeder, C. in C. of the Navy, asking to be allowed to return to the submarine service or to do any other service in the Navy. I heard nothing for several months, and then a reply came, not from Raeder but from Keitel, head of the Wehrmacht. He thanked me, but regretted I could not be employed on active service.'

Such honesty was not calculated to endear Niemöller to those who had just fought a weary war against Nazi Germany. But the pastor had more to say. His country now needed help, not punishment. 'Germany is going to suffer a very hard winter', he pointed out. 'My hope is that through Christian churches in England and the United States some food supplies can be sent. I do not believe the governments are able or willing to do sufficient for our German people.'

Finally, Niemöller made a comment about the rise of Hitler which was misconstrued by many. Hitler misled a good number of Germans simply because of his hypnotic power, explained Niemöller. But he also came to power because the Weimar constitution had not given the German people the kind of authoritarian regime that they craved. He added that he himself had never quarrelled with Hitler over political matters, but purely on religious grounds because Hitler had wanted man's body and soul as well.

The response of the *New York Times* was milder than many. Under the heading 'A Hero with Limitations' its leader observed that Niemöller's press conference in Naples 'does not suggest that he can be a leader in the moral reconstruction of his country', since he neither thought the Germans yet fit for democracy nor had opposed Hitler's politics. Niemöller, declared the *New York Times*, 'is a singularly ineffectual figure in a country and a world crying out for justice'.

As George Bell nicely observed, 'When a hero ceases to be a hero, he becomes a problem.' (Bp. 10. 334) The Revd David Ostergren tried to comfort Niemöller. 'I am awful sorry that the reporters so misconstrued your interview in Naples', he wrote. 'I wrote back to our Church Press trying to give them a correct account of yourself.' (ZEKHN 62, Vol. 525/2507) Others, however, took up the attack. 'It will not do if we allow our pro-German pacifists to make a hero of this brutal ex-officer', screamed the *National Review* in July. Sadly enough, pacifists themselves were also attacking the ex-officer. Pastor D. Meyer-Klugel of Birmingham wrote in *Christian Pacifist* in the same month criticizing Niemöller because he did not lead the Confessing church to fight Nazism as such, 'but only demanded a quiet corner in which to practise rites and confessions'. As Kingsley Martin noted in *New Statesman* after Niemöller's interview, 'The Bishop of Chichester, who builds so much on Niemöller and the Lutherans, has an awkward case to answer.'

These attacks, unfair though they were, deeply affected Niemöller, who was now physically and emotionally exhausted. Pastor Harold Ludicke reported to Bell in October that Niemöller was 'somewhat disturbed by the attacks made on him, which occasionally occur in the press of this country and America'. He added that Niemöller was also deeply worried about his son in a prisoner-of-war camp. (Bp. 10. 329) In Naples (as Dorothy Thompson had reported in *The Observer*), he had still appeared fit: 'He is a man from whom fear has forever flown. Boyishly slim, wiry, nervous but disciplined, he is full of simplicity and humility. His brown eyes look steadily at you as he speaks, and when he smiles his face lights up with kindness and peace.' As ever David Ostergren displayed a sympathetic understanding of what Martin had gone through, and he tried to cushion the blows aimed at Martin by some of his supposed liberators. 'War is an awful thing. Transition periods of reconstruction are also very bad. We have lost so many men in the fight against Nazism that our leaders are bound to be bitter.' In some ways, he added, the German people seemed now like the Children of Israel, punished for following the wrong leaders. 'History continually repeats itself', said Ostergren. But he offered more than sympathy. Would Martin like sweets, for instance? Martin replied that he would, revealing too that he was physically ill. 'Sweets would do me a lot of good as the doctor tells me because I have much less sugar in the blood than I ought to have. And there are some other deficiencies with my health: the pulse is too slow by far and the same thing with blood-pressure, besides I have gone through some infection of tuberculosis but that is over by now.' (ZEKHN 62, Vol. 525/2507)

David Ostergren was not the only American chaplain to help Niemöller in his distress. Another, an old acquaintance from Berlin, offered to go about with Niemöller in his car, to get round the problems of permits and far from friendly occupying powers, especially if he wished to visit Berlin. But he was continually fighting against bureaucratic restrictions. In Caserta he had been promised permission to return to Naples, where some of his belongings had been left, but now this permission was refused. He hoped to go to Switzerland to convalesce, but again permission was not forthcoming. Seeking that permission involved frustrating visits to Frankfurt, with nothing to show at the end. Even David Ostergren was harassed by petty restrictions in his efforts to help his friend. He was given 10 dollars to buy goods Niemöller wanted, and then was refused permission to send them. In September Niemöller told another clergyman friend from the Naples days (the Revd Charles Cranfield) 'Now I am just waiting, as my health has given way and I have lost another 6 pounds since my "liberation" from the Nazis.' (Ibid. and ZEKHN 62, Vol. 393/2442)

Niemöller was also deeply worried about his family. On his arrival at the Lempp's house in Leoni he had expected to find his elder daughter Brigitte, as well as Else, Dora, Hertha, and Martin, but Brigitte was lost somewhere in northern Germany. The family could be fairly confident that she was able to look after herself. But his two sons were lost and in far greater danger in Russian-occupied territory, if not in Russia itself, with no news coming through of either. 'Things are pretty enervating and oppressing', Niemöller told Cranfield, 'and my poor wife is in the worst state of health and spirit by now.... My general impression is that life today is not worthwhile under the present conditions.' In a letter to his concentration camp ally Richard Stevens he confessed that his hopes for the return of his two sons were fading away. The time he spent with the sympathetic and kind Field-Marshal Alexander in Caserta now seemed to have been 'the last happy day of my life'. So depressed was Niemöller that he even looked back with longing to the years he and Stevens had shared in concentration camp. 'I feel rather lonely and hopeless', he wrote, 'and far worse than in the "happy" days when we were together. The old acquaintances of Dachau have been scattered all over the world.' (ZEKHN 62, Vols. 393/2442 and 414/2445e)

In such a physical and mentally depressed condition, Niemöller realized that he was not able to withstand as once he had done the onslaughts of those who disliked what he had to say. When a Miss Cecil Baines of Chelmsford, England, wrote offering her sympathy, he replied, 'Your letter has been a great comfort for me, the more so as I had no good press in America and England for the last months as you know owing to many misinterpretings which took place at an interview held at Naples in the beginning of June' – to which, he added, he 'was not able to adjust in a proper way'. (ZEKHN 62, Vol. 393/2442) The solution was rest, and Niemöller retired to a sanatorium in Bavaria.

The furore caused by some parts of his Naples interview did have the positive value of clearing the air over two aspects of his struggle under the Hitler Reich: his attempted enlistment in 1939 and the precise significance of his fight on behalf of the Jews.

Even before he received Niemöller's long letter explaining his action on 7 September 1939, Bishop George Bell was fairly sure that his friend *had* offered to serve again. In December 1944 he told a correspondent, 'I do not think there is much doubt that Niemöller did first volunteer to return to the Navy when war broke out, and that his offer was declined.' He added shrewdly, 'The situation is very complicated with a man like Niemöller.' (Bp. 10. 283) Niemöller's behaviour had not compromised him in the eyes of the bishop. But others among the pastor's non-German admirers found the episode hard to believe. In May 1945 the distinguished nonconformist Dr Maude Royden wrote to the *Daily Telegraph* suggesting that the story of his alleged offer to serve was 'one of the lies circulated about him by Nazi propagandists to whom the victory over Niemöller would have been a triumph to be trumpeted to the world'. After the Naples interview, she was honest enough to write again conceding that the allegation was true. Others came to terms with it in their own ways. Another correspondent of the *Daily Telegraph* observed on 8 June 1945 that 'Niemöller was ready, perhaps too ready, to give Caesar his due, but he eloquently, and finally almost alone proclaimed the limits of Caesar's authority.'

The truth is that in Hitler's Germany patriotism was still a powerful emotion even among the Führer's most determined opponents. Niemöller's behaviour is paralleled, for instance, in that of another opponent of the Nazis, the diplomatist Johnnie von Herwath, who was technically 'non-Aryan' (his grandmother was a Jewess). Von Herwath left the diplomatic service for a cavalry regiment. 'Early in 1942, Hitler was told that the officers of our First Cavalry Division were a gang of old-fashioned anti-Nazis', von Herwath wrote. 'He cynically replied that, as long as we were willing to die while performing our duties, he would postpone the question of our ultimate fate until the end of the war. It was a characteristic answer and a clever one, too, in that it went to the heart of the dilemma of those officers who opposed Hitler but remained loyal to their duty.' Hitler was not willing even to let Niemöller die serving his country. For all that, Niemöller remained a patriot. He had opposed the 'German Christians' for being first Germans and only secondly Christians, instead of Christians first and only then Germans; but this by no means implied that he regarded being German as without significance. In the years after 1945 a good number of people would find it difficult to cope with Niemöller's intense love of his own country.

The question of Niemöller's attitude to the Jews was more complex and he faced it with his customary honesty. In the autumn of 1945 he and Else revisited Dachau. They visited his cell and then, what he had never seen before, the crematorium of the concentration camp. Nearby had been affixed a white-painted board, with the words, 'Here in the years 1933 to 1945, 238,756 persons were incinerated.'

Niemöller was profoundly moved. In the years to come he preached on this again and again. At Rendsburgh church, for instance, on 23 September 1946, he told the story, and then said: 'The guilt has become anonymous and nobody will share the responsibility. Everybody says, "Go and ask my neighbour. I am innocent."' Niemöller's was an unwelcome voice because he insisted on sharing the guilt which many hoped to push to one side. He now identified the sufferings of communists as well as Jews with those of Jesus Christ himself. As he told his fellow-countrymen, in refusing to speak out for them, German Protestants had again betrayed their Lord. Who knows, asked

Niemöller, what the course of German history might have been, had the churches only acted differently? 'In 1933 and the following years there were in Germany fourteen thousand Protestant pastors and nearly as many parishes', he reminded the German churches.

If we had then recognized that in the communists who were thrown into concentration camps, the Lord Jesus Christ himself lay imprisoned and looked for our love and help, if we had seen that at the beginning of the persecution of the Jews it was the Lord Christ in the person of the least of our human brethren who was being persecuted and beaten and killed, if we had stood by him and identified ourselves with him, I do not know whether God would not then have stood by us and whether the whole thing would not then have had to take a different course.

Niemöller after 1945 consistently refused to evade responsibility himself, in spite of his own sufferings under Hitler. Asked in 1962 to take part in a BBC broadcast on behalf of prisoners of conscience, he wrote his script in his own hand. Again he recalled his visit to Dachau with Else. His mind, he said, groped for an alibi, but the only one he could think of was an indictment of himself by God. 'My alibi only began on the 1st July, 1937, when I was arrested, and held good until the middle of 1945, but this notice said: "1933 to 1945".' There was, said Niemöller, no way out. 'In 1933 I had been a free man, in 1933 when Göring proudly proclaimed that the danger of Communism had been eradicated because now every Communist, not previously in prison, had been thrown behind the barbed wires of the new concentration-camps.' God's question, put to him by the figures of the dead on the notice board in Dachau, was 'Martin Niemöller, what were you doing then?' Only after his visit to Dachau in 1945 did he properly understand, he said, Jesus's words: 'I was hungry and you did not feed me; I was thirsty and you did not give me anything to drink; I was in prison and sick, and you did not visit me.' Through all those who had been suffering in Germany in 1933, Niemöller now believed, God in Jesus Christ had been saying to him: 'Are you prepared to save me?' 'I turned that service down!' Niemöller confessed. (ZEKHN 62, Vol. 396/2442c)

This new understanding of the solidarity of all suffering people with the crucified Jesus forced Niemöller to jettison much that had been traditionally taught in Christendom about the Jews. In

1962 he was sent an article suggesting that Jesus on the cross was far more closely identified with the Jew in the gas-chamber than with those Christians who still told the story of the crucifixion in a fashion that fixed 'upon the Jewish people of today responsibilities which belong to our corporate humanity'. Niemöller wrote to the author: 'I wish to express to you my sincere thanks. I read your article with great interest and as I think with real consent.' (ZEKHN 62, Vol. 400/2443a)

He had no desire to conceal his past. In 1956 he received a letter from Dr Alfred Wiener, who had built up one of the largest and most complete collection of books on Nazi Germany. Begun in 1933 in Amsterdam with anti-Semitic books bought by Wiener in Berlin, the collection included, for instance, copies of *Mein Kampf* in nineteen languages. For safety Wiener had moved his library to London. By 1953 he had built up a classified collection of press cuttings numbering over 40 thousand items, many of them concerned with Niemöller himself. Wiener asked him outright if it was true that he came from an anti-Semitic background and shared its presuppositions. In reply Niemöller wrote, 'I have never concealed the fact and said it before the court in 1938 that I come from an "anti-Semitic" past and tradition.' He pointed out that his father, in so far as he was interested in politics at all, was a friend and disciple of the social reformer Adolf Stöcker, who happened also to be virulently anti-Semitic. 'I was brought up in the German nationalistic spirit and have tried to build on this for my whole life', Niemöller continued. 'First during the Weimar Republic and then very suddenly with the coming to power of the National Socialists I began to think about this matter and as a result to think differently.' But, he wrote, he did not ask for praise. He remained ashamed of his old ways. 'I ask only that you look at my life historically and take it as history. I believe that from 1933 I truly represented the Lutheran-Christian outlook on the Jewish question – as I revealed before the court – but that I returned home after eight years' imprisonment as a completely different person.' (ZEKHN 62, Vol. 424/2449) The letter is all the more impressive because in truth it underestimates the differences between Niemöller and many of his Lutheran-Christian colleagues during the days when Hitler's Reich was ruthlessly persecuting its Jewish citizens.

Niemöller's depression in the autumn of 1945 was not,

however, solely due to his physical condition after long years in concentration camp or his concern about his family. Nor was it either simply due to the absurd harassment he had suffered and the delays involved in getting home, nor to the unexpected hostility shown by some of the world's press.

He was also deeply despondent at the developments in the German church since the defeat of the Nazis. In Naples he had spoken of the future role of the churches in a reconstructed Germany. 'The German people are entirely adrift', he judged. 'They have lost confidence in everything. All their leaders, political, economic, intellectual, military, and even the scholars and the great institutions of learning went on their knees before Hitler, and the Reich army, which once stood for some sort of morale of the state, threw out or assassinated the ablest leaders for Hitler's sake.' There had remained, he believed, 'one institution that never yielded up faith: the Christian church.' Now that church would play a central role in the moral and spiritual rebuilding of the German nation.

These hopeful words ignored how grievously some of the church leaders had let him and the Confessing church down during the struggle against Hitler. Niemöller was soon reminded of the divisions and animosities of the past. When he finally reached his wife and children at Leoni, which was in the diocese of Bavaria, he expected a welcome from its bishop, Hans Meiser. Over thirty years later he remembered angrily that 'It took Meiser, Bishop of Munich, five or six weeks to come to see me.' (MN/jb)

Far from working for a united German Protestant church that would help to renew the country spiritually, Meiser was secretly working to divide it. He belonged to a number of large Lutheran churches (Bavaria, Hanover, Hamburg, Saxony, Thuringia, and Mecklenburg) that had never shown much enthusiasm for the movement towards unity with the Calvinists, which had started in the nineteenth century. If Meiser could manage to persuade those Lutheran churches that had united with Calvinists to break away again, he could then lead a new great Lutheran body, representing eighty per cent of German Protestants.

Power-politics in church affairs such as this seemed appalling to a man like Niemöller at this time of crisis in the life of his country. He had no time for denominational wrangles. Throughout the struggle against Hitler, his Confessing church had tried to push the German churches into a greater unity. Meiser had broken that unity then and was planning to do the same again.

Moreover, his antipathy to Calvinists extended to Niemöller's great friend and ally Karl Barth. When Meiser finally appeared at the Niemöllers' temporary home, they began to speak of the relationship between the churches in the era after Hitler. 'Meiser was an intransigent Lutheran and an intolerant one', Niemöller recalled. 'I said that Karl Barth was needed for the reconstruction of the Protestant church. He said, "You must concede and acknowledge that we are closer to the Roman Catholics than to the Calvinists." I said, "Thank you", and showed him to the door.' (MN/jb)

Otto Dibelius believed that Meiser really wanted the United churches to break up completely in the chaos after the fall of Hitler. Certainly Meiser would not support Niemöller's hopes to reconstruct the churches along the lines of the Confessing church, in which membership depended on genuine commitment rather than merely willingness to pay the church tax.

In the end Meiser did not manage to split the churches, though he welded the Lutherans into a huge power block. The septuagenarian Bishop Wurm invited all the available church leaders to a conference at the Hessian town of Treysa. 'Having no information about anything', Niemöller recalled, 'I was astonished to find Theophil Wurm heading a unity movement.' He did not really believe that Wurm much acknowledged any greater authority than the state, though he knew him to be a brave man, and was pleased that his diocese had sheltered pastors of the Confessing church who were in trouble with Hitler. (MN/jb)

In preparation for the Treysa conference, such members of the Council of Brethren of the Confessing church as were available met in Frankfurt. Barth arrived and (as he recorded) 'sat far into the night with my friend Niemöller'. The two of them were elected among the twelve delegates of the Confessing church to Treysa.

There were, of course, no 'German Christians' to speak of at Treysa, save those that had seen the error of their ways. But many of the old supporters of Barth and Niemöller had been killed during the war, as Barth noted with anxiety as well as sorrow. For, he wrote, to my astonishment I found in the official church roughly the same structure, grouping and dominant tendencies in which I had seen it hastening to its ruin in 1933. The progressive elements – those who had truly resisted between 1933 and 1945 and now wanted to translate into actuality the teachings of those years (Niemöller was one of the best among them) – were still on the scene and at work, but they were still a minority compared with the really dominant and determinative groups and authorities.

Of the eighty-eight delegates present at Treysa about half had in fact suffered imprisonment or house arrest under Hitler. But only a minority wanted a truly new start for the church. They knew that the church was a refuge for 'nominal' Nazis throughout the years of the Reich, and had not seen fit to try to expel them. Some hankered still to preserve that spirit which had supported Bismarck, Kaiser Wilhelm II, and Imperial Germany. And August Marahrens, who in November 1934 had deemed Karl Barth to be the greatest danger to the German Protestant church, Marahrens, who had allowed a 'German Christian' to serve on the governing body of his diocese, was sitting there, not conscious of having erred, perfectly determined not to resign as Bishop of Hanover.

Not surprisingly, the debates at Treysa between 27 August and 1 September were often stormy. The aged Bishop Wurm frequently was too tired to keep control. But, as Otto Dibelius put it, 'the sensation at Treysa was that Niemöller was with us again . . . nervous, excited, but present'. He was there – 'this is the only word to use', wrote Dibelius – as the 'antagonist' of Meiser. Niemöller also appeared to be ill. Some observers believed he suffered two small strokes during the proceedings. Nevertheless, he passionately argued that before the church could call for repentance to the whole German nation, she must cleanse herself and undergo a complete spiritual conversion. He also pleaded for a positive role for the church in seeking justice in society. 'If the Christian church has a place and is to be heard, then as a church we have an interest and a responsibility in preserving justice and the freedom of man in civic and public life.'

The meeting did not, however, adopt the Confessing church as its model for the future Protestant church of Germany. Dibelius was scathing later about its competence. 'The Confessing church had never known what it was to administer a whole ecclesiastical organisation', he wrote. 'It simply did not know what was involved – in the spiritual, juridical, economic, organisational and other fields.' This was certainly debatable. Dibelius well knew that the Confessing church alone had managed to organize a coherent opposition to Hitler's church policies. And even after Niemöller's imprisonment, the Pastors' Emergency League had continued to function properly right until the end of the war, when the positions of the dismissed pastors were finally regularized again.

Dibelius also had less worthy reasons for wanting something much more like a state church that a Confessing church in 1945. Quite simply, he was afraid that the Confessing church movement was not strong enough to stand up to the occupying powers. In his own words, 'above all – and this was the crucial point – things would never have moved smoothly had the Confessing church simply said: "Our Council of Brethren is taking over the direction of the church." Within three months dozens of pastors hostile to the Confessing church would have lodged a protest with the occupation authorities.' Dibelius was particularly concerned to have no such protest where he ran the church. Perhaps, he noted, the Confessing church could have got away with it in Rhineland and Westphalia, but not in Berlin under the nose of the Russians. So at Treysa Dibelius put his weight against Niemöller.

In one important respect the delegates at Treysa realized that whatever their personal relationship they sorely needed Niemöller to represent the German church abroad. They set up an executive council of twelve laymen and pastors, with the seventy-six-year-old Wurm as president and Niemöller not only vice-president but also responsible for the foreign (including ecumenical) affairs of the German Protestant church. As Dibelius put it, 'He alone could represent our church in a world still bitterly hostile to all things German.' Niemöller himself also put the appointment down to the fact that he could speak some English. 'In so far as I was being used as propaganda material addressed to the victorious nations', he said, 'I never was fond of my fame.' (MN/jb) In fact, the post seemed to offer him a worthwhile task at a time when he appeared to be needed nowhere. Sadly, in the next few months, it only served to add to his frustration. In November he told Franz Hildebrandt of his new responsibility for ecumenical affairs, adding that with no secretary, no office, a motor car but no petrol, he could scarcely even make a start. (ZEKHN 62, Vol. 394/2422a)

Late that month he wrote a memorandum on the state of the German church. He and his friends, he said, were striving to stop the Lutherans breaking away from the other Christian denominations involved in the new united church, for if that should happen the unity achieved by the Confessing church would be lost. He listed the disadvantages under which the Confessing church worked, compared with such 'official' churches as those of Hanover and Bavaria. They possessed offices and staff, money, materials and files, all because, paradoxically, they had been recognized by the Nazis. The Confessing church on the other hand was never acknowledged by the Nazis and possessed no such organization. Perhaps the church should have deemed itself a 'free church' at Treysa. But, Niemöller decided, 'nobody would assent voluntarily to such a measure', even though, in his opinion, the financial problems could soon be solved. In any case, a 'free church' would lose the right to take part in the religious education of children in schools, which would be a real loss.

As he pointed out, the new church at Treysa, planned to serve post-war Germany, had been set up, entirely without elections, by church bodies constituted during the time of the Nazis. Proper elections as soon as practicable were vital, he believed, to supply among other things a strong lay element in the new German church. (ZEKHN 62, Vol. 525/2501)

Elections and a strong lay element were not matters foremost in the minds of some of Niemöller's opponents at Treysa. Some of them had been inspired by the German high church movement and were seeking to revive what they considered the submerged Catholic elements of Lutheranism. And this involved exalting the office of a bishop. When one of them, Wilhelm Stählin, was appointed Bishop of Oldenburg after the war, he hoped that a 'validly' ordained Swedish Lutheran bishop would be present at his consecration, to make sure that Stählin was in the true line of succession from the Apostles. When Otto Dibelius took charge once again of the church of Berlin-Brandenburg, he decided that his former title, General Superintendent, was inadequate, and took the title 'bishop' instead. (Since there was no one to consecrate him, he therefore dispensed with a consecration and simply took the title.) Niemöller acidly informed Hildebrandt that 'Dibelius has made himself a bishop and naturally rules according to the Führer principle.' (ZEKHN 62, Vol. 394/2422a) 'Dibelius', Niemöller later recalled, 'was for authority. He did not see the church as growing from the local congregation, as we did during the struggle against National Socialism.' Niemöller's concept of the church was, in contrast, inspired by an image of his father's: 'If you want to *clean* a staircase, you must begin at the top. I regret that you cannot *build* a staircase from the top.' (MN/jb) Niemöller believed in the 'congregation' rather than the 'church', whereas Dibelius had made his name with a book heralding what he called 'The Century of the Church'. He remembered Niemöller once reproaching him with never having been a member of the Confessing church but only a man of the church. 'But what else should I want to be', Dibelius asked, 'than a man of the church?'

'These high churchmen – Asmussen, Lijle, Stählin – were bemused by the office', Niemöller judged. 'I never thought a bishop was what I or the church wanted. I wanted most of all, after I became a pastor, to be in a congregation.' His dislike of the office of bishop extended to its outward manifestations. Hanns Lilje, after he had become Bishop of Hanover, once appeared at an ecumenical gathering wearing a purple stock and clerical collar. Niemöller remembered with glee the reaction of Bishop Berggrav of Norway. ' "Hannsie," cried Berggrav, clapping his hands to his knees, "what is this trousseau?" Lilje could say nothing.' (MN/jb)

Niemöller's objection to bishops and their regalia was in part simply a strong reaction to the autocratic rule of the 'German Christian' church leaders of the Third Reich. He never tired of reminding pretentious or authoritarian church leaders that 'the Nazi bishops all went round with a great cross on their chests'. He tended not to mind foreign bishops at all. When he was elected church president of Hessen and Nassau, he explained to an English correspondent, Oliver Tomkins (later Bishop of Bristol), 'I have not accepted the title of a Bishop, but instead of a President, the history of German bishops not being very encouraging whereas you have a good old tradition, like other places abroad.' (ZEKHN 62, Vol. 401/2443b)

The German high church movement, in all fairness, had

provided some staunch opponents of Hitler's religious policies. The notion of a supernatural church, independent of earthly powers and drawing authority from its spiritual office, enabled some German Christians to resist the encroachments of the Hitler state. When Otto Dibelius was dismissed from his position as General Superintendent of the Kurmark he agreed to suspend his administrative duties. 'But', he continued, 'the kernel of my office is the spiritual leadership of my district. Here the functions of bishop and priest are in question. These functions can only be conferred by the church and are withdrawn by the church . . . On this fact rests the independence of the spiritual office.' In 1923 Wilhelm Stählin had set up a group of high church Christians known as the *Berneuchener* (because they met at Berneuchen), aiming specifically at reviving the Catholic aspects of Lutheranism. When the centre of the church struggle in 1937 moved for a moment to Lübeck, seven of the nine pastors put under house arrest for opposing their 'German Christian' bishop were members of the inner council of the *Berneuchener*.

Yet at Treysa Niemöller and his friend Barth regarded the high church elements at the conference, with what Barth called their 'fanciful' preoccupation with clericalism and liturgy, as likely to hamper 'the simple proclamation of the gospel to the sorely tried people of Germany'. After the meeting Niemöller went so far as to tell Hildebrandt that 'Within the Confessing church at this moment exists the danger that very many people and churches are recommending a sacramental line, in the style and spirit of the *Berneuchener*, instead of concerning themselves with the public life of the church and its public witness.' (ZEKHN 62, Vol. 394/2442a)

So Niemöller was disappointed with Treysa. Looking back in 1958, he observed that the twenty-seven separate Protestant churches that came together in August 1945 did not experience an 'awakening', an 'inner animation'. Writing to a British correspondent on 9 September 1945, with the Treysa conference fresh in his mind, he said, 'The church of Christ in this country is now going through a deep and dark valley of sorrow and misery with our whole nation, and yet we cannot see any sign of improvement and recovery. So we are in the need of prayers more than at any time before.' (ZEKHN 62, Vol. 393/2442)

Yet at his gloomiest, Niemöller did not despair. He told

Hildebrandt at the end of the month that he felt like saying, with Elijah of old, 'It is enough.' But, he immediately added, 'it does good to know that the Lord Christ lives, and that all power, even on earth, has been given to him'. He had good reason for gloom. In Leoni nine people were crammed into three little rooms, scarcely bigger than attics. He could afford to heat only one of them. 'Now I am sitting here at Leoni and am just waiting, for what I don't know', he told Richard Stevens in a letter of 3 October. 'My family is here too; only my two sons have not yet returned from Russia, and the time is going. I have no ministry at all, and things are pretty miserable with the winter coming and neither food nor fuel nor room. So we will have to part from here to the north, not knowing whether we will find better conditions there.' (ZEKHN 62, Vols. 394/2442a and 414/2445e)

That same month came a huge boost to his spirits, with the news that his second son Heinz Hermann had escaped from Czechoslovakia and was in Berlin. With the help of his friends in the US army chaplains' department, Niemöller managed to drive to Berlin and bring his son home, without papers and without falling into the hands of the Russians. Not until May 1948 was he able to write of the joy experienced by himself and Else because Jan was back, safe and sound after four years' internment in the USSR. But Niemöller's health and strength were returning. Soon too he solved the problems of both housing his family and setting up a proper office for the church's foreign affairs department. Rescue came from one of his old Dahlem parishioners. In 1936 Niemöller had married Fürst and Fürstin von Isenburg-Büdingen, who now offered him a home. In December he, Else, Dora, and the children moved from three rooms in the Lempp's holiday home in Bavaria to Schloss Büdingen in Hessen. 'I couldn't get a freighter', he recalled, 'so I took our tiny belongings by car.' (MN/jb) There he set up the offices of the foreign department of the German Protestant church, appointing as his second-in-command Gerhard Stratenwerth, his old ally in the campaign for Bodelschwingh in 1933.

Many supposed that Niemöller would wish to go back to his old parish in Dahlem. Dibelius later claimed that if this had happened, he would shortly have stood down as leader of the church in Berlin-Brandenburg in favour of Niemöller. Dibelius liked power, and one may perhaps doubt whether he would have done so. But Niemöller was unwilling to return to Berlin. He believed that the Russians might kidnap him. He had learned that in a single week over 200 persons had committed suicide in Dahlem alone, as a result of the appalling conditions in Berlin. Scarcely a house had been left unplundered. Occupying troops had ravished women, from eleven-year-olds to eighty-year-olds. Twenty Berlin pastors had killed themselves in despair. Recounting these facts to Hildebrandt, Niemöller added 'Dibelius seems to set no value on my return. So I have in West Germany so far neither a job nor any call to a job.' (ZEKHN 62, Vol. 394/2442a)

Niemöller needed to achieve one other change in the German Protestant church before he could begin work as its foreign representative. Somehow the Christian world had to be convinced that Germany, and its church, had undergone a change of heart. At Treysa he told the assembled delegates, 'We must walk in a new way. We must speak differently from the way the church has hitherto spoken.' On 28 September Karl Barth wrote him a long and urgent letter from Basel. 'People wish to help Germany', he said. But before that could happen it was necessary for the Germans to say, 'frankly and clearly, without any qualifications or modification: We Germans have erred – hence the chaos of today – and we Christians in Germany are also Germans!' Barth was convinced that only Niemöller could force this admission on the German church. 'How I wish that you would make this cause your own', he wrote. 'A great deal could hang on whether or not you will take it up.'

The executive council set up at Treysa was due to meet at Stuttgart on 18 October, in the presence of representatives of the nascent World Council of Churches. On Wednesday the 17th, in a truck belonging to the French occupying forces, these representatives arrived. They included Willem A. Visser 't Hooft (secretary of the provisional World Council of Churches since 1938), Samuel McCrea Cavert (general secretary of the Christian churches of North America), Alphons Koechlin (president of the Swiss Federation of Protestant churches), G. C. Michelfelder (president of the council of Lutheran churches in the United States), Pastor Pierre Maury (representing the Calvinist church in France) and Marcel Sturm (Protestant bishop of the French occupying forces in Germany). The following day

Professor Hendrik Kraemer (representing the Dutch Reformed church) met them in the Graf Zeppelin Hotel. That evening Bishop George Bell of Chichester, who had been delayed by fog, arrived at Bishop Wurm's house in the rubble-strewn Staffelgasse. The eyes of the Protestant churches of the western world were turned on the Germans assembled at Stuttgart.

Driving to Stuttgart from Leoni, Niemöller discovered in a newspaper that he, Dibelius, and Wurm were all expected to preach at a service to open the meeting of the executive council. He preached extempore, on a text from Jeremiah chapter 14: 'the virgin daughter of my people is broken with a great breach, with a very grievous wound . . . Hast thou utterly rejected Judah? hath thy soul loathed Zion? why hast thou smitten us and why is there no healing for us? . . . We acknowledge, O Lord, our wickedness and the iniquity of our fathers: for we have sinned against thee. Do not abhor us, for thy name's sake. . . . '

'The German churches must do penance and no more behave as idiots', Niemöller said in the course of his sermon. 'Not only is Germany suffering because of her own sins, but also Holland, France, Finland, and Poland. . . . The churches too often were silent.' Then, at the meeting of the executive council in the Stuttgart Bible Institute, he addressed the ecumenical representatives. He acknowledged that the church, along with the German people, had taken a wrong way, and thus grievously afflicted the future of the whole world. 'We pray that God may forgive us', he said. But he also hoped that this admission of guilt could bring in a new start and give Germany a new and better role in the world.

Specifically in the presence of the ecumenical representatives, the twelve leaders of the German Protestant church signed a declaration of guilt. 'Through us endless suffering has been brought to many peoples and countries', the Stuttgart Declaration admitted. 'True, we struggled for many years in the name of Jesus Christ against a spirit which found its terrible expression in the National Socialist regime of violence, but we accuse ourselves for not witnessing more courageously, for not praying more faithfully, for not believing more joyously, and for not loving more ardently.' Now a new beginning was to be made, the Declaration went on. 'It fills us with deep joy that in this new beginning we may be aware of the wholehearted unity with other churches of the ecumenical fellowship.'

It was a courageous declaration. Some complained that nowhere did the admission of guilt specifically mention the sufferings of the Jews. Niemöller, who (as he said later) 'spent two years doing nothing else but preaching this Declaration of Guilt to people', made it clear that he at any rate believed that the Germans had sorely wronged the Jews. In Erlangen, for instance, in January 1946 he spoke of meeting a German Jew who had lost everything – parents, brothers, and sisters too. 'I could not help myself', said Niemöller. 'I had to tell him, "Dear brother, fellow man, Jew, before you say anything, I say to you: I acknowledge my guilt and beg you to forgive me and my people for this sin.' Niemöller's stance was by no means entirely welcome to the 1,200 students to whom he was preaching. They shouted and jeered as he preached that Germany must accept responsibility for what had happened in Poland, for the sufferings of Russia and for the five or six million murdered Jews. Students in Marburg and Göttingen similarly heckled him. But Niemöller insisted that 'We must openly declare that we are not innocent of the Nazi murders, of the murder of German communists, Poles, Jews, and the people in German-occupied countries. No doubt others made mistakes too, but the wave of crime started here and here it reached its highest peak.' In an address at Frankfurt on 6 January he said, 'The guilt exists, there is no doubt about that – even if there were no other guilt than that of the six million clay urns containing the ashes of incinerated Jews from all over Europe. And this guilt lies heavily upon the German people and the German name, even upon Christendom. For in our world and in our name have these things been done.'

Niemöller had no desire to see the students that heckled him disciplined in any way. (As he pointed out, in his youth he himself had once actually walked out of an unwelcome sermon.) He was well aware that many Germans, suffering deprivation in 1945 and 1946, were not ready to hear about the deprivation they had brought upon others. As he told Bishop Bell, 'The newspaper reports on the Nuremberg trial and the documentary pictures of the horrible atrocities of the SS in the various concentration camps and extermination camps command little credence.' (Bp. 10. 303)

Some perceptive critics judged that the declaration of guilt was untimely. Helmut Thielicke, who had been part of the resistance to Hitler and became a professor at the university of Hamburg, observed that 'Instead of the preaching of repentance and salvation we had the proclamation of a collective guilt and a hysteria of self-accusation which was in need of psychological understanding rather than having any theological justification, and this led to a hardening of men's hearts.' But Niemöller judged that 'the renewal of the church and the declaration of guilt hung together'. Without the declaration, Germany would not have been welcome amongst the churches of the world. After it, Pierre Maury, speaking on behalf of the ecumenical representatives at Stuttgart, said, 'We cannot take away your misery, but we can see that Germany has a proper place in a new beginning for the world.' At a time when there was no place for Germans either in the international Red Cross or among the United Nations, the World Council of Churches invited the German church to send two delegates to its meeting in Geneva in 1946.

As Niemöller put it, 'the church is the one mouth left through which our poor German people can speak to the outside world'. And he now could begin work as the representative abroad of that church. He and Bishop Wurm were elected delegates of the German Protestant church to the provisional World Council of Churches.

This would mean visiting Geneva the following year. First, however, Niemöller decided he would visit Great Britain. To his surprise, he found that he was far from welcome.

12. THE GOOD GERMAN

THE OBSERVER correspondent in Rome, Dorothy Thompson, wrote on Niemöller's release in 1945 that he embodied 'a spiritual authority possessed perhaps by no other individual in Protestant Christendom'. This was not a view shared by every Britisher. At his press conference in Naples Niemöller announced, 'Now I would like to have my wife and two children to join me and then go to England and America to talk to the Christian leaders, for I too have a spiritual hunger to satisfy. Then I would like to return to preach the gospel of the living Christ to my own people. I have had a long time to meditate on the meaning of life.' He knew, he said, that the German people were suffering great deprivation, and his plan was to try to organize relief for them in countries abroad.

The plan did not appeal to many in Great Britain. Tom O'Brien of the TUC General Council wrote sharply to the *Daily Telegraph* as soon as he heard of it, 'I sincerely hope he will not be allowed to come. If he is, it will be the first overt move of the Germans to "organise sympathy", as they did so successfully and so hypocritically after the last war.' Niemöller, he pointed out, was no pacifist. 'He commanded a U-boat in the last war and, with his brother commanders, was responsible for the drowning of many unarmed British merchant seamen. In this war he volunteered to serve under Hitler. He was (and may now be) as nationalistic as any of his congregation at the fashionable Berlin church to which he ministered.' Another letter (written from the Dorchester Hotel by Philip H. Morton) expressed indignation at Niemöller's plan to collect money for the starving people of Germany. 'Could there be a clearer instance of German failure to realise responsibility?' asked Morton. 'What Niemöller should be doing is collecting in Germany for the starving people of Holland.' Capt. R. W. Keay (Retd) wrote from Eastbourne to remind *Telegraph* readers that though Niemöller denounced Hitler's attempt to subordinate the German church, there was 'no record that he ever denounced Hitler's crimes against humanity or condemned the war'. Another correspondent (Helen Beveridge Thomas) expressed the typical feelings of many who had learned to hate Germany during the war. 'Although it is true that we have still many things to learn,' she wrote, 'no German has anything good to teach us.'

Even some myopic British churchmen opposed Niemöller's proposed visit. The archdeacon of Lancaster wrote to the *Telegraph* on 31 May, 'In my opinion the pastor's visit at this time can do nothing but harm, for the one thing needful is to present a united front to the German people, and to demand proofs of repentance from the whole nation before we can enter into any fraternal relationships'. If Niemöller comes, he added, 'the Nazis will think they have found an easy method of working their passage home'.

Such views were not universally shared in Britain, and certainly not by George Bell and his circle, for whom news of Niemöller's safety brought unadulterated joy. Hearing the pastor broadcast in 1959 brought back memories of that time, Henrietta Bell wrote, 'And especially of one Sunday evening when I was alone in the house in Chichester and the telephone rang and a voice said: "This is Colonel Stevens. Tell the Bishop, Martin Niemöller is safe. He is free and has gone to Sicily. I have seen him." It was the answer to so many prayers, prayed by so many and with no greater faithfulness than by my husband.' (ZEKHN 62, Vol. 393/2442) The dean of Chichester, A. S. Duncan-Jones, tried to counter the adverse propaganda against Niemöller's visit. 'There is, of course, naturally a good deal of misunderstanding and prejudice in many circles here', he told Niemöller, 'but I am doing my best, so far as I can, to clear the way.' (ZEKHN 62, Vol. 394/2442a) But so great was the outcry against the pastor's proposed visit, that even Bell himself felt the need for caution. On 6 July he wrote as tactfully as he could to tell Niemöller so. Bell offered friendship, help and hospitality at Chichester when Niemöller came to Britain. 'But', he added, 'in order that your visit may bear the greatest fruit, it is necessary that it should be rightly timed. I hope the time may soon come, though it is not yet.' (Bp. 10. 322)

Clearly the task of representing Germany abroad would be a daunting one, as Niemöller was beginning to realize. The Revd Dr Leslie Weatherhead had invited him to preach in the City Temple in London. On 9 July Niemöller told him, 'I don't know whether and when it will be possible for me to go abroad and to come to England, and on the other hand it seems to be very unlikely that it may do any good, as the papers in the last few weeks took a rather decisive turn to influence public opinion.' (ZEKHN 62, Vol. 398/2442e)

It soon became clear that the British Home Office was far from co-operative about the proposed visit. Bell had written to his friend Maxwell (who was permanent secretary in charge of the Home Office), asking his help. But Maxwell replied that Niemöller fell into none of the normal categories that would permit a visit to the UK and therefore such a visit was for the time being out of the question. (Bp. 10. 338) By the end of the year Niemöller had decided that both the Swiss and the British authorities would take a long time to issue the papers he needed to do his job for the German church. On 26 November he wrote to his friend Charles Cranfield, 'For myself I got an invitation from the Lord bishop of Chichester to come over and be his guest for several weeks. I and my wife too. But I don't know, whether we shall get the permit, the more so as the permit for Switzerland never was granted – but we have learned to wait anyhow, and shall go on waiting in the same way.' (ZEKHN 62, Vol. 393/2442)

The behaviour of the British authorities now turned into a bureaucratic farce, which was also deeply offensive to Niemöller and made him absolutely determined never again to allow himself to be similarly insulted. Permission came from the Swiss to attend a meeting of the leaders of the World Council of Churches in Geneva. Because the faithful Dora was able to care for the Niemöller children, Else was able to go with her husband. Their plan was to fly on to England with a British visa that would be supplied by the British Consul in Geneva. The Germans had agreed to this, and Bell had persuaded the Archbishop of Canterbury to intervene with the Home Office to get permission for Niemöller to come.

At the appointed hour, 12.15 on Saturday 5 August 1946, Niemöller arrived at the British Consulate in Geneva. His identification was a sheet of paper issued by the German authorities, to which the Swiss had attached another piece of paper bearing their visa, stamps, and seals. The consular official told Niemöller that as there was no space on the document for a British visa, he would not issue one.

According to a letter written to Visser 't Hooft (with a copy to George Bell) by Stewart W. Herman, an American working in the Reconstruction Department in Geneva, 'Niemöller apparently became very upset and called up the World Council office at once, saying that he was fed up with the whole business and would return to Germany.' Herman did his best to get round the idiocy of the British Consulate, but the official (whose name was Bloor) was 'polite but absolutely uncooperative'. Bloor argued that the *Swiss* should have added space for a British visa. Herman observed that the Swiss had no authority to add anything to German passports, but he asked whether Bloor would issue a visa if he could persuade the Swiss authorities to add another piece of paper to Niemöller's document. He told Bloor that the Archbishop of Canterbury, Bishop George Bell and the British foreign office were all in favour of Niemöller's visit, adding, 'Niemöller is deeply offended and embittered by the whole business'. At this point Bloor declared the matter was no concern of his, but really was the problem of the British Consul General, Captain Barrat who was at the Hôtel des Familles. Barrat proved unobtainable. Niemöller persisted in saying that he would not go to England now even if a visa were granted. 'Although Niemöller was upset and not too cooperative', wrote Herman, 'I honestly feel that the British Consulate is largely to blame for a most unfortunate technical obstruction.' (Bp. 10. 364)

'What a great disappointment . . . for you and for all of us', Richard Stevens wrote. At Croydon airport, he said, he had met every plane from Switzerland, 'smiling broadly (at first) in great and pleasurable anticipation, and laden with pipes and tobacco to give you a pleasant little surprise. I can well understand your disgust and bitterness and disappointment, and I sympathise very deeply. We are bound, in this country, by a bureaucratic imbecility which passeth all understanding and belief.' (ZEKHN 62, Vol. 414/2445e)

Niemöller was very angry indeed. 'All went wrong and I shall not come to England in the near future', he said, in a telegram to Stevens. 'The British Consulate in Geneva which had information to provide me with a visa did not acknowledge my passport. Time, money, and strength were lost and the hard work of four months into the bargain.' The affair had very much cast him down. If the allied powers were to continue hampering him in this way, his work abroad for the German church would be made impossible. 'I think now I shall leave all sort of ecumenical work', his telegram continued, 'and retire to Dahlem and settle down there for good, hoping that eventually my experiences with the Russian Army may prove better than those with the Western powers.' (Bp. 10. 367)

Stevens, for one, was determined that this should not happen. Niemöller's telegram added, 'I shall stay in Switzerland for another fortnight.' Without further ado Stevens decided that if his friend could not come to England, he should go to Switzerland. Within a few days he and his wife Moja flew out to meet Martin and Else. Their holiday together was a huge success. 'It was really a great joy, at long last to see you again and to meet your lady wife of whom I had heard so much', wrote Stevens afterwards, 'I do not think that in all my travels all over the world I have ever packed so much pleasure, good fellowship and interest also into as small a time, and our dash round and round Switzerland will remain with me as one of my happiest and most cherished memories.' He hoped the fishing rod they had taken out for little Martin kept the Büdingen table loaded with fish. But his visit had a further purpose too: to persuade Niemöller that he should still come to England. The British control commission for Germany and Austria was trying to smooth over the absurd incident at the Geneva Consulate. Bell instantly set to work arranging another visit, if possible for November. 'I am quite sure, my dear fellow, that his kindly invitation is one that you should accept.' As a bait he added that he had just received a letter from a fellow-prisoner in Dachau, Count Alexander Lamoyski, saying that he too expected to be in London soon. 'What fun it would be', wrote Stevens, 'if we could have a real Dachau reunion here, all together!' (ZEKHN 62, Vol. 414/2445e)

Niemöller wrote back a letter of thanks. *En route* to Büdingen, he had fitted in a two-hour conversation with Karl Barth, who had, he said, urged him to return to Dahlem and make that the basis of his work. 'But', said Niemöller, 'no decision has so far been made.' (Ibid.)

In his letter to Niemöller Stevens had expressed his happiness 'to find that im Grossen und Ganzen [by and large] and in spite of Strapazen [strains] you are full of beans and (given the right atmosphere) good spirits.' But to George Bell he wrote that, 'As in Dachau he is still living very much on his nerves. We all suffered from the same complaint – an inability to accept minor irritations with equanimity. Petty arrogance roused us to a wholly disproportionate fury!' He told the bishop that driving through Basel Niemöller had almost 'piled his car up' because a policeman, in his view wrongly, held him up. But, Stevens added, the pastor was in excellent spirits and willing to come to England after all, if he were invited to do so without any restrictions. (Bp. 10. 369)

Stevens had done good work, and Bell used Niemöller's poor health as a further lever on the British authorities. Niemöller's 'heart gives him trouble', he told R. Wilberforce of the British control commission, 'and I know his wife is anxious about him'. (Bp. 10. 370) But Niemöller had no intention of coming to Britain merely to meet old friends and recuperate. In spite of his anger at what had happened in Geneva, he had a job to do. On 8 September he wrote to Bell saying how much he had enjoyed Stevens's visit and that his enforced stay in Switzerland had been made less of a burden by the chance of being present at the baptism of Stewart W. Herman's twin children. He also said he was now again willing to come to Britain – but not just for a rest. He wished 'to learn what is going on in parishes, camps, institutes, etc.' (Bp. 10. 373) The 'camps' he referred to were prisoner-of-war camps. On 9 September Chuter Ede, the British Home Secretary, authorized the visit.

Niemöller was deeply concerned about the treatment of German prisoners-of-war after 1945. Some of them, he believed, had no right to be held prisoner at all. He sought the release of General von Falkenhausen, who had been with him in Dachau and after and had been sentenced without trial, at the age of 71, to five years' imprisonment in Belgium. (ZEKHN 62. Vol. 413/2445a) This imprisonment was manifestly unjust. But Niemöller also worked to ease the punishment of ex-Nazis too. In October 1948, for instance, he appealed to the Revd Paul Kingdon, of the religious affairs branch of the British occupying forces, on behalf of sixty-year-old Otto Kuehne, a former Lieutenant General in the Luftwaffe. His wife and three children, Niemöller explained, had no means of subsistence. The former general was suffering from glaucoma and an ulcer in his bowels. If the British continued to confine him in Adelheide camp near

Delmenhorst, the health of the prisoner would become precarious. In the same letter Niemöller asked the authorities to release another sixty-year-old German ex-general, Friedrich Wilhelm Neumann. 'He is suffering from a gall-bladder infection and trigeminal nerve'. The general was passing his time in hospital, racked with pain, wrote Niemöller. 'The healing process probably will succeed only by individual nursing at home.' (ZEKHN 62, Vol. 395/2442b) Niemöller left the German Inner Mission to become a pastor, because, he said, 'I hated to be *chef* of a *bureau*'. (MN/jb) Now he headed the foreign office of the German Protestant church. But he remained also a pastor.

He visited dozens of prisoner-of-war camps in Denmark. But the majority of German prisoners-of-war were confined in Britain. By 1945 nearly half a million men and women were interned in 1,500 British camps. Only slowly did the British realize that although almost every German had joined the National Socialist party, not every German prisoner-of-war was an evil monster. Eighteen months after the war fraternization between the prisoners-of-war and the British people was still illegal. Little was done at first to see to the prisoners' emotional needs. Two hundred German generals were interned near Bridgend. These distinguished men, who included Field Marshall von Runstedt, Hitler's commander in the west, were guarded by ill-educated and ill-trained soldiers. Elsewhere, in Camp 18, Featherstone Park, for instance, ex-members of the Waffen SS were beaten, stripped, and made to stand in the cold, in contravention of the Geneva convention. In other places more humanity was shown. About 150 women prisoners were interned in Wildestone Hall, County Durham, which was the family home of Anthony Eden. Others were less fortunate. Five thousand men, for example, were imprisoned in a requisitioned cotton mill in Oldham.

In the atmosphere of the immediate post-war years, Niemöller's determination to alleviate the lot of such men and women was not well-received by many of the victorious allies. The British government made it as clear as possible that Niemöller was an unwelcome guest. When George Bell raised with the Home Secretary the possibility that Niemöller might make some public speeches, Chuter Ede replied churlishly that while he could not prevent liberty of speech, any public utterance by

Pastor Niemöller would be 'undesirable'. Niemöller would be regarded by all the 'sensational' newspapers as offering the opportunity for a 'write-up', he argued, adding, 'I cannot myself believe that the consequences would be beneficial.' (Bp. 10.389) Niemöller's visit was therefore announced as a private one. When Bell gave a reception for him at Mary Summer House, no public announcement was made and the press was excluded.

Even so, some sections of the British press did give Niemöller a hostile 'write-up'. The William Hickey column in the *Daily Express* was headed 'Guest from Gestapo'. 'While Pastor Martin Niemöller remains in England he will preach no sermons, make no speeches. And he is wise', said the column. 'That he should be here at all is the subject of mixed feelings. The admiration expressed by some people for this vigorous critic of Hitler, who has spent eight years in a concentration camp, is offset by others who are wholly allergic to the idea of any "good" Germans, and recall with some venom Niemöller's first-war role of U-boat commander.' Hickey then proceeded to attack Niemöller's host. 'With his wife, the pastor is the guest of Dr. George Kennedy Allan Bell, Bishop of Chichester, a cleric who takes pride in outspokenness and relishes criticism. This time the bishop has shown commendable regard for public opinion by insisting on privacy for his guest.'

Others, however, welcomed Niemöller. Richard Stevens of course met Martin and Else at the airport and took them for a drink at his club before putting them on the 7.15 train for Chichester. He, Moja, the Niemöllers, and a couple of German pastors living in London spent two happy days together. Stevens hoped that Martin would at last have a good rest. 'I urged on him the desirability and wisdom of having a real lazy time', he told George Bell, 'and from the way he deferred to your probable wishes, you will find him (I think) for once amenable to discipline!' (Bp. 10. 390) Niemöller, however, had no intention of having a lazy time. German prisoners-of-war had already written to him asking for visits. Those in Camp Crocker Hill added that they had prayed daily for him when he was in prison. (ZEKHN 62, Vol. 169/3057) Niemöller had time to visit only four camps, but he used that time well. 'My visit to the camps has proved a real experience', he wrote to Bell afterwards, 'and has aroused some ideas, how to prepare our POW men for the task which is awaiting them at home. I think we ought to send over a team of pastors who know something of the situation in today's Germany.' (Bp. 10. 393)

The British authorities did not take up his suggestion. But soon treatment of German prisoners-of-war in Britain improved. The British authorities perceived that it was possible to use them as cheap labour, and contact with ordinary British people built up friendships. Public opinion ended the ban on fraternization. In the end 24,000 German prisoners-of-war decided to stay in Britain and 800 of them married British girls. Niemöller had made contact with a remarkable Jewish refugee from Germany who played a large part in transforming the treatment of prisoners-of-war after 1945. Captain Herbert Sulzbach, who had served as a lieutenant in the Kaiser's army, had become a naturalized Britisher, and served in turn nine years in the British army. He now took the opportunity of turning internment camp 18 at Featherstone Park, Haltwhistle, Northumberland, into a centre of reconciliation between German prisoners-of-war and their British captors. In 1946 Niemöller spent a day there. In the end 25,000 German officers, 4,000 at a time, passed through the hands of this British officer with a Frankfurt accent, during the course of their political 're-education'. Sulzbach wanted the returning prisoners-of-war to act as peace envoys between Britain and Germany. The Swiss head of the International Red Cross in London described Sulzbach's work as 'a model of how to treat a defeated enemy'. When camp 18 closed in 11 May 1948, Sulzbach was demobilized, and Niemöller helped to find him a good job in Germany. (ZEKHN 62, Vol. 413/2445a)

Slowly, hostility changed to understanding, as Niemöller's efforts to serve his country abroad began to succeed. One small sign was a letter from the Revd L. E. Addicott, a Baptist minister in the industrial town of Ripley. During the war he had served as padre to British troops stationed at the prisoner-of-war camp one-and-a-half miles away. His repeated requests to hold services for German prisoners finally succeeded at the beginning of 1947. Addicott and his wife entertained Germans in their home when the men were free from duties at Swanwick and Nether Heage camps. He began to hold services in German and English, and begged Martin Niemöller for messages of encouragement to read at some of these. He also urged Niemöller to tell the German

Christians 'that we know that we share the sin which has brought catastrophe upon the world of our time and that in the presence of the cross we stretch out the hands of brotherhood'. (ZEKHN 62, Vol. 393/2442)

Niemöller similarly won over Americans who initially showed hostility to himself and his cause. Shortly after he arrived in Germany after his detention in Naples, he was asked by a US army chaplain to lecture in Frankfurt on 'the responsibilities and opportunities of the Christian church'. Before the lecture took place he annoyed some of the American authorities with the remark, 'A German does not ask in time of war if war is right or wrong . . . A German wants to fight and die along with his fellow-Germans.' The lecture was cancelled, on the grounds that 'the political character of some of Pastor Niemöller's recent remarks have made him an unsuitable speaker'. One high-ranking American civilian in Germany was quoted as saying, 'There is a feeling that Niemöller has said some very stupid things. He has been in a concentration camp for eight years and isn't in focus with the times. It is like Rip Van Winkle trying to discuss New York politics.'

At the end of the year Niemöller flew to the United States, taking Else with him. Whatever the criticisms made against her husband, she adored travelling with him. (In Seattle she once said, 'having been separated from my husband for the eight years he spent in Hitler's concentration camps, I feel that a trip like this is a kind of second honeymoon'.) But their first trip to the United States was attacked by no less a person than Mrs Eleanor Roosevelt, who in her syndicated newspaper column wrote, 'I cannot quite see why we should be asked to listen to his lectures'. This time another of Niemöller's US army chaplain friends came to his defence. The Revd Robert W. Anthony wrote to Mrs Roosevelt, enclosing a copy of the Stuttgart Declaration of Guilt and observing of his time with Niemöller that 'No one who was with him then and has known of his courageous actions in Germany since that time would fail to be impressed by his marvellous Christian spirit and good judgment.' (ZEKHN 62, Vol. 976/3027) To her credit, Mrs Roosevelt later become one of Niemöller's allies in the fight against racism.

Other Americans stood up for him. Professor Reinhold Niebuhr of Union Theological Seminary, New York, drew attention to his sufferings under Hitler and observed, 'There is a certain pledge of integrity in such a record which deserves respect.' The Chicago journal *Christian Century* published a long leader under the heading 'Fair Play with Niemöller' mocking those who were timid enough to say 'the time has not yet come when it is safe for the American people to be permitted to know that many thousands of Germans fought tyranny as courageously as did the citizens of any other country'.

Part of the problem was that Niemöller brought an unwelcome message: that Germans were starving. In a memorandum he wrote on 28 November 1945 Niemöller analysed the response in Germany to the Stuttgart Declaration of Guilt. People were saying, certainly Hitler and his gang had been criminals, but the new situation is worse. 'In fact,' he noted, 'people are suffering from hunger, and it is well known that people are literally starving in the Eastern Provinces. People are suffering from cold, and it is well known that people are freezing to death in the Eastern parts.' (ZEKHN 62, Vol. 525/2501) On 18 May 1946, in an introduction to a book by his friend Stewart Herman, he wrote, 'We Christians in Germany are indigent. The era of suffering which lies behind us ate up all our resources.' The poverty was spiritual as well as physical. But Niemöller insisted that something must be done to relieve both, for, he wrote, 'we are wholly destitute to-day and must stretch out our hand for help.' Wherever he and Else went outside Germany, he appealed for help.

Very many responded, and both Martin and Else wrote back countless letters of thanks. On 9 October 1945 Mrs Alma Penheiter of Evanston, Illinois, wrote to him, 'It is terrible to sit here with plenty of food and know Germans are starving, and wishing to help and not be able to know where to send the money so it will get there.' She and her Christian friends sent money and gifts. On 30 November Martin wrote to thank her, giving an account of his day to day activities and the German situation in general. 'I should like to use these gifts from you for members of my parish at Berlin-Dahlem', he said. 'Several weeks ago I was able to visit them there, and I found great misery and hunger and cold, but no despair. Circumstances are terrible if you see them with your own eyes as I did. But at the same time this visit has been a great experience for me, in what way faith and love are capable to sustain people, who surely would break down without this help of God.' He told Mrs Penheiter that in the western parts of Germany 'things are not as bad as in Berlin and the Eastern districts which doesn't mean that there is no hunger and no epidemics. But we have to bear these distresses silently, knowing that we have had our share in causing them'. Mrs Penheiter continued to work for the relief of the Germans. She sent money to Niemöller (by way of Visser 't Hooft in Geneva) with which he bought insulin and penicillin. 'Our Christian women are sewing every day for German children', she told him. 'We get new goods and also make dresses and underclothes and seal them in boxes waiting for the day when we can send them across. We have blankets to send and much medicine. May the Lord give us a chance to send them soon.' (ZEKHN 62, Vol. 526/2501a)

Generous support came from the Revd Albert J. Kissling, minister of Riverside Presbyterian church, Jacksonville, Florida, and his congregation. Kissling, who had spent two years in Germany, sent parcels which the Niemöllers gratefully acknowledged. Martin sent one parcel to an old parishioner in Cecilienallee, Berlin-Dahlem, who wrote back describing the gift as 'like sunshine in the darkness'. Kissling also sent parcels to the Russian occupied zone, trusting that the pastors would see that the gifts got through. When, later, the Russian authorities began to restrict the weight of parcels sent into the zone, the Niemöllers broke down gifts into smaller parcels and sent them in that way. (ZEKHN 62, Vol. 73/3222a)

In 1949 Albert J. Kissling and his wife visited Germany to see conditions for themselves, calling on the Niemöllers. Afterwards he wrote, 'We had a very delightful trip in many respects, except that our hearts were saddened by the great need on every hand.' They were not able to visit the Russian zone, but the Niemöllers kept them informed of the great difficulties there. In August 1949 Else passed one of Kissling's parcels on to a pastor and his family in the East. 'His wife's health is seriously weakened by undernourishment', she explained. 'As a pastor his salary is too low to enable him to buy the needed foodstuffs on the free market.' (Ibid.)

Conditions were made much worse in Germany by the long drought of 1947. 'We are facing the winter without potatoes and a good deal of the cattle stock will have to be slaughtered, which means a fat ration reduced considerably under the present normal amount of 50 grams a week', Niemöller told an American correspondent on 31 August. 'No wonder people are more despondent than ever before.' Towards the end of November he sent a long letter describing conditions to Mrs George Gillespie of Eldorado, Texas. The first snows of winter had just fallen. 'Never before in my whole life had I the precise feeling that the snow is a winding sheet for dead people, leaving no hope for the future', he wrote. There was not enough coal – none at all in the country towns. Hardly anyone had woollen clothing or rugs. Soon there would be a shortage of potatoes. But most of all, fat and flour were urgently needed. 'Mrs Niemöller will send you ten letters of people who are in great need', he promised. Even if Mrs Gillespie sent packages immediately, they would not arrive before the end of January, but that would be the time of greatest calamity. (ZEKHN 62, Vols. 503/2488 and 509/2492)

Adding to these troubles was the constant flow of refugees. In 1949 Niemöller regarded this problem as the most urgent and at the same time the most difficult facing the churches in Germany. He racked his brains to find some solution to the problem of twelve million persons, mostly Protestants, who had lost their homes in the Eastern provinces. In 1951 he wondered, in a letter to Hildebrandt, whether a reasonable solution might be to absorb some of them in the underpopulated lands between the Oder and the Elbe. (ZEKHN 62, Vol. 394/2442a) But in the meantime they needed feeding and clothing.

In all this work Else Niemöller was of enormous help to her husband. The clergy throughout Germany sent addresses to both of them. By now he had obtained questionnaires, on which the needy wrote their personal details and requests. They wrote asking for coats, shoes, and underwear, for bed-linen, curtains, handkerchiefs, table cloths, and stockings. Women drew on paper round their shoes, to show what sizes they needed. Niemöller would sign the questionnaires to indicate his approval, and then he and Else would write to England, New Zealand, Australia, and the USA, begging for gifts. They also passed on the names of Germans who wanted pen-friends abroad. Americans offered to adopt German orphan children, but Niemöller was obliged to write saying that this was still forbidden, except for American families living in Germany. (ZEKHN 62, Vol. 65/2501a)

Apart from the obviously Christian and humanitarian aspects of this work, Niemöller conceived of it also as part of his spiritual duty towards the Germany nation. Unending poverty led to despair with, he believed, the danger of Nihilism. 'The uncertainty of industrial life becomes a great sorrow for all of us', he wrote towards the end of 1945. 'This economic situation is pressing upon the minds and souls, the more so as the family-life is broken down.' At first the allies were seen with thankfulness and even hope. That feeling could no longer be found. Instead people's souls had hardened, 'nearly unto despair'. (ZEKHN 62, Vol. 525/2501) Ten months later he judged the spiritual condition of Germany to be much worse. On 1 September 1946 he wrote to the Revd D. J. Hill of Iserlohn, 'the spiritual situation all over our country is developing to the worse in a tremendous manner. Really there is one loud cry for help, not only physically, but even louder spiritually, because we are drifting into despair and Nihilism, fighting each other and charging God with cruelty and injustice.' One year later, on 23 November 1947, he told Mr Raymond E. Gloria in the Philippines, 'For the present moment it is very difficult to recognise what the way in the future may be for Christian endeavours in Germany; the sufferings from hunger and cold are very oppressing, and people have no spiritual powers or interests left, because the whole day is filled with the primitive problems of food and shelter.' (ZEKHN 62, Vols. 394/2442a and 509/2492)

In the face of widespread poverty, starvation, and despair, Niemöller was appalled that the allies were punishing his country by dismantling its industries. The pretext was that Germany could no longer be trusted with anything that might be useful in any future war. The means of making radio transmitters or heavy industrial tractors were deemed to come under this heading. As the policy was increasingly put into effect, German workers resisted. In June 1949 there was passive resistance to the dismantling of synthetic oil plants in the Ruhr. The allied powers in the face of resistance elsewhere, had reduced the number of industrial plants they planned to destroy, but the Fischer-Tropsch oil plants were considered dangerously useful in the event of war. Herr Heinrich Kost, chairman of the German Coal Management at Essen, now declared they were also essential for the coal industry. Nearly three thousand workers demonstrated against the closure. All this was to no avail. The British occupying powers gave 48 hours' notice that the plants would be dismantled.

Niemöller intervened by sending telegrams to the British Council of Churches, the Church Commission for International Affairs in London, and the Federal Council of the Churches of Christ in America, asking them to use their influence to stop the destruction of German industry. The politicians took no notice. In the British House of Lords, Lord Beveridge had said, 'I am sure that not one British voter, if he really knew what was happening in Germany, would want this to continue.' He argued, 'If you insist on the elimination of everything that could be used for war, you must eliminate the whole of industry.' In his view, proper control was needed, not destruction. George Bell spoke in the same debate. He had just returned, he said, from an extensive tour of the Ruhr, where he found conditions much worse than a year before, i.e. 1945. Niemöller obtained copies of both speeches, and underlined phrases of Bell's such as 'complete prostration of Germany', 'the scarcity of the food situation,' and 'want of confidence' in the British authorities. He underlined a whole sentence: 'the real danger is lest by unwise actions and policies on our part we should renazify the German people'. (ZEKHN 62, Vol. 169/3057) But the British government was implacable. In the House of Commons, Ernest Bevin, the foreign secretary, said, 'I have to consider those who have suffered German attacks, and this House must always bear that in mind when dealing with these war industries.' He added, 'I am not going to be led into a position, after months of negotiation, that German pressure and propaganda can make me alter my mind.'

Niemöller was intervening in the political field and inevitably provoked opposition. After a visit to the United States, where he made his views forcibly clear, Edwin Sears, attorney officer working with the Council for War Crimes, wrote to the *New York Herald Tribune* to say that in attacking the plans to ruralize Germany and in complaining that Germans in the British zone lived on no more than 800 calories a day, 'to both America and Germany no German is at this time doing greater harm to either than Pastor Niemöller'. Niemöller was in the eyes of some an annoying trouble-maker. But Major General S. C. M. Archibald (Retd) MC, religious adviser to the British occupying power, wrote in confidence to C. O'Neill, the head of chancery, UK High Commission in Germany: 'Dr Niemöller may well be unable to see facts as they are, and he evidently does not appreciate political realities, but his views are coinciding with those of many who are dissatisfied with Western policy. Therefore, watch this trend carefully.' (Bp. 10. 440)

Niemöller had also clashed politically with the occupying powers over their policy of denazification, which the allied powers were carrying out in an incredibly ham-handed fashion. An allied joint chiefs of staff paper, no. 1067, had called for denazification in 1945. The worst area in terms of injustice and absurdity turned out to be the American zone, where Niemöller now lived. The US authorities issued buff questionnaires containing 133 questions, to be answered by everyone over the age of 18. Twelve million of these were completed. The major war criminals had been tried at Nuremberg at the end of 1945. Yet the Americans managed to find another 130,000 persons guilty of Nazi crimes in the US zone alone (whereas the British found no more than 22,000 such criminals in their zone).

Martin Niemöller was not the only German to find denazification ludicrously unfair. Helmut Thielicke pointed out that in Württemberg every employee whose job ended in the syllable '*rat*' (that is, 'senior official') was dismissed, including schoolmasters and vets. To get their jobs back, these people had to persuade proven anti-Nazis to give them testimonials, which soon began to be known as '*Persilscheine*', after a well-known washing powder which was said to wash whiter than white.

As he wrote from the USA to Pastor Forrell of London, Niemöller was continually perplexed by the mixture of warmth and vengeance towards Germany shown by the allies. (Bp. 10. 414) Denazification seemed to issue out of sheer vengeance. The executive council of the German Protestant church, meeting at Treysa in May 1946, cautiously but firmly warned against it. 'By the so-called denazification is meant the cleansing of the German people from the corrupting influence of National Socialism', the council said. 'The need for such a cleansing is recognized by the church.' But the council went on to claim that the questionnaires inevitably were answered with lies and deceptions. The harassing of former members of the Hitler Youth (who had been given no choice in the matter) was absurd and led to feelings of hopelessness. 'In expressing these anxieties', the council members maintained, 'the church is not defending the spirit of National Socialism.' But renewal of the German people could come only through the word of God, not through the denazification trials. Only through the word of God 'can the German people find a new relationship with the rest of the people of the world'.

Niemöller thought that imposed denazification of the kind practised by the occupying powers was basically undemocratic. (MN/jb) He also believed it to be unnecessary. The German people had seen through the lies of the Hitler era themselves. Fourteen months after his release, he said, he still had to find a single German who had not recognized its madness. Unfortunately, the occupying powers did not share this view. 'In the circles of the occupying powers', Niemöller wrote, 'and particularly the Western occupying powers, as well as among the political parties in Germany, the question of "Denazification" is still regarded as the key to the whole problem. That is a fundamental error, for any recrudescence of Nazism is quite out of the question.' Moreover, the denazification process, which was cumbersome and slow-moving, threw men out of work at a time when many in Germany were starving. Niemöller told Bell in November 1946 that it seemed likely to be twelve years before everyone in Hamburg had been denazified and eight years before Bavaria had been cleansed. Meanwhile whole families suffered because the head of the house was compulsorily idle. The suspected Nazis had been divided into four categories. Since what Niemöller called the 'heavy' criminals had already been dealt with, he suggested that the two last categories of minor offenders – the *Minderbelastete* [less incriminated] and the *Mitläufer* [fellow-travellers] – should be granted an amnesty. 'There is no doubt that the weight of moral strain and hopelessness, of which the denazification difficulties form an important part, press heavily upon our population, causing frictions and all sort of dissatisfaction', he told Bell, 'hampering every chance of new spiritual life and revival.' (Bp. 10. 304 and 396)

The following year the synod of the Protestant church of Hessen, Nassau, and Frankfurt-am-Main elected Niemöller as its first president. The job was exacting, since it involved bringing together three separate smaller churches with their own highly individual traditions. But Niemöller also made it an instrument for promoting his own Christian convictions. The church of Hessen and Nassau adopted the church of Saxony in East Germany and sent there food, clothing, and medicine. Niemöller, refusing the title of bishop, sought to involve the local congregations in the wider work of the church. He, Else, Dora, and the younger children moved from Büdingen to Wiesbaden the following year. At last Else had her own home again. 'We have moved to Wiesbaden, Brentanostrasse 3, because here is the office of the Church Board,' she told her American friend Albert J. Kissling. 'And we like it here.' (ZEKHN 62, Vol. 73/3222a)

Now Niemöller had another platform, and in 1948 he used it for a powerful attack on the whole denazification programme. At the beginning of February every pastor in the province of Hessen and Nassau read from the pulpit a statement by Niemöller declaring that the whole spirit of denazification was one of revenge, since it inspired even Germans to take vengeance on their fellow-countrymen. 'In their hundreds of thousands, people are constantly pressed to tell lies. Now the former system of arresting the entire family of an offender is being revived.' Countless people were still interned, unable to earn a living while they awaited sentence or release. 'In these circumstances every Christian must ask whether it is his responsibility to go along with these judicial processes or not.' Niemöller counselled Christians no longer to take part in denazification trials, either as judges, prosecutors, or witnesses.

Privately the Niemöllers were extremely friendly with General Lucius D. Clay, the American military governor in Germany since 1945. Clay (as John K. Galbraith wrote) was 'one of the most skilful politicians ever to wear the uniform of the United States Army'. He was certainly shrewd enough to spot the stature of the church president of Hessen and Nassau, and would invite Martin and Else to supper with him privately. (ZEKHN 62, Vol. 31/324a) Now, however, he felt obliged to make a public rebuke to Niemöller. 'It is painful for me to see a representative of religious faith offering himself as barrister for those who disregard and offend against the law.'

But Niemöller was here condemning a genuine grievance of the Germans. Niemöller in no way believed in glossing over the evils of the Nazi era. In 1965, when the secretary of the Defence Committee for Victims of Nazi Persecution wrote to him expressing alarm that the West German Federal Government seemed ready to grant an amnesty for Nazi murderers, Niemöller replied that he deemed it impossible in principle – and was definite about this – that the crimes of the Nazi days in Germany could ever be declared no longer liable for punishment. (ZEKHN 62, Vol. 415/2446) But this did not stop him working for the release of men whose sentences in his view far outweighed their alleged crimes. He co-ordinated, for instance, a campaign for the release of Lieutenant Colonel Erich Killinger, commandant of the Dulag Oberursel camp, and his two deputies, Heinz Junge and Heinrich Eberhard, who had been sentenced by Wuppertal military tribunal to serve sentences of five and three years' penal servitude. Pastor Lutze, a member of the Confessing church and superintendent of the local synod of Solingen, was willing to testify that he had frequently met Erich Killinger at acts of worship in Dulag prisoner-of-war camp, that his conversation had frequently been anti-Nazi, that he did not shrink from disobeying immoral orders and that as an officer he always behaved with due regard to international law. Niemöller collated all the documents in Killinger's appeal, adding to Pastor Lutze's testimony letters in his favour from Professor Gerhard Ritter, two other pastors, a retired rear-admiral, a British Air Vice-Marshal who had been a prisoner at Dulag, five American officers who had also been prisoners, and so on. (ZEKHN 62, Vol. 143/3219) All together, even after he had declard the whole process to be an unjust farce and counselled Christians to have no more part in it, Niemöller filled nine thick files with correspondence over those on trial or imprisoned as war criminals, appealing for Richard Hildebrandt (a former general of the Waffen SS), Erich Kock (former Gauleiter of East Prussia), Johannes Lehmann (former Gestapo officer), Rudolf Lehmann (former chief of the army legal department), Hans Reinhardt (a former tank corps general), Karl Wolff (another ex-general of the Waffen SS), Helmuth von Ruckteschell (ex-commander of U21), and countless others.

He himself would appear in court, to testify for example on behalf of Kurt Gerstein, an SS officer who had worked in Auschwitz and was described by Niemöller as 'an idealist through and through'. In defence of men he considered unjustly condemned, Niemöller used every possible international contact.

On behalf of the ex-submariner Helmuth von Ruckteschell he asked Richard Stevens if he knew a high ranking British Naval Officer 'who would be able and willing to second a petition for pardon concerning an old friend and comrade of mine whom I am standing bail for?' Stevens tried, but found no one. ('Sorry that I rang the wrong bell in asking you . . .', wrote Niemöller a few weeks later. 'In the meantime he passed away in prison.') Soon however Stevens was promising to go to Nuremberg, 'to see if I can help Toni Kellner in his appeal against the vicious sentence passed by the Volkspruch Kammer'. (ZEKHN 62, Vol. 414/2445e)

'The consequences of denazification are felt severely by so called "small people" who went into the party, not by conviction, but to secure their jobs and business', Niemöller wrote in a memorandum of November 1945. They were not Nazis at heart. (ZEKHN 62, Vol. 525/2501) The occupying powers, using the blunt instrument of denazification, seemed unable or unwilling to recognize this. Unlike them, Niemöller had personal experience of the goodwill and basic generosity of men ostensibly in the service of Hitler, such as the official who had tried to comfort him before his trial in 1938. Now he was trying to help them. As he told Professor Hendrick Kraemer, begging his help on behalf of a German prisoner-of-war in Hertogenbosch who was suffering from angina, the man had been commandant of a hostage camp during the war, but he had helped many. (ZEKHN 62, Vol. 437/2445)

In such ways after World War II Pastor Niemöller tried to serve his countrymen. But it was not what people of other nationalities had meant when they described him as a 'good' German.

13. PASTOR, POLITICIAN, AND PACIFIST

IN THE early years after World War II wherever Martin and Else Niemöller went as ambassadors for their country, critics were not slow to accuse him of being a German nationalist. In March 1946 Albert J. Brandt in the New York paper *This Month* wrote, 'For eight years men everywhere have admired Pastor Niemöller. We know now that he has always been and remains a dangerous Pan-German.' Brandt added, 'His statements since his liberation have shocked a great many people who believed sincerely that here was one of the "good" Germans.' Two-and-a-half years later when Martin and Else reached Australia, the Sydney *Jewish News* described him as 'a commercial traveller for German nationalism using religion as his business card'.

Such sentiments, understandable as they might be so close to Hitler's war and the murder of so many Jews, indicate the weight of Niemöller's task as head of the foreign affairs department of the German Protestant church. His aim was to win back Germany's place among the civilized nations of the world. In March 1949 he addressed a packed meeting in Oxford, thanking those present for their generosity towards his country. 'The people of the world today are either giving or receiving nations', he said. 'We in Germany are definitely a receiving nation, and I feel it is my duty tonight to thank you for what you have already done to alleviate the sufferings of the German people.' Then he spoke of what he called Germany's greatest need. Germans suffered 'day after day, month after month' from 'the paralysing idea that they were in some way or other cut off from Christian brotherhood – put into isolation. Our greatest need', said Niemöller, 'is the realisation that we are part of the Christian brotherhood.'

For this reason Niemöller invested many hopes in the first great post-war ecumenical meeting in February 1946 in Geneva. He was not disappointed. Bishop Berggrav embraced him with the words, 'Brother Niemöller, I have been looking forward to this moment for months.' Later that year he told Frank Ballard (British moderator of the Free Church Federal Council), 'There is no adequate expression for my and my brethren's feelings,

which were aroused in Geneva this springtime when we for the
first time met again with the representatives of the Christian
churches of foreign countries and found out that we could really
meet in the brotherhood and fellowship of Christ, notwithstanding all that had happened in the meantime. This fact has given us
new hope and courage for the difficult task ahead after a long time
of suffering and sorrow.' (ZEKHN 62, Vol. 400/2443a)

The leaders of the World Council of Churches made
Niemöller feel for the first time after the Second World War that
Germany was not an outcast. In May 1946 he dared hope that the
church in Germany, in spite of its weakness, might have
something to offer to the other members of the Christian family
throughout the world. 'The Church in Germany to-day may
rightly be regarded as a decidedly feeble member,' he wrote;
'nevertheless, if the Lord ... so wills, her service will be
accounted of use to the whole.' So welcome did he and Else feel at
Geneva, experiencing (as he told Hildebrandt) 'quite wonderful
days, where we lived with the Freudenbergs and where I felt so
well in the circle around Visser 't Hooft's ecumenical working
party', that he had an immediate desire to see if he could find a
permanent post there. (ZEKHN 62, Vol. 394/2442a)

Niemöller remembered one aspect of the Genevan meeting as
symbolizing the world-wide unity of Christendom. 'In Geneva
cathedral Berggrav preached in German; I had to preach in
French; and a Chinese Christian preached in English.' (MN/jb)
His own sermon emphasized the value of Christian solidarity
during his own time of danger. He recalled his father's words to
him in concentration camp: 'My son, the esquimaux of Canada
and the Bataks of Sumatra send messages to you; and they pray for
you.' Then he deliberately spoke of the guilt of the German
church and people. The impulse of self-protection 'makes a man
minimize his guilt, saying, "I myself have not murdered or
plundered or deceived others"'. But, said Niemöller, a people
had to avoid two errors: of refusing to acknowledge guilt and of
giving way to despair. The Christian message of repentance
should enable Germans to say, 'We may, we can reverse our
course.'

Niemöller's wholehearted participation in the ecumenical
movement (which culminated in his election as one of the
presidents of the World Council of Churches in 1961) arose not

solely out of his desire for a new welcome for his nation. It also sprang from the earliest days of the church struggle and from the inspiration of his martyred friend Dietrich Bonhoeffer ('the soul of all our ecumenical connections in the Pastors' Emergency League as well as in the whole constituency of the Confessing church', as Niemöller put it). (ZEKHN 62, Vol. 425/2449a) And, as he said in his notorious press conference in Naples in June 1945, he had learned in the church struggle that 'faith cuts across creeds'. He had read von Galen's pastoral letters from his pulpit in 1937. In Dachau he had been sustained by Catholic priests.

Niemöller's ability to sit lightly on dogma was an asset in his approach to Roman Catholicism. In an interview published in *The Catholic World* he said that Christianity 'should not be a system of principles but a living, personal relationship to the Lord'. In consequence, doctrines about the mother of Jesus which had in the past deeply divided Catholics from Protestants were not for him very important. 'In the concentration camp', he commented, 'Mariology was not a source of controversy between me and my priest friends.' Since he felt 'that any Christian quoting the Gospel has greater authority than a bishop who is not quoting it', the notion of the infallibility of the Pope seemed remote to him; but, he insisted, 'We cannot allow any difficulty to act as an insuperable bar to rapprochement.'

None of this inhibited his own sturdy opinions, however. At the beginning of 1957, for instance, he caused a fair amount of controversy when he presumed to disagree with the Pope's Christmas message to the world. Pius XII, who was Pope at that time, was respected by Niemöller for his diplomatic skills. (Pius XII had been nuncio to Germany before the war.) 'There are such diplomatists in all churches', said Niemöller, 'but the Roman church has the best.' His ecumenical work naturally brought him into contact with post-war Popes and he learned to like them. 'I was very fond of John XXIII,' he remembered, 'and I was rather reserved in my judgment on the acts of Paul VI. I was sad for John Paul I.' (MN/jb)

After the Second World War Niemöller became an internationalist. He and Else travelled together, representing Germany and as part of his work with the World Council of Churches, to Australia and New Zealand, to the USA and the UK, to

Denmark, Norway, Latin America, Canada, and also to countries in the Eastern bloc. In 1948 he met for the first time Metropolitan Nikolai of Kiev, under the auspices of the Moscow-inspired World Peace Movement, and later saw this as a turning-point in his life. 'Because I was an ecumenist, I became a pacifist', he explained. (MN/jb)

But the former U-Boat officer, who had volunteered to fight for Adolf Hitler's Germany in 1939, became a pacifist also out of a deep love and concern for his own country. Even on his liberation in 1945 Niemöller did not trust the victorious allies to govern Germany properly. 'I pray above all that the four powers who administer Germany will be able to agree to work together on a common programme', he announced at his forthright press conference in Naples. 'Should Germany be divided into separate spiritual spheres, it could be the last terrible fate for my country.' All together it would mean no peace, and a breach of the peace would bring the dark ages back again for centuries.

The four occupying powers could not agree. Germany *was* divided, first into zones and then by an iron curtain between east and west. 'In the summer of 1945', wrote Niemöller, 'the general conviction was that all in all the American zone was the best to live in, that the British zone offered, in comparison, the best regulated general conditions, that in the French zone one would be hungry, and in the Russian zone one would starve.' Gradually all hopes of any alleviation disappeared. Instead 'the demarcation line between West and East became more and more a hermetically sealed frontier'. (Bp. 10. 306)

Niemöller strove to persuade his own people not to go along with the division of Germany into two halves. When the three western powers asked the Germans to ratify a constitution for the Federal Republic, Niemöller called a conference on the subject at a Hessian church institute in a castle that had belonged to the Hohenzollerns. 'The polling day was a Sunday', he recalled. 'After breakfast we went to the village church. When the service was over, I went back to the castle. My six deputies went to vote. At dinner afterwards I told them, "Have you not yet discovered that what you are doing means the separation of Germany into two states?"' They should all have realized what was happening when, a year previously, the Deutschmark was excluded as a currency from the Russian zone. (MN/jb)

By 1950 Niemöller was convinced that the Germans were effectively being denied control over their own destiny. 'We Germans since 1945 have become objects', he stated, 'objects for the plans and doings of other powers. We have become objects and not a nation.' Only if the occupying powers stepped back could the German people begin to live again as full citizens of the world. Niemöller sought the help of sympathetic people abroad. One such was the English peer, Viscount Stansgate. When they were in London, Stansgate entertained Martin and Else to lunch in the House of Lords. And on 23 June 1950 Martin told the Viscount of his desire 'to speak to you about quite a number of our problems which, I find, are becoming more and more serious, by a continuing policy tending to cut continental Europe definitely into two halves'. (ZEKHN 62, Vol. 416/2446a)

The British, the Americans, and the French no less than the Russians had, Niemöller believed, set up 'puppet states' in Germany. In consequence, he argued, Germans in both camps lived under an inadequate form of democracy. He had little time for the established political parties, believing (as he said in 1946) that the individual would be better represented not by national parties but by another individual. 'I visualise future representation based on local professional groups rather than on political parties,' he said. In any case, as he pointed out two years later, most people supposed that the political parties were 'shams'. They agitated, argued, and voted, and then the military government took a quite different decision. As a result Germany had experienced 'the failure of our great democracy'. Now was the time to set up new, more representative political groups. Several times in these years Niemöller tried to participate in such tentative new groups (with the SPD leader Dr Kurt Schumacher and with Dr Gustav Heinemann) but with little electoral success.

Although (as he said in a broadcast from Glasgow in 1959) Niemöller believed that 'Any form of government can be tolerable for a Christian', in his view 'democracy is a form of government with which Christians can find their peace in the easiest ways.' He added, 'I think our German people need democracy'. (ZEKHN 62, Vol. 821/3795) He continued to feel that German democracy did not achieve what, for example, British democracy had: a politics in which 'the elected member of parliament is responsible not to his party but to the population.

Even now nobody knows those people whom we elect to be our representatives in parliament. We don't know the people who really act in our name, and we are very little inclined to acknowledge what they do in the name of our people.' (MN/jb)

He combined these attacks on the unrepresentative nature of western democracy as he saw it with a conviction that Christianity could survive in East Germany under communism. His was a markedly different stance from that of Otto Dibelius. 'After long reflection, I learned, as a man of seventy, to say "No" to Communism and to everything it thinks and does', wrote Dibelius. 'I learned it not on political grounds but for the sake of the Christian religion.' Niemöller by contrast had learned that one reason for the rise of Hitler was an over-extreme reaction to the dangers of bolshevism. He had seen that communists shared his sufferings in the fight against Hitler. And he believed that the church had a responsibility to communists as well as to capitalists.

After a visit to the Russian zone in July 1959 Niemöller reported that 'The Russians have not touched the church in Germany, save to bar all religious services and gatherings in the open air.' After he had visited the USSR itself he came to believe 'the Russians recognise that they cannot make Russians out of Germans'. He was willing to give the Russians the benefit of the doubt. In 1953 rumours were circulating that the Russians had no wish to come to an arrangement with the western powers leading to a peaceful reunion of the two Germanys. 'Personally I am not convinced that this view is correct', Niemöller told Lord Stansgate. 'I think that everything which the Russians and the Eastern German government are doing at this time can be explained . . . as preparations for the negotiations which are due to come. [The] Russians and [the] Eastern German government have examined their present position and mustered the pawns which they have in hand.' As for the condition of the church in East Germany, although the 'situation is far from being settled', Christians who had been imprisoned were being freed 'and a great church institute in the province of Saxonia which we believed would never be given back to the church, has been turned over to the church authorities even this week'. (ZEKHN 62, Vol. 416/2446a) This willingness to trust the good intentions of the East German authorities led to some disappointments; but it also persuaded the East German prime minister,

Otto Grotewohl, that (as he said) 'it would be a mistake to throw all pastors into one pot with Bishop Dibelius. The bishop does not represent the church'.

Fear of communism blinded people in the west both to what was actually going on in East Germany and to the defects of their own society, Niemöller believed. In January 1958 he concluded an address at Augsburg with a trenchant analysis of western society in its response to communism. 'We are told we are free', he said. 'We are allowed to repeat what we read in the government papers this morning. Certainly, we have the right to hold meetings: but only because there are so few of us. If there were several millions of us, that would be the end of our freedom.' He also asked what freedom was for. 'Ask the first man you meet what he means by defending freedom, and he'll tell you privately he means defending the standard of living. I cannot accept communism, but I must admit that its ideals are very different from ours, which are all tangled up with the most sordid materialism.' Niemöller was not a communist, nor a convinced socialist in the fashion of his friend Karl Barth. He spoke in socialistic terms, he explained, only because the political choice offered was seen simply as between that or capitalism. In such a context, he said, 'I would have to say a word in favour of socialism. The corner-stone of my thinking is that the root of every evil development is money.' (MN/jb)

In 1951 Patriarch Alexi invited him to Moscow as the guest of the Russian Orthodox church. Niemöller knew the risks he was running in accepting the invitation. 'By 1951 you could see East and West drifting apart – in a way intended perhaps by both sides', he recalled. 'Everybody going from West to East was regarded as a suspicious person. I've always known that faith and suspicions cannot go together.' (MN/jb)

In 1951 the so-called cold war was beginning. In the USA Senator Joseph McCarthy was vigorously pursuing suspected communist fellow-travellers. Niemöller was aware that Otto Dibelius would be livid with anger. ('He was so cross with me', Niemöller said later, 'because I went to Russia before he did.') (MN/jb) And his position on the executive committee of the World Council of Churches could cause complications if he were regarded as in any way an official representative of that body. Niemöller therefore kept his preparations as quiet as possible, informing Visser 't Hooft that his visit was a personal and private one only ten days before he (with Hertha as interpreter) flew out from Berlin.

Niemöller believed they were the first civilians to visit Moscow since the war. He was also the first Protestant ever to set foot in the six-hundred-year-old monastery of Zagorsk, which the Russian authorities had confiscated and then returned to the church in 1945. He met Patriarch Alexi, and also Metropolitan Nikolai again. He preached to two thousand Russian Baptists. He returned convinced that the Russian Orthodox church should join with the other parts of Christendom through the World Council of Churches. Already, he recalled, he had become convinced that Russia, though part of the United Nations, was in reality excluded from that body. As for the Russian church, 'I believed', he said, 'that in Russia there are millions and millions of Christians who need their allies in the non-bolshevik world. I wanted the Russian church in the ecumenical movement; and I worked very hard for it.' (MN/jb)

Back in Europe Niemöller spoke of the 'spiritual vitality' he had seen amongst the Russian Orthodox and the Russian Baptists. He insisted that the Patriarch of Moscow and Metropolitan Nikolai were doing their best to preserve the church under difficult circumstances. 'Clearly the church in Russia is a patient and not a privileged institution in any way', he reported. Yet, in no church and in no act of worship that I visited there did I have the slightest doubt that here I had joined a Christian congregation.'

Niemöller's visit completely transformed the relationship between the Russians and the World Council of Churches. Even though he had gone to Moscow entirely on his own initiative, he reported to the executive committee of the World Council in London at the beginning of February. 'The basic question with which I went to Moscow was: is there really a church there or only a propaganda incident? To put the matter another way, is the Russian church a servant of Stalin first or of Christ first?' He reported his belief that 'the state clearly tries to use the church, and today especially, for purposes of peace propaganda'. But he also reported his conviction that the Patriarch would willingly join the World Council of Churches, if only his government would allow it.

Niemöller's advocacy overcame opposition in the west to the entry of the Russians into the World Council of Churches. Bishop Berggrav had advanced four reasons to George Bell why they should not be allowed to join: 1. the Russian church had abandoned the right to preach the law of God to the Russian people; 2. it had so allowed itself to support state policies that it had become a political tool; 3. a 'true Christian church' was likely to exist underground in Russia; and 4. it was the duty of the west to foster that 'true' church. Niemöller's testimony countered such doubts. By 1961 the Russians had become full members of the World Council of Churches. As he continued to visit Russia, Niemöller grew to admire the Russian church still more, especially its patterns of spirituality. In 1982 he said,

I am now convinced that the Reformation of the church will come from the east. In the west there is no spiritual life. (I'm speaking of the Protestant church and not the Roman Catholic church.) We have civilisation and we try to keep up culture, but we have no spiritual life. The east has a spiritual life. They know that colour influences the spirit more than black lines. In Russia there is still the notion that art is nearer religion than thinking in lines and logic. All abstract rationalising needs to be filled out with sensual thinking and feelings. In Russia there is still a strong impression of colour. (MN/jb)

As Niemöller specifically insisted, he went to Moscow as a man of the church, not as a politician. But the political cold warriors were still angry. The West German Chancellor, Konrad Adenauer, described Niemöller's visit as a stab in the back for the government. In response the Swiss Protestant press service commented that in the west the freedom of the church was taken as a matter of course and the churches were not to be expected to conform to government foreign policy. Niemöller himself observed that the Protestant church does not allow any earthly authority to prescribe what it should or should not do. But Otto Dibelius agreed with Adenauer. He wrote angrily to tell George Bell that Niemöller should not have gone to Moscow, adding, 'All operations of Dr Niemöller have an astonishing power of division. Whatever he does, one group will agree passionately and the other will reject passionately as well.' (Bp. 10. 461)

The British government too was apparently displeased with Niemöller's Russian visit. In January when he applied for his visa to come to London in order to report to the executive committee of the World Council of Churches, he was asked to fill in a form giving details of his 'movements and activities' since he last came to Britain. Niemöller had never been asked to fill in such a form before in order to obtain a visa. He was, however, by now well used to British official bureaucracy. Without more ado he sent the form to Bell, asking him to sort out the matter. Bell did so by a personal intervention with the assistant head of the visa office. By this time Niemöller had flow off to Paris by way of Berlin. The hapless authorities were obliged to pursue him with the message that he could pick up a visa at any time, in Frankfurt, Paris, or Berlin. (Bp. 10. 457f. and 473)

Holding such views about the Russians, their churches, and their policies in East Germany, Niemöller found abhorrent the notion that communism could be countered by force. 'To reproaches that I have described Russian occupation as bearable, I say: I am only against the often-heard statement that a war against bolshevism is necessary to save the Christian churches and Christianity. But it is unchristian to conduct a war for the saving of the Christian church, for the Christian church does not need to be saved', he said. 'The church is not afraid of bolshevism. It was not afraid of Nazism. The church has to serve the communists as well as all human beings. While the church rejects communism as a creed, just as it rejects all other creeds, communism must and can only be fought and defeated with spiritual weapons. All other powers will fail.'

These views were enormously reinforced by fear for his own land. Addressing 1,100 Protestant clergymen at a service in 5th Avenue Presbyterian church, New York, in 1947 (while Else addressed 800 women at St Bartholomew's church, Park Avenue), he said, 'The question today is whether the eastern and western worlds will find a way of living together in peace. It cannot be solved by Germany and the central European nations.' The key to the future lay in the question: 'will Germany and central Europe be a bridge or a barrier between east and west?' Already such opinions were unwelcome in some political circles. Niemöller was due to address a group of US senators just before he left New York in May 1947. The meeting was cancelled. He sent a copy of his intended speech to George Bell. Had he been allowed to give it, he would have said, 'The problem of Europe cannot be solved in gaining over Europe for bolshevism nor in gaining over Europe for the western American type of democracy.' At all costs Europe must not become the centre of an ideological struggle between the two ways of life. Instead, 'Europe has to become an entity of its own in order to function as a bridge between east and west.' He acknowledged that for this to happen, America would have to give up part of its 'sphere of influence', but as he saw it, 'the only hope for the future of the world, . . . is a re-Christianised Europe which, as a cultural centre and link between east and west, may bring about the understanding and collaboration of the two "ways of life" which otherwise would have to meet their fate of fighting each other to death.' (Bp. 10. 404–6)

In the following years, as Europe and Germany in particular, far from becoming a 'bridge' between east and west, became a bone of contention between the super powers, Niemöller grew increasingly apprehensive. In March 1948 he told Richard Stevens that he hoped to preach a sermon in Cambridge the following June, '*if* there will be no new war until then'. He noticed that many shared these fears. In November 1951 he spoke (in Bloomsbury Baptist church) of his recent trip to the USA, comparing it with his first visit: 'in 1947 I had not met anybody there who did not look forward with hope, whereas in 1950 I did not meet anyone who was not full of anxiety.' (ZEKHN 62, Vols. 414/2445e and 407/2444c) His great fear was that if the German people could not become a bridge between east and west, 'then the land must become a battlefield between them'. (Bp. 10. 309)

Under these anxieties, Niemöller was horrified late in 1950 to learn that the West German chancellor, Konrad Adenauer, was contemplating West German rearmament. Niemöller had never believed that Adenauer was committed to democracy after the war. (MN/jb) Now he addressed an open letter to the chancellor, asking him if it were true that he had introduced rearmament without consulting his parliamentary colleagues and demanding fresh elections before any decision were made on such an issue. Niemöller's letter roused Adenauer to a fury. Niemöller, he told his cabinet, was 'an enemy of the state'. He added, 'What Niemöller is now doing is little short of treason.'

The following week at a synod in Frankfurt Niemöller alleged that a former general of the Wehrmacht had taken over an office at Würzburg in order to set up 'German contingents for a West European army'. The synod agreed that 'rearmament should be rejected in the present circumstances'. It was announced that Gustav Heinemann had resigned from the government on the issue. And the following day an American spokesman in Heidelberg stated that a Lieutenant-General Paul Mahlmann had been employed for the past three weeks in connection with a labour service centre at Würzburg, but that there was no intention of incorporating any German contingent in a European army.

Niemöller was now deeply incensed with Adenauer, who he believed had no sympathy with the plight of Protestants living in the heart of East Germany. As a Roman Catholic, it seemed that Adenauer might even relish the fact that West Germany, bereft of these Protestants, might easily soon contain a Catholic majority. Twenty years later Niemöller conceded that although 'Adenauer had his ear close to Catholic public opinion, I would not say he was ruled by it'. In 1950 he was less charitable. Adenauer's policy seemed not only to justify Niemöller's accusation that West Germany was a mere puppet in the control of the Americans; the chancellor also seemed to be behaving as the tool of Catholicism. At a synod in Lund Niemöller claimed that 'The Federal Republic was conceived in Rome and born in Washington.' He denounced Adenauer's remilitarization policy, insisted on his right to speak out against it, and said that if he was disciplined for doing so he could always take a small country parish in East Germany.

Adenauer's press office now described Niemöller as 'an impossible person in public life'. But the church president tirelessly argued that Germany could not rely on the former allied powers for aid. In his old Dahlem pulpit on 19 November he said that the only true 'neighbours' to East Germans were West Germans. Russians, Poles, Czechs, were all indifferent to the fate of East Germany. France would be 'very glad if these Germans were dead, for then the French would sleep more soundly'. As for the British and the Americans, they recognized no neighbours but themselves.

'You will have heard that this noise arose when I wrote an Open Letter to Dr Adenauer asking for an answer whether or nor rearmament had been started already in Western Germany', Niemöller wrote to Lord Stansgate the following January. 'There was no answer, but the public became wide awake and the question of rearmament was discussed everyday and everywhere to the effect that plans were withdrawn, officers dismissed and the whole procedure revised.' He went on to say that his whole point had been 'to make clear that rearmament in Germany pending the present state of division cannot amount but to suicide, and that we are not allowed to think of ourselves only . . . leaving the 20 Million people behind the Iron Curtain to the Bolshevics.' (ZEKHN 62, Vol. 414/2446a)

In February Stansgate wrote back arranging a meeting in the Kingsway Hall, London, to be addressed by Niemöller. People in England, Stansgate said, are anxious to allow the German people to 'determine their own place in the European structure. It becomes therefore of paramount interest to us to hear from his own lips the opinions on all these matters of one who is so universally respected in this country as you yourself'. (Ibid.) Niemöller addressed the meeting on 23 February, arguing that the rearming of half of Germany would imperil the safety of the world. Great standing armies did not stay still. They had their own momentum and marched. Yet he believed that the Russians shrank from a war in Europe. They should be fought with better propaganda, aimed at promoting peace, unity, and freedom.

To many church people Niemöller now seemed to be abusing his spiritual office by dabbling in politics. Their anger that a church president who was also the official representative of German Protestantism overseas should take up these stances was all the more exacerbated in so far as Niemöller's political opinions were not theirs. Bishop Wurm believed that the nation had the right to protect itself by force of arms against communism, and attacked Niemöller for preaching politics when he took the opposite view. Dibelius, as Niemöller said, 'looks upon war as upon something which ought not to be . . . On the other hand he has never been a "pacifist", and as a member of Adenauer's Christian party he has been and is a strong supporter of German rearmament and a "policy of strength" over against Russia and her allies.' (ZEKHN 62, Vol. 399/2443) Inevitably, they clashed over the correct public stance of the churches. Niemöller's gift of invective both brought prominence to his opinions and provoked hostility. In November 1950 *Die Welt Woche* dubbed him 'The Aggressive Pacifist' (though he was not yet a pacifist). When he declared that a united Germany even under communism was better than a permanently divided country, others believed he had taken leave of his senses. After his attacks on Adenauer in 1950, for twelve hours the Protestant church leadership argued with Niemöller at a specially convened meeting in Berlin-Spandau. Finally a compromise resolution drawn up by Dibelius declared that the question of rearmament should be treated with the greatest circumspection. The resolution regretted the 'acrimony' of many of Niemöller's remarks. Niemöller for his part regretted the manner in which the Federal chancellor had presumed to criticize him. There was, however, no question of depriving him of his office. As the independent *Tagesspiegel* observed, it was doubtful whether such a deprivation would persuade Niemöller to keep quiet. For that very reason it was foolish to try to curb him.

Niemöller next had to face a storm in his own synod of Hessen and Nassau. By 97 votes to 54 the synod reaffirmed the right of churchmen to express political opinions, still counselling restraint and discretion. 'I got off with a two-thirds majority,' Niemöller told Stansgate, 'which was "near enough".' (ZEKHN 62, Vol. 416/2446a) Throughout the 1950s he faced much sharp criticism. The churches were not used to taking political responsibility of this kind. Nor were politicians keen to welcome it. 'It would be extremely good if Herr Niemöller would remember the old saying, the shoemaker should stick to his last', commented the *Süderländer Tageblatt* in 1957. 'His duty is to preach the gospel, not play the small-town politician.' Dr Kreutzer of Wiesbaden wrote to say he was no longer fit to serve as church president in Hessen and Nassau. Niemöller replied that he should make his complaints to the synod itself. (ZEKHN 62, Vol. 935/3288a) Occasionally when a complaint was factually inaccurate, he would take some pains to correct it. On 3 October 1958 he wrote to John F. C. Green of McKeesport, PA, USA, 'Your letter of August 30 arrived a few days ago with a stamp "Pray for Peace". I think that the stamp of your mail really is a good expression of what I am and what I stand for; but to label me as "the constant leftist" certainly is a caricature. And I really should like to know when and where you ever have heard me propose "that the church people should engage in treason – in Germany – by betraying defense positions to the Communists".'

It is not the age of treason but the age of the big lie, Niemöller commented. (ZEKHN 62, Vol. 510/2492a)

Within the German churches Niemöller's political opponents did from time to time score victories. In 1956 they even managed to secure, in his absence, his dismissal from the office of foreign representative of the Protestant church. Niemöller took the matter surprisingly calmly. The office now scarcely mattered to him. He continued as before, using his prestige as a world figure and his position in the World Council of Churches, to follow his Christian conscience and make its demands known to others. He also lost the fight not to give any apparent religious blessing to West German rearmament. In 1957 the decidedly political Otto Dibelius in the name of the council of the German Protestant church signed an agreement in Bonn with Konrad Adenauer to provide the German forces with army chaplains.

During the early 1950s when he was campaigning against West German rearmament, Niemöller was inexorably moving towards pacifism. The catalyst was the atomic bomb. 'We had been frightened of atomic weapons since 1945', he observed. 'In those days I became convinced – and remain convinced now – that, after Hitler, Truman [who ordered the atomic bombing of the Japanese cities of Hiroshima and Nagasaki] was the greatest murderer in the world.' (MN/jb) Two scientists brought him to the centre of the movement against atomic weapons in the 1950s. The first was Professor Otto Hahn.

On 6 June 1954 Otto Hahn visited the Max Planck Institute in Wiesbaden where Niemöller lived. Niemöller asked him if the danger of atomic destruction was as great as some people supposed. Otto Hahn answered, 'Herr Pastor, it is not only as bad; it is a great deal worse.' Hahn explained that it was now possible to produce an atomic device that would end not only all human life on earth, but also the life of every higher organism. Niemöller wondered out loud what would have happened had Hitler possessed such a device in the Berlin bunker in April 1945. He returned home and re-read the Sermon on the Mount. Then, carefully explaining that he was speaking only for himself, he declared that henceforth he could no longer justify the use of force.

As disturbing was the testimony of Professor Linus Pauling, the atomic chemist of the university of Pasadena in Colorado, that to test a simple water-bomb would cause the premature deaths of 15,000 human beings, not to speak of a similar number of aborted babies.

These men pushed Martin Niemöller faster along the road on which he had already started. In February 1954 he had written for a Japanese publication: 'The renunciation of war as expressed in the Japanese Constitution has given a first ray of hope to a world in darkness and despair, and men today cling to this hope passionately. Can we really do something about it or are we to stand aside as idle onlookers, unable to contribute for better or for worse?' In April of the same year he sent a message to the British National Campaign against the Hydrogen Bomb, to be read publicly in the Royal Albert Hall in London. 'I am convinced', the message began, 'that only a strong pressure from the side of public opinion will be able to stop the avalanche which is threatening in an ever increasing way not only the civilisation but also the survival of mankind.' (ZEKHN 62, Vols. 35/2433c and 416/2446a)

Niemöller had also been drawn into the world-wide peace movement launched by the remarkable Frenchman Frédéric Joliot-Curie in the cities of Paris and Prague in 1949. Joliot-Curie had been a French bureaucrat, politician, Gaullist minister, delegate of the French Communist party and French high commissioner for atomic energy. In July 1952 Joliot-Curie invited Niemöller to join the World Peace Committee and serve on its council. The following year Niemöller attended the first three days of the council's session in Budapest. On 10 March 1955 Joliot-Curie solicited his signature for an appeal against atomic weapons, with the comment, 'I think your public approval of our Appeal will have a great weight.' (ZEKHN 62, Vols. 795/3179 and 797/3179a)

All the aspects of Niemöller's peace work were now coming together. The World Peace Committee was implacably opposed to German rearmament, and the council, meeting in Paris on 15 January 1955, praised those Germans who were trying to prevent it, commenting that 'The remilitarisation of Germany will inevitably lead to the madness of an armaments' race between east and west, between France and Germany.' But the committee also, like Niemöller, saw the problems of Germany in a world-wide perspective. Unable to attend the council meeting in Stockholm in November 1954, Niemöller sent his apologies to Joliot-Curie with the hope that 'divided peoples – in Korea, Indochina and here in our Germany – might through the committee's work be peacefully brought together again.'

The third aspect of his life in connection with the World Peace Committee was his fascination with Russia. As well as French, Czechs, Americans, Germans, and the British, the committee sought the help of communists, atheists, and also Russian Christians. On 22 April 1955 Metropolitan Nikolai wrote to Niemöller happy that they would soon meet again at the forthcoming Helsinki congress of the WPC. 'Every meeting with you is a source of joy to me', wrote Nikolai. 'How I am looking forward to being with you in Helsinki on 22 May! There we shall set up a Christian front against war.' (Ibid.)

Niemöller used his position in the World Council of Churches to spread his views on nuclear weapons. 'I personally can imagine no situation in which to the question, "Lord, what do you wish me to do", I received from God the answer, "Drop an atomic bomb!",' Niemöller told the executive council at its meeting in Denmark in 1958. But it was from Britain that he now drew inspiration for a further initiative towards peace. In 1957 Canon L. J. Collins of St Paul's cathedral had just completed a successful campaign against capital punishment. A group of nuclear disarmers asked him to direct his energies to running a campaign against atomic weapons. The distinguished philosopher Bertrand Russell was invited to become president of the campaign.

The idea was conceived of an Easter march of protest from London to the atomic weapons research establishment at Aldermaston. At the beginning of April 1958 Martin Niemöller joined the first of these. 'I walked from Windsor to Aldermaston in rain and wind', he recalled. 'I stood in water up to my knees and spoke.' (MN/jb) The personal context of his speech was the proposal to rearm his own nation's soldiers with nuclear weapons. He said that there now existed the possibility of one-tenth of the world's population destroying the rest. Defence measures had become a form of aggressiveness, 'an ever-growing provocation'.

Once again Niemöller was a marked man in Britain. On his next visit, in November, instead of walking as usual through the customs' formalities, Niemöller was called aside by an immigration official. Niemöller turned on his heels and took the next plane back to Germany, leaving an embarrassed Home Office to cope with hostile questions about the incident in the House of Commons and angry letters from clergymen.

None of this harassment forced him to give up the fight. The issue was of too great importance. He had no qualms about the accusation that he mixed with fellow-travellers and communists. On 22 May 1959 he wrote, 'I am certain that in the ten years of its existence the World Peace Committee has opened the eyes of millions of people to the seriousness and to the importance of the endeavour to achieve a stable peace, not only as the goal but also as the presupposition of all reasonable politics in the atomic era.' (ZEKHN 52, Vol. 796/3179a) This and his own integrity enabled him to work alongside those whose other presuppositions he did not share. As he wrote in a message to a nuclear disarmament mass meeting in the Free Trade Hall, Manchester, on 13 May 1960, 'We are all in the same boat; nuclear disarmament is more than a problem of politics; we must achieve it for mankind's sake and fight for it in the name of right, of humanity, of God himself.' (ZEKHN 62, Vol. 415/2446)

But it *was* also a political issue of great sensitivity, especially in his own country, and some right-wing German politicians were deeply irritated by Niemöller's speeches and activities. On his return to Germany from the first Aldermaston march Niemöller had declared that 'those who favour the production, stockpiling and use of atomic means of mass destruction were acting, wittingly or unwittingly, as materialists, nihilists, and atheists, even though they might describe themselves for political purposes as Christians.' As a result he was refused permission to preach in a Bavarian church in August. This was not the only German Protestant pulpit from which he was barred for such reasons. But on 28 January the following year he was threatened from a more powerful direction, when Herr Franz-Joseph Strauss, the West German defence minister, filed a suit for defamation against him after reading reports that he had told a pacifist meeting that military training for positions of high command must now be considered a 'high-school for criminals'. Under West German law it was considered possible to defame the army collectively. After some time Strauss was advised to drop the suit, and did so. But it had been a serious threat. Long afterwards Niemöller said, only half-jokingly, that if Franz-Joseph Strauss ever achieved political power in West Germany as a whole, he would leave the country and go to live in Switzerland. (MN/jb)

Niemöller denied that he had defamed the army. None the less, the April synod of the church of Hessen and Nassau insisted on passing a resolution stating that a soldier has 'a particularly heavy responsibility towards God. He has therefore a special claim to the sympathetic understanding and continual intercession of the church. The more the church shares his burden, the sooner will attention be paid to the church's warnings, which the development of modern weapons and the international situation have made necessary.' Niemöller commented that the resolution would be interpreted as a certificate of honour for the armed forces.

He resolutely refused to join in the cold war, especially when, as it seemed to him, men like Otto Dibelius were promoting it. In the middle of 1961 he reluctantly refused to take part in the *Kirchentag*, which Dibelius and others had managed to arrange in Berlin. To induce thousands of West German Christians to demonstrate their faith in that free city deep inside East Germany seemed to Niemöller unduly provocative. As he explained to Mark Gibbs of the *Kirchentag* ecumenical committee, he would dearly love to have felt able to take part. 'I have cancelled this appointment not because I am afraid of meeting with opposite views and tendencies in Berlin, but because this *Kirchentag* is being held in Berlin under the political tensions as they are now. The *Kirchentag* in Berlin will be a whole supply of ammunition for the cold war.' (ZEKHN 62, Vol. 410/2445a)

In August Niemöller had decided to go on holiday. During the past six months he had suffered anxiety and a few blows, but nothing so great as that which was to strike him now.

Else had begun to suffer from multiple sclerosis, and was more and more dependent on Dora – as indeed the whole family were in one way or another. The plan was for Martin to visit an international meeting of Methodists, while Dora and Else holidayed in Denmark. (MN/jb) On 7 August the three left Büdingen. At 2.30 in the afternoon, north of Flensburg near the Danish town of Aabenraa in south Jutland, the car left the highway on a hill curve and hit a tree. Niemöller was seriously injured. He was unconscious for two days. When he came to in hospital, he found that the wife with whom he had shared so many hardships and triumphs, and their faithful companion from the years in Berlin, were both dead.

Ach Elslein, liebes Elslein, wollt Gott, ich wär bei Dir!
So fliessen tiefe Wasser wohl zwischen Dir und mir!

14. TO PROVOKE PEACEFULLY

BY THE time Martin Niemöller left hospital his wife and Dora had been buried together in Wiesbaden. (MN/jb) For the rest of his life he kept in his study the last photograph of himself and Else in the fatal car. In no way could he give up the work they had done together. But it now seemed much harder. On 12 October he wrote to Saint Louis, Missouri, to thank an American who had sent his sympathy, and said, 'Life has become rather difficult, since I do not know how to work and to live without my wife who for forty-two years has been my companion, and I do not know either whether I can rely on the strength of my body which has enabled me ever since I was young to do what I wanted to do or what I felt necessary to be done.' (ZEKHN 62, Vol. 449/2485a)

At the end of the year he was present at the conference of the World Council of Churches in New Delhi. Its significance was twofold. First, the Russians were participating. And even more significant, perhaps: as Niemöller told his fellow-Christians in Germany afterwards, 'New Delhi in 1961 was the first ever meeting of the world's churches to take place in a non-Christian land.' Niemöller's notions of the solidarity of mankind were still widening. He had first visited India with Else in 1953 and had been brought to understand the possibility that Christianity and the teaching of Mahatma Gandhi might converge in many important ways. If there could be Christianity without Christ, the teachings of Gandhi were Christianity. Later he inevitably took up Gandhi's techniques of non-violent protest.

But Niemöller was also extending his attacks on racism, as he found a wider constituency than Germany alone. By now the suspicions which Jews had sometimes held against him had disappeared. As early as 1949 Dr W. S. Matsdorf of the *Australian Jewish Herald* (once he had learned from Niemöller himself that the Stuttgart Declaration of Guilt involved guilt over the murder of the Jews as well as a general guilt for the evils of the war) was sending Niemöller details of such obscenities as the desecration of Jewish cemeteries in Germany, and Niemöller gladly investigated them. (ZEKHN 62, Vol. 3/3236). Niemöller stood for the deliberate, careful cultivation of friendship between Christians and Jews. (MN/jb) He found it began to illuminate his own faith. As he told the Frankfurt-am-Main society for Christian–Jewish co-operation in 1964, he had come to see both Christianity and Judaism as the creeds of revolutionary minorities within society. (ZEKHN 62, Vol. 128/3560).

He also perceived racism as a threat to world peace. In 1957 he signed a 'declaration of conscience', at the request of a committee chaired by Mrs Eleanor Roosevelt (who once had not wished him even to visit her own country), calling on South Africa to uphold human rights and protesting against the policy of *apartheid*. Martin Niemöller did not lightly give his name to causes, however appealing they might appear. He wrote to the secretary of the committee: 'It is only with considerable hesitation that I can give my consent. The Declaration of Conscience expresses fully my own conviction and still I should have preferred to go to South Africa personally and tell the responsible people of that country what the world and especially the Christian church is thinking of this attitude and behaviour.' He signed such declarations, as he explained to another correspondent on 27 December 1963, because of his conviction that 'it is our most urgent duty to fight all sorts of racialism, because otherwise we shall not be able to escape a catastrophe of inhumanity; and our children's children will have to pay for that'. (ZEKHN 62, Vols. 499/2485a and 416/2446a)

For this reason he was willing to sign another appeal to South Africa, this time for political prisoners there, and in September 1966 he managed to visit the country himself. There he met the Nobel Peace Prize winner, Albert Luthuli, former leader of the banned African National Party. He courageously declared that the South Africans needed to break through the barriers they had erected to isolate themselves from the rest of the world, when they would learn that racism was anti-Christian – and also that they were part of the whole of humanity. 'I think we in Europe and people in the United States are today far more aware that the whole world is interrelated – that the fate of the white man in South Africa cannot be isolated from the fate of the white man anywhere,' he said. 'The thing I have found strangest, coming as a stranger to this country, is that there are whites here who think that their fate is their own affair – that it will not be affected by the rest of the world.' But he did not approve of a policy of rejection. Germany had needed acceptance by the rest of the world. He had fought to win it. Now in South Africa he said that the most important thing to him was that people outside South Africa should help her to come to feel part of humanity as a whole.

Racism he perceived to be connected with powerlessness and poverty. When the Revd Martin Luther King was murdered in America after campaigning for black rights in a non-violent way, Niemöller's thoughts instantly flew to the murder of Gandhi twenty years previously. The death of both men, he said, spoke about the relations between Christians and Jews as well as whites and blacks.

Increasingly Niemöller preached that we lived either in *one* world or in a world with no future. In 1964 he entitled a volume of his collected speeches and broadcasts *Eine Welt oder keine Welt* [One World or No World]. As he had insisted at the Hamburg *Kirchentag* ten years earlier, to act solely in the interests of one's own nation had become questionable behaviour. This was a conviction especially valuable, he preached, 'to Germans on the frontier between east and west', who had their own important contribution to make to those living on both sides of that frontier. No doubt, he said, 'our nation belongs to the western world and we have little desire for confidence in or a relationship with the east. But because we have a neighbour in the east, we have to make the attempt to see whether a peaceful relationship as neighbours is possible. If we want peace – and who does not want it? – then we must desire also understanding with our opponent: and to effect that we must speak with him.'

In this spirit Martin Niemöller continued to travel the world after the death of Else, and in particular to travel to Russia. In 1964 he retired as president of the church of Hessen and Nassau. It made little difference. (He told one correspondent after his first year of 'retirement' that he had spent more than two hundred days out of the 365 outside Germany.) (ZEKHN 62, Vol. 396/2442c)

In 1964 he visited Russia to celebrate the fiftieth anniversary of the consecration as bishop of Patriarch Alexi. Niemöller's successor as president of the church of Hessen and Nassau went 'officially'. Niemöller went in a personal capacity. The visit boosted his spirits in a totally unexpected fashion.

The two Germans in Russia had between them one interpreter, whom Niemöller had known for many years. 'I was already hard of hearing then, and so I asked for a second one', Niemöller recalled. 'I got one. She was an interpreter between Chinese and Russian. She couldn't speak German, but she'd learned enough English to translate Russian into English. Now she worked for the Russian foreign office.' Niemöller had mourned Else for two years. 'In the meantime', he said, 'I didn't believe I was an old man. (I was sixty-eight or so when Else died.) All my life I had been in love with somebody.' Between him and the interpreter developed a dear friendship. 'I wanted to bring her back to Germany', he related. 'There was no possibility. All my efforts to bring her failed. Soon we had to give up this idea.' But they wrote lots of letters to each other. Later he got his chauffeur to remove them from his collected papers. 'You wouldn't want them in the archives', he said with a smile. (MN/jb)

A letter he wrote to Metropolitan Nikodim reveals the transformation in Niemöller. 'When I look back on the wonderful days in Moscow, Odessa, and Sotschi', he wrote, 'then I must say I have not experienced such a lovely holiday since I became a widower; and I thank God that I could spend this holiday in Russia and on the Black Sea.' (ZEKHN 62, Vol. 497/2484a) Niemöller kept the tickets he'd bought for the Moscow circus and elsewhere during his holiday.

In another letter he told Nikodim, 'I continue to pray for the unity of Christendom.' (Ibid.) He also continued to work for the unity of his own country. At a meeting of the World Council of Churches' executive committee in Paris in August 1962 he had declared, 'I am no nationalist and did not claim any rights for my country in 1945.' None the less he now pointed out that then Germany had surrendered unconditionally and seventeen years later was still waiting for a reply from the victorious powers to her surrender. Now was surely the time for Russia and the USA to come together with a reasonable answer to the hopes of the Germans. He continued to regard democracy as much less than perfect in the west, and in 1964 went so far as to suggest that the next elections should be boycotted by the Germans, since all they could vote for was a dictatorial regime, bent on obtaining nuclear weapons when the rest of the world wanted peace. Some of the generous remarks made on his retirement were now forgotten or taken back. Herbert Wehner, for instance, the chairman of the SPD, described the suggestion as 'eccentric, misleading and malicious'. Niemöller, he said, 'had not yet understood democracy'. Niemöller readily defended himself. 'Of course the whole political path of the German nation interests me', he wrote, 'but I speak out in politics only when some essential issue arises that the politicians are not discussing. Of course I may break taboos, but I have no need to ask what I'm allowed to say. Instead I say what my conscience tells me.' He continued to regard politicians with suspicion, saying half-humorously, 'I doubt whether medical practitioners lie as much as politicians. For politicians truth and falsehood are unimportant. So I never could become a politician – not even a church politician.' At the age of ninety, he was even more impatient with European politics. 'I began my political responsibility as an ultra-conservative. I wanted the Kaiser to come back; and now I am a revolutionary. I really mean that. If I live to be a hundred I shall maybe be an anarchist, for an anarchist wants to do without all government.' (MN/jb) And he continued to hold that spiritual bonds transcend political boundaries. It was an important assumption in divided Germany. As he had said in 1964, 'I go to East Germany to show that we in West Germany as Christians do not allow ourselves to be separated by political ideas.' Niemöller's work in the 1960s was based on a conviction he put to Gustav Turs, archbishop of the Lutheran church of Lettlands, remembering their days together in Riga in 1961, that 'Jesus Christ does not recognise boundaries or fronts'. (ZEKHN 62, Vol. 407/2444c)

Niemöller's impulse to dedicate himself to peace and disarmament in a divided Germany and then in a divided world began with a religious conviction after World War II and was still enormously strong in the 1960s. The reconstructed Protestant church had declared that it must remain unthinkable for Germans to shoot at Germans. Niemöller deeply deplored not just the loss of that determination but a process of education which actually reversed it. 'We have now been influenced to see the "other side" as the enemy. Each side uses the same slogan. For more than twenty years we've been educated to use the special slogan: "The enemy is the east/west".' (MN/jb)

In his determination to try to reverse this process and regard the 'enemy' as his friend, Niemöller inevitably risked exploitation. In trivial ways this involved appearing in East German newspapers such as the *Neue Deutsche Bauern Zeitung* billed as 'An upright Man' when he had said something acceptable to the East German SEPD. This was not particularly irksome or serious, since it merely paralleled the vicissitudes of Niemöller's reputation in the western press.

But Niemöller was particularly careful not to have his name exploited for purposes that he did not approve of or by those who were willing to put propaganda before facts. In July 1965 Niemöller went as a representative of the clergymen's emergency committee for Vietnam to visit that country. The Vietnam war increasingly horrified the imagination of the west. When Lyndon Baines Johnson become president of the United States of America, there were 16,000 US advisers in Vietnam. When he left the White House, 536,000 US troops were fighting there and another 30,000 were dead. Niemöller himself passionately wished to see an end to the war, but he was deeply annoyed when he discovered that the secretary of the committee, Alfred J. Hassler, had produced a report suggesting that members of the delegation had actually visited both sides in the conflict. Niemöller had not, and he did not suppose the others had either. He wrote a sharp note querying Hassler's report. 'I must confess that during my stay in the countries of Indochina', the note ran, 'I have not met with nor spoken to anybody who belonged to the "other side".' (Hassler lamely replied that some delegates met 'supporters' of North Vietnam on an occasion when Niemöller was not present.) (ZEKHN 62, Vol. 506/2491) In fact Niemöller's largely agreed with Hassler's views; but he was not willing to sacrifice his integrity or the truth to bolster up his case.

The following year, together with the Anglican Bishop Ambrose Reeves, the American Presbyterian minister A. J. Muster, and the Canadian Rabbi Abraham Feinberg, the seventy-four-year old Niemöller went to North Vietnam as guest of the Hanoi government to see for himself conditions there. There they were joined by Monsignor Georg Hässler, Roman Catholic secretary-general of the German branch of the relief agency Caritas. The clergymen, said Niemöller, were able to move around quite freely, in so far as the war allowed. For one-and-a-half hours they spoke with Ho Chi Minh in his Hanoi residence.

'The meeting was carried out in complete frankness', said Niemöller at Rome airport *en route* home. 'One thing is clear', he added: 'the president of North Vietnam is not a fanatic. He is a very strong and determined man, but capable of listening, something that is very rare in a person of his position.' Niemöller reported that Ho Chi Minh's position was very clear: 'The Americans must leave Vietnam. When they have done so, the rest will be very easy. The first premise for any negotiation is that the bombardments cease'. In Niemöller's view the desire for peace shown by Ho Chi Minh and all those he had met in North Vietnam was obvious, but they would continue to fight so long as the Americans continued to bomb them. Niemöller went on to say that he had investigated how a grant from the German Protestant churches of 300 thousand Deutschmarks in relief had been spent. He had investigated the need for further aid. And he had seen the air raids. The party, he said, went to Phu Ly near the Chinese border and found the small town 'almost totally destroyed by American bombings and abandoned by its inhabitants'.

Such news and opinions were unwelcome in many western political circles in 1966. Niemöller's strength, however, lay in two things. First he was willing to go to great trouble to ascertain his facts. Although he was frequently accused of naïvety in politics, he filled his house with newspaper cuttings, annotated in detail. Secondly, once he had come to his opinion, he was fearless in expressing it.

Having become a convinced pacifist, he was uncompromising in his determination to foster the peace movement in Germany. He was also willing tirelessly to travel and speak wherever he could outside Germany in favour of peace. Canon L. J. Collins asked him to speak in London on an inconvenient day in 1961. Niemöller replied, 'if by any chance you have a real lack of theologians, please let me know, and then I shall try after all to get rid of my [other] obligations'. On 17 April 1962 Linus Pauling asked him to write immediately to President J. F. Kennedy, urging him to postpone the US atmospheric tests until after the Geneva conference. Niemöller instantly agreed. In May he was in Budapest, and broadcast the message: 'The best means of securing coexistence is through the removal of mistrust, which can be best achieved and most speedily by general and ceaseless disarmament, where each side is given unlimited control over the other.' In June he took part in an anti-nuclear arms convention of the Gandhi Peace Foundation. (ZEKHN 62, Vols. 602/2444c, 526/2501a, 492/2483 and 821/3795)

In all this activity Niemöller was deepening both his own knowledge of the technical and political problems involved and also his awareness of the enormity of it all. On 20 May 1963 Bertrand Russell wrote to him, 'out of a profound concern and anxiety with regard to the rapid development of a rocket and nuclear arms race in the Middle East'. He asked Niemöller to sign an appeal for a halt to this. Martin replied, 'I felt rather ashamed that up to now I have never contemplated even the idea that the situation in the Middle East demands not only our concern but our own activity.' (ZEKHN 62, Vol. 416/2444a)

In spite of all this Niemöller continued to run his church until his retirement, and even after that he continued to help many individuals who sought his aid. Above all he was concerned with the danger of nuclear destruction in his own land. He believed this danger to be growing, not lessening. 'I used to say we were an American colony', he observed; 'now we are merely an ammunition dump.' (MN/jb) For this reason he seized on and greatly encouraged the German Easter marches inspired by the British campaign for nuclear disarmament. By October 1981 he judged them a huge success, and set out plans to broaden their base, creating a huge extra-parliamentary pressure-group. (ZEKHN 62, Vol. 821/3795) This provided a new platform for dissidence. In 1967, after reminding his hearers how the Easter marches had grown in the past nine years since they were imported from Britain, Niemöller used the occasion of the Christian feast to speak of Vietnam. 'Still today Vietnam seems a far country and a small one, whose fate has little to do with us', he said. 'But the thirty-two million people who have had to suffer there for years and decades are human beings like ourselves, and they suffer fearfully and bitterly, men and women, the old and the children: human beings who are not responsible for this suffering.' He linked the human aggressiveness that had caused this suffering with the aggressiveness of Germany's Third Reich. The people of Vietnam, said Niemöller, were 'human beings such as those we old ones came to know in Poland, in Holland, in Norway, in Denmark, in France, in Russia, people who have no great desire save to be left in peace and allowed to see to their own concerns.' How long would it be, he asked, before the Asian people began to see the white race – Russian socialist as well as American capitalist – as their opponent and enemy? On the Easter march 1967 he called for an end to a war that could help no one and bring only disaster to both sides.

Niemöller was not so sanguine as to suppose that disarmament would of itself solve the dangerous political tensions of the world. It would, however, serve to reduce enormously the peril involved in those tensions. When in 1961 a correspondent asked whether he held rearmament responsible in the main for the political complications of the time, he replied, 'Though rearmament has not generated the present political complications it certainly has magnified them.' As he saw it, a constructive approach to easing the tension between the nations was to propose a disarmament-zone in Central Europe including both Germanys. (ZEKHN 62, Vol. 509/2492) As Niemöller approached the age of ninety, he was heartened by the growing influence of the anti-nuclear 'Green' movement in Germany – though here again he did not believe that the 'Greens' could produce a programme that would serve as a political panacea to all the ills of his country. 'The peace movement must concern itself with things that belong to the next step', he said: 'the neutron bomb, the middle-range bomb and the rockets. If these are introduced into West Germany, we must make a revolution.' (MN/jb)

Niemöller's technique from the 1950s onwards was, as he put it at the Genevan world conference for church and state in 1966, 'to provoke peacefully'. In 1951, after his open letter to Konrad Adenauer had so powerfully provoked the Federal chancellor, Niemöller had told his friend Lord Stansgate, 'The Bonn Parliament may have even now a small majority favouring rearmament in the way of participation in a West European Defense Program; but the people are against it, at least three quarters of them.' (ZEKHN 62, Vol. 416/2446a) Twenty-one years later, in the year of Niemöller's eightieth birthday, he could take some pleasure from the fact that 120 thousand protesters, mostly young people, at a Hamburg church congress in the presence of chancellor Helmut Schmidt and defence minister Hans Apel, were opposed to the stationing of NATO missiles on German soil.

But Niemöller at eighty was not looking back with complacency. On the contrary, he said: 'I am interested only in what could and should happen tomorrow. I want my entire generation and the ones that follow to strive for tomorrow without losing the wider outlook that not only our fate is at stake but that of all mankind.'

15. PORTRAIT OF A HUMAN BEING

IN JUNE 1945 an extremely intelligent US army officer tried to sum up Martin Niemöller's character in an official report. His assessment was extremely complimentary. Asked to read it, Niemöller dismissed the report with the comment, 'approved "as far as it goes"'.

Any attempt to assess the character of a giant among human beings is bound to end in failure. The US army report described Pastor Niemöller as 'a man capable of high organisation and clear cut execution of his programs, as they relate to his own activities... He is physically a dynamic and electric character possessed of extreme nervous energy and ability to express himself forcefully and clearly to a question no matter how searching. He obtains his refreshment and stimulus from association with people.' (ZEKHN 62, Vol. 976/3027) He could also relax, and sometimes in the midst of all his burdens longed to get away. 'Here everything is well except for the amount of work which certainly is much too much', he wrote to his friend Richard Stevens in 1949, '(you understand for somebody who is dreaming everyday of the happy laziness of the Hawaiians).' (ZEKHN 62, Vol. 414/2445e) But he could never have achieved so much without prodigious powers of hard work. Even at the age of eighty-seven he still bristled with energy and authority, smoking cigars, pressing them on me when I visited him, refusing to be interviewed by the BBC until he had got to know his interviewer properly and denying that the ticking clocks would ruin the sound-recording, poring over newspapers and consulting *Who's Who* to make sure of a stray biographical fact. (MN/jb)

Throughout his career he displayed such energy. Between 17 and 21 October 1957, for instance, on a brief visit to the German Protestant churches of northern England, he managed to preach in Huddersfield and Wakefield, take coffee with the Huddersfield pastors over a morning's discussion, lunch with the Bishop of Bradford, preach in Bradford cathedral, attend a conference of the British and Foreign Bible Society in Ilkley, lead two Sunday services in Bradford, before going on to address the Eastbrook

Hall Methodist Mission that same evening. (ZEKHN 62, Vol. 404/2444)

Yet he always insisted on making time for individuals as well, representing this incidentally as a favour to himself. In 1949 he wrote to Pastor Walter Kurtz, who ministered to a refugee congregation in Britain, that on his next visit he would love to take tea with him and his fellow-pastor Julius Rieger. But he begged Kurtz not to fill the house with others. 'Don't invite fifteen people, please', wrote Niemöller. 'I shall drink my tea better with your dear wife, Rieger and you alone.' (Ibid.)

Martin Niemöller did not forget the favours people had done to him. A year after Richard and Moja Stevens had speedily flown out to comfort him in Switzerland conditions for the Niemöllers were still not good. But Martin, writing to Richard, still remembered to mention the fishing rod they had brought from England. 'Else is not in too good a condition, and we are waiting for Jan all the time; we had no news from him for several months, and I begin to doubt whether we shall see him again after all. Herta and Hermann are going on with their study-work, and we don't see much of them both; only little Martin is staying with us, but normally invisible as the angler and fisherman strolling about in Büdingen and [the] vicinity.' When he could, Niemöller seized the chance to repay such favours. In the case of Richard Stevens he had to wait till 1965, after the Germans had decided to offer some reparations for those grievously ill-treated during the war. The authorities ludicrously tried to reject Stevens's claim on the grounds that he had suffered not inside the concentration camp proper but in a special camp outside. Stevens was able to appeal to Niemöller for corroboration of the true facts. (ZEKHN, 62, 414/2445e)

Niemöller put himself out for the trivial as well as the weighty problems people brought to him. In December 1959 the secretary of a tour party wrote asking if he could possibly get them all tickets for the Oberammergau passion play. Martin tried, but failed. When the Oldham and district council of churches wrote asking for a message to introduce their pageant (which was mounted to raise money for refugees), Niemöller responded with the same alacrity as he did to a request for an interview by the Japanese publisher Mr Genzaburo Joshino, editor-in-chief of

Iwanami Shoten. Since his secretary was away, Niemöller wrote the Oldham message on his way home and sent it off himself.

But in the midst of a hectic life, his solicitude took much out of him. In May 1950 Else wrote to a scholar who complained that Niemöller did not answer his letters: 'since we left England life has been an awful strain for him. There were two big synods in Germany in which he took an outstanding part and on May 2nd he left for South America and will not be back before June 3rd.' She added, 'I am very much looking forward to his coming home.' Martin, she said, had not liked being without her, seemed quite worn out and could not get on with his work. (ZEKHN 62, Vols. 395/2442b, 355/2433c and 416/2446a)

Niemöller's dealings with others, especially on a pastoral or personal level, display an unconscious humility. He himself took a mischievous delight in being better informed than most. 'My ambition is only human', he once said: 'to know more than the others. I have always enjoyed showing that they didn't know everything.' (MN/jb) But, as at school he never needed to appear to be top in everything, so he never looked on his authority in the church as a prize to be grasped at. 'There are no ranks in the Prussian church', he would explain. 'Superintendent-generals, yes, but no archbishop.' He restored the church of Hessen and Nassau after World War II on as democratic a basis as possible. This attitude was nurtured in his youth. At the age of seventeen or so, Niemöller learned from a boy in his class called Herbert Loewen that he had been baptized by his own father – a layman – the previous Sunday. 'I felt for that kind of church', he said later, 'free, but with some kind of order and rules, such as a family needs.' Indeed, he believed that 'we need anti-clericalism in Christendom, to keep Christianity in order'. Quakers such as Fox and Penn, who did not believe in removing their hats before human authorities, offered, he came to believe, 'not the fulfilment of the gospel, but a correction to a gospel that was hopelessly deformed'. (MN/jb)

But Niemöller took some time to work out his attitude to the question of legitimate authority in the state if not in the church. 'We Germans have this notion that society must be ranged in ranks', he explained. 'Just four weeks ago I had a meeting with a general. He is half my age, but as soon as I met him I had the feeling that I must stand to attention. It is an innate feeling and not a rational concept, for authority must be *lived* – it doesn't belong to an office.'

Niemöller went so far as to suggest that one problem in dealing with Hitler was the difficulty of getting rid of the innate feeling that because of his office he must possess authority. 'I was a small subordinate among 60 million German people', Niemöller explained. 'Who was I to speak to the one who represented 60 million German people.' He added, 'maybe after my nearly ninety years of experience, if I had to go through the same fight again, I would be much less respectful'. (MN/jb) In fact the struggle against racism under Hitler and afterwards convinced Niemöller of the basic equality of human beings. As he put it in 1959, 'Races are diverse. They are different from each other, but certainly every human being has the same value in the sight of God . . . There is no such thing as a monster man or a super man.' (ZEKHN 62, Vol. 821/3795) He would never consider himself any kind of hero. And certainly the many honorary doctorates he received – the Lenin Peace Prize, the coveted bronze medal of the university of New York (offered to 'Martin Niemöller – courageous churchman') – did not in his view remotely sum up who he was. *Pastor* Niemöller remained his preferred designation.

Yet in his correspondence and still more in his presence Niemöller made an extraordinary impact. In 1981 I asked for some of Niemöller's writings in a Würzburg bookshop. The manager's face lit up as he remembered and began to speak of a visit paid to him by Niemöller in Ripon prisoner-of-war camp thirty-five years earlier.

Part of Niemöller's impact on others depended obviously on his sense of conviction as well as his ability to devote himself to others' needs. Niemöller often combined this with a great deal of charm. His skill at choosing the most provoking words when challenging an opponent did not conceal its reverse side: considerable wit. His grasp of language enabled him to speak both American English and English English (distinguishing, for instance, between 'railroad' and 'railway' with ease). A straightforward joke in his conversation ('An American, if he likes you, will always put one of your cigars in his top pocket before leaving') was likely to be topped by a better one ('If he is a courteous American and there are three cigars in your box, he'll take two and put the third in *your* top pocket'). Without vanity, he could delight in telling jokes at his own expense ('We have a German saying, "Cold coffee makes you pretty". That's why I always drink the first half of a cup warm and leave the rest to go cold').

One effect of his wit is that the best descriptions of his contemporaries – especially of those with whom he sometimes clashed – are often his. 'The greatest moment in Dibelius's life, to my mind', he once said, 'was when he was deposed and became the curate of Jacobi. He simply obeyed.' This, Niemöller believed, also illustrated a difference between the two of them. 'I never could obey just like that, even as a sailor. Always I had to question orders and ask why – though I would obey some captains because their orders were so clear.'

When it came to describing Hanns Lilje, with whom Niemöller got on better than with Dibelius, Niemöller also poked gentle fun at himself. 'Hanns Lilje was ten years younger than I was,' he pointed out. 'If you always regard somebody as a young man, you get the idea that if only he had your experience, he would think differently! When I was thirty Lilje was working for the Christian students' movement. I was a pastor when he was a student, and I had my naval career behind me.' Niemöller added: 'Lilje was the successor of Bishop Marahrens, whose pupil and curate he was, with whom he did not agree in the least. But he always succeeded in concealing this from Marahrens. This was Lilje's political gift. He could make you believe he was in agreement with you. He could prevent disagreements coming to light, unless it was absolutely necessary.' (MN/jb)

Here Lilje differed markedly from Niemöller, who never concealed his political disagreements from anyone, though if he wished he made sure they did not damage his friendships. (When Richard Stevens took a post with the Eisenhower administration, for instance, Niemöller urged him not to be distressed whenever he found his Dachau friend in conflict with his new master.) (ZEKHN 62, Vol. 414/2445e) But politics inevitably divided many from Martin Niemöller. Frequently he was told to choose between being a pastor or a politician, to which he would reply, 'Christ is the conscience of the nation as well as the church'. In Niemöller's experience politicians were all too prone to forget the demands of morality. During his long struggle, with Else's help, to obtain relief for a starving Germany, the assistant general secretary of the nascent World Council of Churches, Oliver Tomkins, had admitted that 'political considerations hamper much that we wish to do'. (ZEKHN 62, Vol. 410/2443b) In the perilous times through which Niemöller lived, a church that kept silent about politics was failing in its duty. 'In the midst of a world in fear we are tempted to become a church in fear, a church without real faith, a church thinking first of her own safety.' (ZEKHN 62, Vol. 407/2444c) To that temptation Niemöller never succumbed, in spite of abuse for the stances he took. When he attacked the power of others, it was never to exalt his own. He argued from 1945 onwards that the great powers of the world must relinquish some of their world-wide roles; but this was out of a desire to see the emergence of a better world government. In 1951 he wished the occupying powers to leave Germany to run her own affairs, supervised by the United Nations. Whatever the faults of UNO, it was not so much motivated by self-interest as the so-called great powers, in his view. In his desire to find some solution to the sufferings of Indochina in 1966, he wrote that he earnestly desired to get the United Nations into the whole business and problem, 'because my sure impression is that no state government or population of Indochina will ever enter into negotiations with the United States of America.' If this was harsh on America, it was Niemöller's considered opinion at a time when he believed that 'The hour of the day in history is much later than we have supposed it to be hitherto.' (ZEKHN 62, Vol. 506/2491)

Nations, Niemöller judged, could become greedy, and not only the USA but also his own. He became increasingly critical of what he called 'the Europe of the rich'. Although he still believed in the hope of a united states of Europe, stretching from the Atlantic to the Urals, he ceased to think that this could ever be based with justice on the European economic community. (MN/jb)

Having come to perceive racism as closely bound up with the ill-treatment of the poor of this world, Niemöller in the 1970s began to attack the economic policies of the west. 'The front of the rich must be smashed', he said in 1973, 'in order to build human brotherhood.' It was a Christian insight, but like many of Niemöller's political judgements, not an entirely welcome one.

Niemöller himself underwent a long and arduous political

development, before finally deciding where he stood before God. The experience of Hitler, of post-war Germany and finally of the international needs of mankind, transformed him. When he wrote *From U-Boat to Pulpit* in 1934, he knew nothing about copyright, so that an English translation appeared in 1936 without any major collaboration from himself. (MN/jb) He did, however, add a preface, praying for peace in the future between Germany and Great Britain. The book was bought by Hugh Macnaghten for his remarkable war library in Eton College. Macnaghten's habit was to send every book he bought back to the author, begging a signature and a *pensée* summing up the message of what the author had written. By the time *From U-Boat to Pulpit* reached Germany in 1937, Niemöller was in gaol. The book was returned to Eton and marked 'No signature available for this volume'.

In 1983 I took out to Germany the Eton College copy of *From U-Boat to Pulpit* in the hope of at last obtaining Niemöller's *pensée*. On 12 March he inscribed the book, in English:

> With my kindest greetings and best wishes to Eton College, which I came to know from outside only, when I saw it from the height of Windsor Castle in 1908, a boy of 16. The next time was in the fifties when we members of the World Council of Churches were presented to the Queen and then – a last time – at the last day of the Aldermaston march! Martin Niemöller. (ECMN)

Without this gloss, Niemöller's memoir of 1934 gives a completely misleading picture of the man he had become. In 1938 A. S. Duncan-Jones had called his extended version of the book *From U-Boat to Concentration Camp*. A new title would be needed to sum up Niemöller's remarkable development from World War I to 1983: *From U-Boat to Pulpit to Pacifist*.

Yet the later Niemöller is also found in the memoir of 1934, above all when he speaks of the influence of his early years. 'It is becoming increasingly clear to me', he wrote there, 'how strongly the first recollections of my early childhood in my parents' rectory of Lippstadt have impressed themselves on my memory and how their influence on me is increasing with the passing of the years.' In his study, as well as a ship-mobile and photographs of himself as a naval cadet and officer, he kept – along with the last photograph of Else – a portrait of his father and a picture of himself as a boy at school. And, conscious of the deep influence of a Christian family, he sought to give this to his own children in spite of the enormous difficulties of the Hitler years.

Nathaniel Micklem, Principal of Mansfield College, Oxford, from 1932 to 1953, once wrote that 'when Martin Niemöller came to stay with us in Oxford, I was entirely sure that being busy I could leave him happy with the children. For of such is the kingdom of heaven.' How strongly Martin cared for his seven children can be glimpsed in the letters he sent home from Moabit gaol. On 4 January 1938 he sent from prison 'a hearty kiss' for Else 'and seven more for the young Niemöller generation: vivat, crescat, floreat!' Before he was free, two of the seven had died. Else and Martin decided to adopt two more in their places. 'My youngest son was only 10 when I came back', said Niemöller. 'He and our adopted son grew up together. We took a foster daughter of a widow in Berlin whose husband was lost in Russia. Now there are still seven children in our family.' (MN/jb)

He relished family life, and in 1971 married again. Sybil von Sell had been a girl in Sunday school when they first met. She shared his faith. She also shared his love of good wine ('I prefer French food and German wine – we used to prefer French food and English sanitation', he averred, 'and I don't get down my coffee without first having opened my throat with Sekt') as well as his fondness for American musicals. The first time he saw a German operetta – it was called *Frau Luna* – was in 1909. He never visited New York without seeing a musical comedy, his favourite being *My Fair Lady*. ('I've seen it I don't know how often', he said happily, 'and can't get enough of it.') When I asked him why he accepted the post of foreign relations officer of the church, since, as he had asserted, it was all a mistake, he sang 'I'm just a girl who can't say no', from *Oklahoma*. (MN/jb)

As for his faith, although he was, so to speak, born with it, it undoubtedly developed under the influence of Karl Barth. Barth sharpened his awareness of the subtleties of denominational Protestant differences, though he never thought they much mattered and once said that in the early years of their relationship he did not know that he was Lutheran whereas Barth was Calvinist. He and Barth would often joke about each other, while fundamentally agreeing over most things. On Niemöller's sixtieth birthday, Barth observed, 'Not so long ago a conversation between Martin Niemöller and myself went like this. Barth: "Martin, I'm surprised that you almost always get the point despite the *little* systematic theology that you've done!" Niemöller: "Karl, I'm surprised that you almost always get the point despite the *great deal* of systematic theology that you've done!" '

What Barth did teach him, as Niemöller himself said, was 'finding the simple formula'. (MN/jb) A British headmaster wrote to Niemöller in 1948 to say how much his boys admired his resistance to Hitler and asking for 'a line from you saying how you got your strength to resist'. Niemöller's reply quoted Jesus's words recorded in Matthew chapter 6, verse 34, about not being anxious for tomorrow, since there is enough evil to be anxious about in the present day. He had tried to eliminate anxiety for the future and simply prayed for enough strength to face each day as it came, and this prayer was always heard. He added, 'It's just a simple truth . . . as everything of Christian life is basically simple.' (ZEKHN 62, Vol. 419/24447) He had come to see that the 'German Christians' against whom he had fought in the 1930s threatened to eliminate precisely the central if simple element on which he relied. They and Hitler's own supposed 'positive Christianity', he told an American correspondent in 1953, 'developed into something in which for Christ there was only very little space left and then into a movement in which Christ was abolished and outlawed'. The final result was the naked idolatry of a nation instead of Christ. (ZEKHN 62, Vol. 505/2488) Karl Barth had shown him that the answer to the question, 'What do you think of the National Socialists?' was 'There is only one person to whom we listen.' (MN/jb)

Niemöller remained a man of prayer. When he finally resigned from the synod of Hessen and Nassau in 1968 (for he had become an ordinary member on retiring as church president) he said it had been a Christian gathering because in it 'people were speaking to each other – and also praying'. But he did not claim that he possessed any great mystical experience (notwithstanding his ability to respond to the spirituality of Russian Orthodoxy), nor did he claim any esoteric Christian knowledge. He derived his belief in a future life solely from faith. When the widow of Captain A. Hunter, one of Niemöller's British opponents in World War I, got in touch with the former U-Boat commander in 1959, Niemöller wrote to her, 'We hope to meet in a better

world where our Saviour will reign as the Prince of Peace.'
(ZEKHN 62, Vol. 410/2445a)

Captain Hunter's widow did not claim in any way to have
made contact with her husband after his death, but other
correspondents of Niemöller's did make similar claims. In
replying to one of them in April 1953, Niemöller took the
trouble to spell out for her his own faith. 'I am sorry to say that I
have not spiritual experiences of that kind and never have had
any', he wrote. 'Therefore I cannot follow your thoughts and
deliberations.'

For me as for many simple-minded people the Bible and the Message of
Christ just must do and I have not the feeling that I am missing anything
because of these facts. And I am quite willing to labour on in this life
and to wait with confidence that I shall be given eyes to see if only I am
given ears to hear in this present life so that I see in my fellow men
Christ is visiting me and asking me whether I will recognise him.
Wherever that happens I really lack nothing and have a full day's work
to do. (ZEKHN 62, Vol. 420/2447a)   .

SELECT BIBLIOGRAPHY

Articles

Anonymous (Hanns Lilje), 'Suspendierung – Aufhebung – Suspendierung – Aufhebung', leader in *Junge Kirche*, Verlag Junge Kirche, Göttingen, 1. Jahrgang, 1 December 1933, pp. 348–64.

Bentley, J., 'British and German High Churchmen in the Struggle against Hitler', *Journal of Ecclesiastical History*, vol. xxiii, no. 3, July 1972, pp. 233–49.

——'The most irresistible temptation', *The Listener*, vol. 100, no. 2586, 16 November 1978, pp. 635–7.

Church of England Council on Foreign Relations, 'Survey on the Affairs of the Continental Churches', May 1934.

——'Second Survey on the Affairs of the Continental Churches', November 1935.

——'Third Survey on the Affairs of the Continental Churches', March 1936.

——'Fourth Survey on the Affairs of the Continental Churches', June 1937.

Conway, J. S., 'The Struggle for Peace Between the Wars', *The Ecumenical Review*, Geneva, vol. 35, no. 1, January 1983, pp. 25–40.

Lilje, H., 'Lasst uns Kirche sein', *Junge Kirche*, 1. Jahrgang, 19 October 1933, pp. 224–6.

Meier, K., 'Kirchenkampfsgeschichtsschreibung', *Theologische Rundschau*, Neue Folge, J. C. B. Mohr, Tübingen, 46. Jahrgang, Heft 1, March 1981, pp. 19–57; Heft 2, May 1981, pp. 101–48; Heft 3, September 1981, pp. 237–78.

Niemöller, M., 'Auch "Deutsche Christen" wählen "Evangelium und Kirche"', *Junge Kirche*, 20 July 1933, p. 67.

——'Die Jungreformatorische Bewegung und die Kirchenpolitik. 16 Thesen', *Junge Kirche*, 24 August 1933, pp. 99–101.

——'Eine zweite Antwort', *Junge Kirche*, 12 July 1933, pp. 57–8.

——(with Karl Lücking), 'Eingabe westfälischer Pfarrer', *Junge Kirche*, 17 July 1933, pp. 51–2.

——'Gott der Herr über Kirche und Volk', *Stimme der Gemeinde*, Eisemann, Berlin-Steglitz, no. 16, 1936, pp. 157–65.

——'Kirche? – Kirche! Ein Wort zur Stunde ernster Entscheidung', *Junge Kirche*, 2. Jahrgang, 20 February 1934, pp. 39–143.

——(with Walter Künneth and Hanns Lilje), 'Kundgebung der Jungreformatorischen Bewegung', *Junge Kirche*, 17 July 1933, pp. 45–7.

—'Missionierende Kirche', *Stimme der Gemeinde*, no. 16, 1936, pp. 6–15.

—Predigt über Lukas 12, 15–21, *Junge Kirche*, 19 October 1933, pp. 221–4.

—'Sätze zur Arierfrage in der Kirche', *Junge Kirche*, 2 November 1933, pp. 269–71.

—'Zur grundsätzlichen Beurteilung der kirchlichen Lage', *Junge Kirche*, 1 December 1933, pp. 344–6.

Niemöller, Wilhelm, 'Martin Niemöller', *Junge Kirche*, December 1981, pp. 573–8.

Robbins, K., 'Martin Niemöller, the German Church Struggle, and English Opinion', *Journal of Ecclesiastical History*, vol. xxi, no. 2, April 1970, pp. 149–70.

Newspapers

Daily Telegraph
Der Christ in Unserer Zeit
Die Welt Woche
Frankfurter Allgemeine Zeitung
Manchester Guardian
New York Times
Rand Daily Mail
Sopade Informationsdienst
Sydney Jewish News
The Catholic World
The Christian Century
The Times
The Times Literary Supplement
This Month
Wiesbadener Kurier
Völkischer Beobachter

Books

Abosch, Heinz, *L'Allemagne sans miracle. D'Hitler à Adenauer*, René Juillard, Paris, 1960 (tr. D. Garmen, *Menace of the Miracle, Germany from Hitler to Adenauer*, 1962).

Barth, Karl and Kittel, Gerhard, *Ein theologischer Briefwechsel*, W. Kohlhammer, Stuttgart, 1934.

Batten, J. R., *The Bible in Dachau*, 1951.

Beckman, J., Mochalski, H., *et al.* (eds), *Bekennende Kirche. Martin Niemöller zum 60. Geburtstag*, Christian Kaiser Verlag, Munich, 1952.

Bentley, James, *Between Marx and Christ*, 1982.

Berger, Claus and Neureuther, Karl (eds), *U-Boat Stories*, tr. E. Sutton, 1931.

Bethge, Eberhard, *Dietrich Bonhoeffer*, Christian Kaiser Verlag, Munich, 1967.

Bloch, Ernst, *Politische Messungen, Pestzeit, Vormärz*, Suhrkamp Verlag, Frankfurt-am-Main, 1976.

Bonhoeffer, Dietrich, *Gesammelte Schriften*, Christian Kaiser Verlag, Munich, 1958– (selections translated by E. H. Robinson and John Bowden as *No Rusty Swords*, 1965, *The Way to Freedom*, 1966, and *True Patriotism*, 1973).

——*Letters and Papers from Prison. The Enlarged Edition*, ed. Eberhard Bethge, 1971.

Bosanquet, Mary, *The Life and Death of Dietrich Bonhoeffer*, 1968.

Brüninghaus, Willi, *Die politische Zersetzung und die Tragödie der deutschen Flotte*, Deutsche Verlagsgesellschaft für Politik und Geschütze, Berlin, 1926.

Busch, Eberhard, *Karl Barth*, tr. John Bowden, 2nd revised edition 1976.

Carr, W. G., *By Guesss and By God*, 1930.

Cochrane, Arthur C., *The Church's Confession under Hitler*, 2nd edition 1976.

Conway, John S., *The Nazi Persecution of the Churches 1933–45*, 1968.

Cornelissen, Peter, *Die Hochseeflotte ist ausgelaufen!*, J. F. Lebmann, Munich, 1930.

Dibelius, Otto, *In the Service of the Lord*, tr. Mary Ilford, 1965.

Duncan-Jones, A. S., *The Struggle for Religious Freedom in Germany*, 1938.

Ehrenberg, Hans P., *Autobiography of a German Pastor*, 1943.

Freiwald, Ludwig, *Last Days of the German Fleet*, tr. M. Moore, 1931.

——*U-Boots-Maschinist Fritz Kaster*, J. S. Lebmann, Munich, 1933.

Glenthøg, J. (ed), *Die Mündige Welt V*, Christian Kaiser Verlag, Munich, 1965.

Gordon, H. J. Jr., *Hitler and the Beer Hall Putsch*, Princeton, 1972.

Greschat, Martin (ed), *Die Schuld der Kirche*, Christian Kaiser Verlag, Munich, 1982.

Gutteridge, Richard, *Open Thy Mouth for the Dumb!*, Oxford, 1976.

Haushagen, Ernst, *U-Boote Westwärts. Meine Fahrten um England 1914–1918*, E. J. Mittler & Sohn, Berlin, 1931.

Herbert, Karl and Lembeck, Otto (eds), *Christliche Freiheit im Dienst am Menschen. Zum 80. Geburtstag von Martin Niemöller*, Frankfurt-am-Main, 1972.

Hebly, J. A., *The Russians and the World Council of Churches*, Belfast, 1978.

Henderson, Nevile, *Failure of a Mission. Berlin 1937–1939*, 1940.

Herman, Stewart W., *The Rebirth of the German Church* (with an introduction by Martin Niemöller), 1946.

Hildebrandt, Franz, *Pastor Niemöller and his Creed*, 1939.

Kagelmann, Paul, *Unterseeboots-Minenleger im Weltkrieg*, Anker-Verlag, Berlin, 1934.

Hitler, Adolf, *Mein Kampf*, tr. James Murphy, 1939.

Hopman, Albert, *Das Kriegstagebuch eines deutschen Seeoffiziers*, A. Scherl, Berlin, 1925.

Kittel, Gerhard, *Die Judenfrage*, W. Kohlhammer, Stuttgart, 1933.

Kloppenburg, Heinz, *et al.* (eds), *Martin Niemöller. Festschrift zum 90. Geburtstag*, Pahl-Rugenstein Verlag, Cologne, 1982.

Koch, Diether, *Heinemann und die Deutschlandsfrage*, Christian Kaiser Verlag, Munich, 1972.

Köppen, Paul, *Die Überwasserstreitkräfte und Ihre Technik*, E. S. Mittler & Sohn, Berlin, 1930.

Lauterbach, Julius, *1000£ Kopfpreis tot oder lebendig*, A. Scherl, Berlin, 1918.

Marder, Arthur J., *From the Dreadnought to Scapa Flow*, vol. 5: *1918–1919*, 1970.

Meier, Kurt, *Der evangelische Kirchenkampf*, Vandenhoeck & Ruprecht, Göttingen, Band I, 1976.

—*Die deutschen Christen*, Vandenhoeck & Ruprecht, Göttingen, 1964.

—*Kirche und Judentum*, Max Niemeyer Verlag, Halle, 1968.

Micklem, Nathaniel, *The Box and the Puppets*, 1957.

Mochalski, Herbert, *et al.* (eds), *Der Mann in der Brandung. Ein Bildbuch um Martin Niemöller*, Stimme-Verlag, Frankfurt-am-Main, 1962.

Neu, Heinrich, *Die Revolutionäre Bewegung auf der deutschen Flotte 1918–1919*, W. Kohlhammer, Stuttgart, 1930.

Neumann, Peter, *Die Jungreformatorische Bewegung*, Vandenhoeck & Ruprecht, Göttingen, 1971.

Niemöller, Martin, *Ansprache an die Vertreter der Bekennenden Kirche in Frankfurt-am-Main am 6. Januar 1946*, Evangelische Verlag, Zollikon-Zürich, 1946.

—*Briefe aus der Gefangenschaft Moabit*, ed. Wilhelm Niemöller, Otto Lembeck, Frankfurt-am-Main, 1975.

—*Das Bekenntnis der Väter und die bekennende Gemeinde*, Christian Kaiser Verlag, Munich, 1934.

—*Dennoch getrost. Die Letzten 28 Predigten des Pfarrers Martin Niemöller*, Verlag der Evangelischen Buchhandlung, Zollikon-Zürich, 1939.

—*Die Staatskirche ist da!*, Wuppertal-Barmen, 1936.

—*Ein Briefwechsel statt einer Antwort. Ein Wort zur kirchlichen Lage*, Eisemann, Berlin-Steglitz, 1936.

—*Eine Welt oder keine Welt. Reden 1961–1963*, Stimme-Verlag, Frankfurt-am-Main, 1964.

—*Facing Jesus Christ*, ed. M. Maertens, 1966.

—*First Commandment*, with a foreword by James Moffatt, 1937.

—*Not und Aufgabe der Kirche in Deutschland*, Quellverlag der Evang. Gesellschaft, Stuttgart, 1946.

—*Pastor Niemöller and his Creed*, tr. Margaret Blunt, 1939.

—*Pfarrer Niemöller D.D. an die Göttingen Studenten*, Vandenhoeck & Ruprecht, Göttingen, 1946.

—*Reden 1945–1954*, Stimme-Verlag, Darmstadt, 1958.

—*Reden 1958–1961*, Stimme-Verlag, Frankfurt-am-Main, 1961.

—*Reden, Predigten, Denkanstosse, 1964–1976*, Pahl-Rugenstein Verlag, Cologne, 1977.

—*The Gestapo Defied*, tr. Jane Lynburn, with a foreword by Thomas Mann, 1943.

—*Vom U-Boot zur Kanzel*, Martin Warneck Verlag, Berlin, 1934. (tr. D. Hastie Smith, as *From U-Boat to Pulpit*, 1936; with an additional chapter by A. S. Duncan-Jones, *From U-Boat to Concentration Camp*, 1939).

—*Was will die Bekennende Kirche?*, Eisemann, Berlin-Steglitz, 1934.

—*Was würde Jesus dazu sagen? Reden – Predigten – Aufsätze 1937 bis 1980*, Union Verlag, Berlin, 1982.

—(with Otto Dibelius), *Wir rufen Deutschland zu Gott*, Martin Warneck Verlag, Berlin, 1937.

—. . . *zu verkündigen ein gnädiges Jahr des Herrn!*, Christian Kaiser Verlag, Munich, 1946.

Niemöller, Wilhelm, *Bekennende Kirche in Westfalen*, L. Bechauf, Bielefeld, 1952.

—*Die dritte Bekenntnissynode der Deutschen Evangelischen Kirche zu Augsburg*, Vandenhoeck & Ruprecht, Göttingen, 1969.

—*Die Preussensynode zu Dahlem*, Vandenhoeck & Ruprecht, Göttingen, 1975.

—*Kampf und Zeugnis der Bekennenden Kirche*, L. Bechauf, Bielefeld, 1948.

—*Kirchenkampf im Dritten Reich*, L. Bechauf, Bielefeld, 1946.

—*Macht geht vor Recht. Der Prozess Martin Niemöllers*, Christian Kaiser Verlag, Munich, 1952.

—*Martin Niemöller. Ein Lebensbild*, Christian Kaiser Verlag, Munich, 1952.

Nygren, Anders, *The Church Controversy in Germany*, 1934.

Payne Best, Sigismond, *The Venlo Incident*, 1950.

Reimers, Karl Friedrich, *Lübeck im Kirchenkampf des Dritten Reiches*, Vandenhoeck & Ruprecht, Göttingen, 1965.

Rupp, E. G., *I seek my brethren*, 1975.

Schneider, H., *Die letzte Fahrt des kleinen Kreuzers "Dresden"*, K. F. Koehler, Berlin and Leipzig, 1926.

Scheer, R., *Germany's High Sea Fleet in the World War*, 1920.

Schmidt, Dietmar, *Martin Niemöller*, tr. Lawrence Wilson, 1959.

Schmidt, Jürgen, *Martin Niemöller im Kirchenkampf*, Leibniz Verlag, Hamburg, 1971.

Scholder, Klaus, *Die Kirche und das Dritte Reich*, Propylaen, Frankfurt-am-Main, Band I, 1977.

Schultz, Paul, *Im U-Boot durch die Weltmeere*, K. F. Koehler, Berlin and Leipzig, 1926.

Smith-von-Osten, Annemarie, *Von Treysa 1945 bis Eisenach 1948*, Vandenhoeck & Ruprecht, Göttingen, 1980.

Speer, Albert, *Spandau. The Secret Diaries*, tr. R. and C. Winston, 1976.

Spiess, Johann, *Six Ans de Croisières en sous-marin*, Payot, Paris, 1927.

Spotts, Frederic, *Kirchen und Politik in Deutschland*, Deutsche Verlags-Anstalt, Stuttgart, 1976.

Stählen, Wilhelm, *Via Vitae, Lebenserinnerungen*, Johannes-Stauda-Verlag, Kassel, 1968.

Stein, Leo W., *I was in Hell with Niemoeller*, 1942.

Svärd, Arvid, *Martin Niemöller*, Westerberg, Stockholm, 1967.

Thielicke, Helmut, *Between Heaven and Earth*, tr. J. W. Doberstein, 1967.

Thomas, Lowell, *Raiders of the Deep*, 1929.

Valentiner, Max, *Der Schrecken der Meere. Meine U-Boot-Abenteuer*, J. S. Lebmann, Munich, 1934.

van der Vat, Dan, *The Grand Scuttle: the Sinking of the German Fleet at Scapa Flow in 1919*, 1982.

von Hase, Georg, *Der deutsche Sieg vor dem Skagerrak*, K. F. Koehler, Berlin and Leipzig, 1926.

—*Kiel and Jutland*, tr. A. Chamber and F. A. Holt, 1928.

von Hassell, Ulrich, *Diaries*, 1947.

von Herwath, Johnnie, *Against Two Evils. Memoirs of a Diplomatist-Soldier during the Third Reich*, 1982.

von Reuter, Ludwig, *Scapa Flow. Das Grab der deutschen Flotte*, K. F. Koehler, Berlin and Leipzig, 2nd edition 1921.

von und zu Peckelsheim, Freiherr, *Kriegstagebuch "U 202"*, A. Scherl, Berlin, 1918.

Wright, Jonathan R. C., *'Above Parties'. The Political Attitudes of the German Protestant Church Leadership 1918–1933*, 1974.

—*"Uber den Parteien". Die politische Haltung der evangelischen Kirchenführer 1918–1933*, Vandenhoeck & Ruprecht, Göttingen, 1977.

Zipfel, Friedrich, *Kirchenkampf in Deutschland 1933–1945*, Walter de Gruyter, Berlin, Band II, 1965.

INDEX

Aabenraa, 217
Aachen, 81
Abraham, 18
Academic Defence Corps, 25
Achenbach, 26
Acts of the Apostles, 63, 129
Adam, 125
Addicott, Revd L.E., 187f.
Adelheide Camp, 184
Adenauer, Konrad, 207, 209–12, 227
African National Party, 220
Albertz, Martin, 118
Aldermarston march, 215f., 235
Alexander, Field-Marshal, 157, 162
Alexi, Patriarch, 205f., 221
Althaus, Paul, 24, 43, 99
Anthony, Revd R.W., 188
Anti-Semitism, 44–8, 62–80, 90, 105,
    114f., 120, 166
Apel, Hans, 227
Archibald, Major General S.C.M., 193f.
Argentina, 20f.
Armistice, 13–15, 38
Aryan paragraph, 64–72, 74, 80–82, 95,
    100
Asmussen, Hans, 101, 109f., 120, 122f.,
    128, 158, 172
Atomic weapons, 213–16, 222f., 228
Augsburg, 205
Augsburg Confession, 82f.
Auschwitz, 197
Australia, 191, 199, 201
Australian Jewish Herald, 219
Austria, 154 183

Baines, Cecil, 163
Balla, Profesor D., 90f.
Ballard, Frank, 199
Baltic, 94
Balzer, Bishop Erwin, 124, 173
Barmen, 97, 100–7, 111f., 117
Barrat, Capt., 182
Barth, Karl, 4, 22f., 49–51, 56, 59, 84,
    97, 101–4, 109, 111f., 151f., 168f.,
    173, 175, 183, 205, 236f.
Basel, 104, 111f., 175, 184
Basler Nachrichten, 111
Bataks, 206

Bavaria, 40f., 52f., 77, 83, 88, 97,
    107–9, 119, 150, 158, 163, 167, 171,
    216
BBC, 153, 165, 229
Beatty, Admiral David, 16
Beck, Käthe, 121
Becker, Reinhard, 135
Belgium, 77, 184
Bell, Bishop G.K.A., 71f., 80, 88,
    98–100, 105f., 111, 123, 132, 135,
    137f., 141, 145–7, 149f., 152–4,
    160f., 163, 176f., 180–6, 193, 195,
    207f.
Bell, Henrietta, 180
Bergen, Claus, 18
Berger, Pastor, 112
Berggrav, Bishop Eivind, 145, 172,
    199f., 207
Berlin, 2, 13, 34, 36, 46, 51, 55f., 59,
    62, 66, 69, 71, 73–5, 82–5, 89, 92,
    97f., 100f., 106f., 111, 113, 115,
    116f., 122f., 127, 141, 145, 148, 151,
    166, 170f., 174f., 189f., 206, 208,
    212f., 217f., 236
Bernard of Clairvaux, 28
Berneuchener, 173
Best, Capt. S. Payne, 155f.
Bethel, 25, 28, 34f., 52, 55, 64, 130
Beveridge, Lord, 193
Bevin, Ernest, 193
Bielefeld, 36, 38, 126, 130
Bilheimer, G.S., 141
Birmingham, 161
Blum, Leon, 154, 156
Böhm, Hans, 118, 138
Bonhoeffer, Dietrich, 50, 64–6, 71, 73,
    79–81, 98f., 105f., 119, 122f., 131,
    134, 151f., 155, 201
Bonn, 213, 227
Bradford, 229
Brandenburg, 60, 74, 77, 97f., 101
Brandt, A.J., 199
Breit, Thomas, 101, 109
Bremer, Friedrich Wilhelm, 26
Bremer, Hermann, 13, 18, 32
Bridgend, 185
Bristol, 172

British Control Commission, Germany, 183f.
British Council of Churches, 193
Brown Synod, 60, 63f.
Brüninghaus, Admiral Willi, 17
Brunotte, Heiz, 118
Buchenwald, 152
Budapest, 225
Buddenbrook, Frau, 59, 96
Büdingen, Schloss, 183, 196, 217, 230
Busch, Wilhelm, 127
Buth, Pastor, 114
Buxton, Dorothy, 152

Cain, 67
Calvin, John/Calvinists, 2, 50, 97, 101, 109, 112, 167, 236
Canada, 200
Canon City, Colorado, 141
Carr, W.G., 13
Caserta, 157, 162
Cavert, Samuel McCrea, 175
Chamby, 123
Charles V, Emperor, 83
Chelmsford, 163
Chicago, 200
Chichester, 57, 71, 75, 80, 88, 186
Christian Century, 153f., 189
Christian Kaiser Verlag, 96, 151
Christian Pacifist, 161
Christliche Welt, 73
Church of England Council on Foreign Relations, 105f., 136f.
Cigars, 6, 101, 148, 150, 229, 231
City Temple, 180
Claudius, Mathias, 122
Clay, General Lucius D., 196
Collins, Revd Canon L.J., 215, 225
Cologne, 2
Colorado Women's College, 123
Communism, 14, 17, 25f., 28, 42f., 73, 92, 135, 164f., 204–6, 208, 211f., 214
Communist Manifesto, 34
Confessing Church, 90–2, 101f., 105–8, 110f., 113–6, 119f., 122–4, 129, 131, 136, 169–73, 197
Council for War Crimes, 193
Council of Brethren, 70, 80, 96, 98, 103f., 109f., 117f., 127–9, 168, 170.
Crown Prince, 25
Croydon, 182
Czechoslovakia, 174, 210, 214f.

Dachau concentration camp, 65, 148f., 155, 163f., 183f., 201, 233
Dahlem, 36–8, 41, 44, 52f., 55, 63, 66, 70, 72, 77, 79, 88f., 93, 95, 107–9, 111–14, 117f., 121, 127, 129, 131, 133f., 140, 144, 156, 183, 189f.
Daily Express, 186
Daily Telegraph, 163, 179f.
Defence Committee for Victims of Nazi Persecution, 196f.
Democracy, 95, 195, 203f., 209, 222, 231
Denazification, 187, 194–6
Denmark, 98, 202, 215, 217f.
Dibelius, Bishop Otto, 44, 55f., 58, 118, 122, 126, 131f., 168–74, 176, 204f., 207, 211, 213, 217, 231
Die Welt Woche, 211
Diestel, Max, 138
Diestel, Superintendent, 37
Dinter, Artur, 45f., 114
Diocletian, Emperor, 50
Dortmund, 26, 198
Dulag Uberursel camp, 197
Duncan-Jones, Dean A.S., 57, 75, 80, 136, 138, 140, 153, 180, 235
Dusseldorf, 39

Easter Marches, 226
Eberhard, Heinrich, 197
Ecumenism, 99, 200–2, 206
Ede, Chuter, 184–6
Eden, Anthony, 185
Eden Theological Seminary, Missouri, 92
Ehlers, Hermann, 38
Ehrenberg, Hans, 64, 121, 127, 143, 146, 152, 154
Eidem, Archbishop Erling, 71f., 88
Eine Welt oder keine Welt, 221
Eisenach, 52–4
Eisenhower, Dwight D., 233
Elberfeldt, 3–7, 20, 23, 25, 37f., 45, 51
Eldorado, Texas, 191
Elizabeth II, Queen, 235
Emsmann, Jochen, 18, 27, 152
Erlangen, 66, 177
Essen, 36, 191
Esquimaux, 200
Eton College, 7, 40, 235
European Economic Community, 234
Euten, 77
Evanston, 189

Fabricius, Cajus, 136
Falker, Gustav, 29
Fanø, 98f., 105f.
Featherstone Park camp, 185, 187
Federal Council of Churches of Christ in
  America, 71, 138, 145, 193
Federal Republic of Germany, 202, 210,
  216
Fezer, Karl, 47, 50, 76, 84
Fiedler, Eberhard, 110
Fife, Maxwell, 181
Finland, 176
Fisher, Archbishop Geoffrey, 181f.
Fischer-Tropsch oil plants, 192f.
Flensburg, 8, 217
Foreign Office, German, 71
France, 2, 28, 39, 77, 175f., 203, 208,
  214f., 227, 236
Frankfurt-am-Main, 10, 157, 162, 168,
  187f., 195, 208f., 219
Frau Luna, operetta, 236
Free Church Federal Council, 199
Freikorps, 25f., 48, 139
Freiwald, Ludwig, 15, 40f.
Frick, Wilhelm, 56f., 85
From U-Boat to Pulpit, 9–11, 14, 39, 94,
  235

Galbraith, J.K., 196
Gandhi, Mahatma, 219, 222
Garibaldi, General Sante, 155f.
Geneva, 106, 148, 178, 181–4, 190,
  199f.
Geneva Convention, 185, 225, 227
George V, King, 7
Gerhard, Pastor, 37
'German Christians', 46–52, 54, 56f.,
  59–62, 66, 69, 73–9, 82, 84, 86, 89f.,
  97, 104, 109, 119, 121, 126, 172f.
German Democratic Republic, 204f.,
  208, 210, 223
Gerstein, Kurt, 197
Gestapo, 59, 72, 85, 87, 100, 118, 120,
  128, 141, 145, 148, 150
Gibbs, Mark, 217
Gillespie, Mrs George, 191
Glasgow, 203
Gloria, Raymond E., 192
Goebbels, Joseph, 145, 147
Gollwitzer, Helmut, 51
Goltzen, Herbert, 69
Göring, Hermann, 85–7, 144, 165

Gospel and Church movement, 59f., 64,
  69
Göttingen, 27, 47, 177
Great Britain, 15f., 45, 89, 105, 111,
  121, 135, 149, 154, 160, 163, 178f.,
  183–7, 191, 193f., 201, 203, 207f.,
  210f., 214–16, 229, 235, 237
Green, J.F.C., 212
Green party, 227
Griefenberg, 114
Grossman, Pastor, 55
Grotewohl, Otto, 204f.
Grüber, Heinrich, 148
Grützmacher, Georg, 23
Guderian, General Heinz, 155

Hahn, Otto, 213
Hamburg, 4, 20, 54, 77, 167, 195, 227f.
Hanoi, 225
Hanover, 12, 51, 88, 119, 167, 171
Hassler, A.J., 224
Hässler, Monsignor Georg, 224f.
Haushagen, Ernst, 13
Headlam, Bishop Arthur Cayley, 136f.
Heckel, Bishop Theodor, 88f., 98f.,
  106, 137
Heidelberg, 210
Heiden, 59, 96
Heinemann, Gustav, 203, 210
Held, Heinrich, 77, 127
Helsinki, 215
Henderson, Nevile, 145
Henriod, H.L., 106
Herman, Stewart W., 182, 184, 188
Hertogenbosch, 198
Hess, Rudolf, 132, 146
Hesse, Hermann Albert, 51f., 111f.
Hessen, 172, 174, 195f., 212, 217, 221,
  231, 237
Hickey, William, 186
Hildebrandt, Franz, 64, 66, 71, 79f.,
  130, 134, 141, 151, 154–7, 170–3,
  175, 191, 200
Hill, Revd D.J., 192
Himmler, Heinrich, 112
Hiroshima, 213
Hirsch, Emmanuel, 47, 49, 62
Hitler, Adolf, 1, 4, 8, 28, 33f., 40–54,
  56–62, 65, 67, 73–5, 78f., 83–9, 91f.,
  94–6, 101–8, 110–13, 115f., 120,
  125, 127–9, 131, 135f., 140, 143f.,
  146–8, 151–5, 159f., 163–6,

168–170, 185, 189, 195, 198, 202, 213, 232, 236f.
Hitler Youth, 41, 81, 118, 120, 194f.
Ho Chi Minh, 224
Holland, 24, 149f., 176, 179, 198, 227
Holstein, Horst, 139
Hopman, Admiral Albert, 40
Hossenfelder, Joachim, 46, 48, 55f., 59f., 62, 71, 74, 76–9
Huddersfield, 229
Hundt, Ernst, 56
Hungary, 155

Immer, Karl, 100f., 111
India, 219
Inner Mission, 4, 30f., 33–6, 41, 46, 52, 56, 64f., 185
Inflation, 21, 26f., 29, 35, 38f.
Innsbruck, 155
Italy, 10, 36, 159, 210
Iwand, H.J., 122

Jacksonville, Florida, 190
Jacob, 31
Jacob, Günther, 69
Jacobi, Gerhard, 38, 49f., 69, 71, 75, 77, 80, 92, 98, 100, 113, 122, 124, 127, 233
Jäger, August, 54–7, 59, 78, 97f., 107–10
Jäger, Samuel, 39
Jannasch, Wilhelm, 120, 124
Japan, 214f., 230f.
Jeremiah, 176
Jesus, 3, 6, 31, 33, 47f., 58, 63, 66–8, 72, 74, 89, 93, 95, 101, 104, 107f., 117–21, 124–9, 132–4, 139, 151, 154, 164–6, 173f., 176, 200, 206, 219, 223, 237f.
Jewish News, 199
Jews, 43–8, 61–80, 95, 105, 114, 116, 120f., 127, 129, 139, 159, 163–6, 177, 219f. *See also* Anti-Semitism.
John, St, 144
John XXIII, Pope, 201
John Paul I, Pope, 201
Johnson, L.B., 224
Joliot-Curie, Frederic, 214f.
Joshino, Genzaburo, 230f.
Jugoslavia, 150
Junge, Heinz, 197
Junge Kirche, 50, 61, 67, 90

Kähler, Bishop of Stettin, and Frau Kähler, 22, 29, 31, 36
Kapler, Hermann, 34, 51–4, 56, 60
Kapp Putsch, 25, 139
Kasten, Fritz, 41
Keay, Capt. R.W., 179
Keitel, Field Marshal, 147, 160
Kellner, Toni, 198
Kempner, Robert M., 145
Kennedy, J.F., 225
Kerrl, Hanns, 115–20, 122, 125f., 144
Kiel, 13f., 17f., 20, 144
Kiev, 202
Killinger, Erich, 197
King Martin Luther, 221
Kingdon, Revd Paul, 184f.
Kirchentag, 33, 217, 221
Kissling, Revd A.J., 190, 196
Kittel, Gerhard, 47, 50, 62f., 76, 103f.
Koch, Karl, 60, 64, 84, 87, 96, 98, 100f., 105f., 109, 111, 113, 116, 119, 122
Kock, Erich, 197
Koechlin, Alphons, 175
Kölnische Zeitung, 77
Königs, Ernst, 4, 130, 133, 148
Königsberg, 48
Köpenick, 89
Köppen, Capt. Paul, 11
Korea, 215
Kraemer, Hendrick, 198
Krause, Reinhold, 74–6
Kreuzer, Dr, 212
Kristallnacht, 65f.
Krummacher, Dr, 77
Kube, Wilhelm, 46, 76
Kuehne, Otto, 184
Kuhtze, Fräulein, 36
Künneth, Walter, 50, 57, 84f., 87
Kurmark, 55, 173
Kurtz, Walter, 230

Lamoyski, Count Alexander, 183
Lancaster, Archdeacon of, 180
Lang, Archbishop Cosmo Gordon, 145, 150
Lange, Karl, 123
Lauterbach, Capt. Julius, 24
League of Nations, 78, 99
Lehmann, Johannes, 197
Lehmann, Rudolf, 197
Leiper, Henry Smith, 138
Leipzig, 20

Lempp, Albert, 151, 162
Lempp, Maria, 151f., 158
Lenin Peace Prize, 232
Lettlands, 223
Liberty, 153
Lilje, Bishop Hanns, 50, 172, 223
Lippe, River, 6f., 25f.
Lippstadt, 1–6
Loewen, Herbert, 231
Loewenfeld, 25f.
London, 7, 79f., 150, 166, 180, 186, 193, 206, 209f.
Louis XIV, King, 50
Lübeck, 120, 124, 173
Ludicke, Harold, 161
Lücking, Karl, 60–5, 111
Ludendorff, General Erich, 25, 41
Luke, St., 89
Lund, 210
Luther, Martin, 34, 46, 49, 55, 72–4, 83, 107, 144, 168, 171, 173
Luthuli, Albert, 219
Lutze, Pastor, 197

McCarthy, Joseph, 205
Macdonald, A.J., 137
Macedonia, 150
Macfarland, Revd Charles S., 71f., 83
Macnaghten, Hugh, 235
Mahlmann, Lieutenent-General Paul, 210
Manchester Guardian Weekly, 88
Mann, Thomas, 92, 140
Marahrens, Bishop August, 51f., 59, 69, 84, 87–90, 96–100, 110, 112, 115, 116–19, 124, 169, 232
Marburg, 66, 90, 177
Martin, Kingsley, 161
Marx, Karl, 34. *See also* Communism.
Mary, Blessed Virgin, 201
Mason, John Brown, 123
Matthew, Gospel of, 237
Maury, Pierre, 175, 178
Mecklenburg, 52, 167
Mein Kampf, 41, 43–5, 47, 166
Meiser, Bishop Hans, 52f., 57, 81, 83f., 89f., 96–8, 100f., 107f., 110, 115–19, 130, 167f.
Melanchthon, Philipp, 83
Meyer, Bruno, 124
Meyer-Klugel, D., 161
Michaelis, Capt. 8, 15
Michelfelder, G.C., 175
Micklem, Nathaniel, 136, 236

Middle East, 235
Missouri, 92, 219
Mit brennender Sorge, 125
Moabit prison, 123, 131–4, 140, 152f., 157
Moeller, Reinhard, 34
Moffat, James, 135
Moltmann, Jürgen, 8
Moore, W.G., 138
Morton, Philip H., 179
Moscow, 157, 202, 205f., 222
Moses, 62
Müller, Fritz, 38, 53, 55, 70, 82, 115, 117, 119, 129, 140
Müller, Josef, 155f.
Müller, Ludwig, 48f., 51–5, 57, 59–62, 71–88, 90, 96–100, 102f., 107, 110f., 113f.
Munich, 46, 84, 96–100, 102, 150f., 167
Münster, 22–5, 28, 31, 36, 49, 125f.
Mussolini, Benito, 50
Muster, A.J., 224
Muzzling Decree, 81f., 84, 90
My Fair Lady, 236

Nagasaki, 213
Naples, 156–61, 163, 167, 179, 188, 201f.
Nassau, 172, 195f., 212, 217, 221, 231, 237
National Review, 161
National Socialists, 28, 40, 42, 46–8, 52, 54, 56, 58f., 62, 73–5, 77f., 81, 89f., 93, 99f., 111–13, 120f., 131, 135–8, 148, 153, 156, 162, 166–9, 171, 194f., 208, 237
Navy, German, 7–20, 48f., 148
—, Royal, 7, 16
Nero, Emperor, 50
Nether Hege camp, 187
Neu, Heinrich, 17
Neue Deutsche Bauern Zeitung, 224
Neumann, Friedrich Wilhelm, 185
Neureuther, Karl, 18f., 41
Neustatten, 123
New Delhi, 219
New York, 99, 188, 208, 232
New York Herald Tribune, 193
New York Times, 160
New Zealand, 191, 201
Niebuhr, Reinhold, 188f.

250 Index

Niemöller, Brigitte, 25f., 35, 140, 162, 236
—, Christine, 1, 26
—, Else, v, 1, 13, 20–3, 25–32, 36f., 70, 84, 87, 89, 93, 130–5, 138, 140–7, 151f., 157f., 162, 164f., 174, 179, 181, 183, 188f., 191, 196, 199–201, 203, 208, 217–19, 221f., 230–3, 235f.
—, Gerhard Heinrich, 3f., 6, 236
—, Hans Jochen, 27, 147, 152, 236
—, Heinrich, 1–6, 12, 20–3, 25, 27, 30, 32, 36, 52, 88, 93, 144, 148, 200, 235f.
—, Heinz Hermann, 31f., 94, 147, 151, 157, 161, 174, 230, 236
—, Hertha, 31, 146, 158, 162, 206, 230, 236
—, Jan Heinrich, 31, 147, 174, 230, 236
—, Jutta, 31, 152, 236
—, Magdalene, 3
—, Maria, 3
—, Martin junior, 93, 158, 162, 183, 230, 236
—, Paula, 1–3, 5, 21, 25–27, 36, 144, 148, 235f.
—, Pauline, 3
—, Sybil, v, vii, 236
—, Wilhelm, 1, 3f., 25, 28f., 39f., 60, 75, 114, 129, 131, 133, 146
Niesel, Wilhelm, 128
Nihilism, 192
Nikodim, Metropolitan, 222
Nikolai, Metropolitan, 202, 206, 215
Norway, 150, 172, 202, 227
Nuremberg, 47, 110, 194, 198
Nuremberg Laws, 116, 145
Nuremberg Trial, 177

O'Brien, Tom, 179
O'Neill, C., 194
Oath of loyalty to Hitler, 107, 112
Oberammergau, 230
Oberheid, Heinrich, 83f.
Observer, 179
Odessa, 222
Oklahoma, 236
Old Testament, 3, 47, 74–6, 93, 120
Oldenburg, 77, 93
Olympic games of 1936, 122f.
Ostergren, Revd David L., 156, 160–2
Oxford, 126, 136–8, 149

Pacifism, 73, 99, 202–7, 211, 214
Papacy, 201
Paris, 209, 214
Pastors' Emergency League, 69–72, 75–84, 86–8, 90–7, 103f., 113f., 117, 131f., 170
Paul, St, 22f., 28, 31, 44, 75, 82, 120, 123, 131
Paul VI, Pope, 201
Pauling, Linus, 213f.
Pauly, Irene, 156
Pauly, Richard, 156
Peale, Norman Vincent, 153
Penheiter, Alma, 189f.
Peter, Bishop Friedrich, 75f.
Peter, St, 89, 129, 132
Petersen, Pastor, 92
Phu Ly, 225
Pius XI, Pope, 125f.
Pius XII, Pope, 201
Poland, 56, 176f., 210, 226
Prisoners of war, 77, 161, 184, 186–8
Proverbs, Book of, 138f.
Provisional Church Government, 111, 114, 127
Prussia, 46, 48, 54, 57–60, 62, 66, 69, 72, 82, 96, 110, 115, 118, 197
Psalms, Book of, 94

Racism, 220f., 232
Raeder, Admiral Erich, 147, 160
Railways, German State, 27–30
Rearmament, West German, 209–15, 227
Red Cross, 178
Reeves, Bishop Ambrose, 224
Reich Church Committee, 116f., 124, 126
Reinhardt, Hans, 197
Reformation, 24, 37, 69f., 73, 75f., 82
Refugees, 29
Rendsburgh, 164
Rentdorff, Bishop Heinrich, 52, 54
Rhineland, 91, 97f., 170
Rieger, Julius, 230
Ritter, Gerhard, 197
Röhricht, Eberhard, 37, 53, 55, 112, 118
Roman Catholics, 2, 12, 27ff., 35, 43, 60, 73, 125f., 137, 140, 148–51, 168f., 201, 210
Roosevelt, Eleanor, 188, 220
Rosenberg, Alfred, 145f.

Rothert, Dr, 25
Rothstein, Dr, 23
Royden, Maude, 163
Ruhr, 5, 24f., 39f., 191–3
Russell, Bertrand, 215, 226
Russia, 12, 105, 151, 170, 174f., 177, 183, 189, 202, 204f., 210f., 215, 221f., 227, 236
Russian Orthodox Church, 202, 205–7, 237
Rust, Bernhard, 48, 54, 56

Saarbrücken, 129
Sachsenhausen concentration camp, 1, 120f., 141, 143, 147–9, 153f.
Savings Society, 35
Saxony, 75f., 167, 196, 204
Scapa Flow, 17f., 40
Schacht, Hjalmar, 155f.
Scharf, Kurt, 72, 74, 77
Scharfenberg, Pastor, 89
Scheer, R., 14, 20
Schlageter, Albert Leo, 39f.
Schmend, J., 23
Schmidt, Helmut, 227
Schmidt, Jürgen, 63
Schmidt-Henrici, Walter, 122
Schmidtz, Otto, 23
Schneider, Erna, 92
Schneider, Paul, 152
Schöffel, Bishop Simon, 54, 57, 71, 76f., 87f.
Schumacher, Kurt, 203.
Schultz, Paul,16.
Schulz, Dora Bertha, 96, 133, 151, 157f., 162, 174, 181, 196, 217–9
Schulze, Otto, 139
Sears, Edwin, 193
Seattle, 189
Sennlich, 21
Shakespeare, William, 7
Sicily, 180
Siegen, 112
Social Gospel, 4f., 33–5
Socialists, 38, 105, 203, 205, 227
SPD, 203, 223
Solingen, 197
Sotschi, 222
South Africa, 220f.
South America, 231
Spain, 16
Spiess, Johannes, 16
Sports Palace Rally, 74–7, 88f., 114, 125

Stählin, Bishop Wilhelm, 93, 171–3
Stahn, Julius, 116
Stalin, Joseph, 12, 206
Stansgate, Lord, 203f., 210–12, 227
Stargard, 152
Stein, Leo W., 153
Stevens, Moja, 149, 183, 186, 230
Stevens, Richard, 149f., 155f., 162, 174, 180, 182–4, 186, 198, 209, 229f., 233
Stöcker, Adolf, 5, 166
Strasser, Gregor, 46
Stratenwerth, Gerhard, 52f., 65, 174
Strauss, Franz-Joseph, 217f.
Sturm, Marcel, 175
Stuttgart Declaration of Guilt, 175–8, 219
Submarines, 9–14, 17, 20, 22, 24f., 30, 32, 56
Süderländer Tageblatt, 212
Sulzbach, Herbert, 187
Sumatra, 200
Swanwick camp, 187
Swastika, 93
Sweden, 71, 88, 93, 171
Switzerland, 50f., 56, 103, 122, 162, 175, 181, 183f., 207, 217
Sydney, 197

Tagesspiegel, 212
Tecklenburg, 20–2
Tegel, 152
Teltge, 29
The Catholic World, 201
The Cost of Discipleship, 131
The State Church is Here!, 118
The Times, 88, 135–7, 145
Theological Existence today, 56
Theological Wordbook of the New Testament, 47
Theology, 105
Thielicke, Helmut, 42f., 177, 194
Thomas, General Georg, 155f.
Thomas, Helen B., 179
Thompson, Dorothy, 179
Thuringia, 8, 14, 27, 167
Thyateira, Archbishop, 145
Times Literary Supplement, 10
Tomkins, Oliver, 172, 234
Topp, Karli, 13f., 22
Treysa, 168f., 171, 173, 175, 194
Truman, Harry S., 213
Tübingen, 23, 47, 103

TUC, 179
Tyrol, 155

Ulm, 78f., 105
Union Theological Seminary, New York, 99, 135, 188
UNO, 234
United States of America, 71, 92, 99, 156-8, 160, 163, 179, 188f., 193f., 201, 203, 205, 208-10, 212-15, 222, 224-6, 229, 233
US Army chaplains, 174. *See also* Ostergren, Revd David L.
US Zone, Germany, 154
Universal Christian Council for Life and Work, 98, 100, 105f., 123, 126, 136f.

Valentiner, Max, 79
Van Dijk, J.C., 150
Venlo, 149, 155
Versailles Treaty, 38, 99, 136, 157
Victoria, Queen, 16
Vietnam, 215, 224-7, 234
Villabassa, 155
Visser t'Hooft, W.A., 175, 181, 200, 206
Völkischer Beobachter, 59, 137
Volkskirche, 34, 41, 47-49, 51, 57, 70, 74, 96
Von Bismarck, Otto, 140, 169
Von Bodelschwingh, Friedrich the elder, 34
Von Bodelschwingh, Friedrich the younger, 34f, 52-5, 58, 64f., 111f., 119, 126, 130
Von Bonin, Bogislav, 155
Von der Ropp, Friedrich, 137
Von Falkenhausen, Alexander, 155f., 184
Von Galen, Bishop Clemens August, 125f., 148, 201
Von Hase, Georg, 24, 39f., 45
Von Hassel, Ulrich, 159
Von Herwath, Johnnie, 164
Von Hindenburg, Paul, 25, 41, 56-8, 74, 77, 83-5
Von Isenburg Büdingen, Fürst and Fürstin, 174
Von Kallay, Nikolaus, 155
Von Krosigk, Schwerin, 83f.
Von und zu Peckelsheim, Spiegel, 45
Von Rabenau, Eitel-Friedrich, 72, 74, 77
Von Reuter, Admiral Ludwig, 17, 40
Von Ribbentrop, Joachim, 89, 146

Von Ruckteschell, Helmuth, 197f.
Von Runstedt, Gerd, 185
Von Schirath, Baldur, 81, 84
Von Schlabrendorff, Fabian, 155
Von Schuschnigg, Kurt, 154, 156
Von Schuschnigg, Maria-Dolores, 154f.
Von Selchov, Bogislav, 24
Von Trott, Adam, 195
Von Watter, Oskar, 26, 139

Walter, Ernst, 127
Wandering Jew, 63
Wannsee, 13, 71
Warthegau, 56
Was würde Jesus dazu sagen?, 6
Weatherhead, Leslie, 180
Wehmer, Herbert, 223
Wehner, O., 40
Wehrung, Georg, 23, 49, 96
Weimar Republic, 24, 34f., 40f., 51, 160, 166
Weissler, Friedrich, 120
Werder, Friedrich, 129
Werfels, Franz, 44
Wesen, 1, 21, 26
Weschke, Eugen, 69
Westerkappeln, 2, 20f.
Westphalia, 1, 20, 25, 29-31, 33f., 36, 49, 52, 60, 69f., 76, 84, 90, 97f., 100f., 125, 170
Westphalia, Bank of, 30
Wichern, Johann Hinrich, 4f., 30, 33f., 41
Wiener, Alfred, 166
Wiesbaden, 130, 157, 196, 212f.
Wilberforce, R., 184
Wilderstone Hall camp, 185
Wilhelm II, Kaiser, 3, 8, 14, 23-5, 38f., 41, 44, 73, 99, 169, 223
Wilhelmstrasse, 85
Wilmershaven, 49
Wilson, Woodrow, 16
Windsor, 7f., 215, 235
Wittenberg, 3, 27, 70f.
Wolff, Karl, 197
World Council of Churches, 8, 175, 181f., 200, 205-8, 213, 215, 219, 222, 234
World Peace Committee, 202, 214-16
World War I, 9ff., 19, 39, 45, 48f., 61f., 77, 94, 99, 102, 152, 237

World War II, 27, 63, 70, 93, 141, 149,
   169, 198–200, 223, 231
Wright, J.R.C., 34
Wurm, Bishop Theophil, 54f., 81, 83–6,
   89f., 96–8, 100f., 107f., 110, 112,
   115, 118f., 130, 168–70, 176, 178,
   194
Württemberg, 54, 77, 83, 88, 97, 107f.,
   119, 194
Würzburg, 209f., 231

Young Reformation Movement, 49–55,
   57–61, 64, 69f., 90

Zahn, Pastor, 81
Zänker, Bishop Otto, 110
Zoellner, Bishop Wilhelm, 29f., 33f., 41,
   51, 58, 119, 124
Zwingli, Ulrich, 2